The Vegetarian 5 Ingredient Gourmet

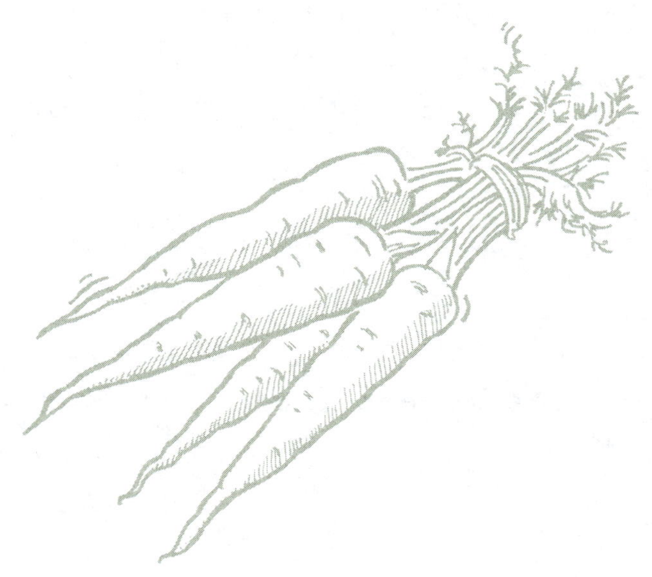

ALSO BY NAVA ATLAS

Vegetariana

Vegetarian Celebrations

Vegetarian Soups for All Seasons

Vegetarian Express
(co-authored with Lillian Kayte)

Great American Vegetarian
(formerly *American Harvest*)

Pasta East to West

The Vegetarian 5 Ingredient Gourmet

250 Simple Recipes and Dozens of Healthy Menus for Eating Well Every Day

Nava Atlas

BROADWAY BOOKS NEW YORK

Broadway Books titles may be purchased for business or promotional use or for special sales. For information, please write to: Special Markets Department, Random House, Inc., 1540 Broadway, New York, NY 10036.

Visit our website at www.broadwaybooks.com

Library of Congress Cataloging-in-Publication Data
Atlas, Nava.
The vegetarian 5-ingredient gourmet : 250 simple recipes and dozens of healthy menus for eating well every day / Nava Atlas.—1st ed.
p. cm.
Includes index.
1. Vegetarian cookery. 2. Quick and easy cookery. I. Title.
TX837 .A8474 2001
641.5'636—dc21

00-045537

FIRST EDITION

Book design by Pei Loi Koay
Illustrated by Nava Atlas

ISBN 0-7679-0690-X (pb)

20 19 18 17 16 15 14 13 12

For Jennifer Josephy

Contents

Acknowledgments

It's ironic that a book on simplified cooking took longer to write and required more eagle-eyed editors and talented hands than some of my other books put together. I'm grateful to everyone who took part in this project, helping to bring it to a more satisfying fruition than I could have imagined.

Thanks for help in polishing the manuscript in its early states go to Carol Wiley Lorente and Jen Jeglinski. Thanks to Jen also for sharing a family recipe for creamy zucchini soup. The origin of this recipe is credited to Helen Horvath. I'd also like to thank a few others for sharing ideas that became recipes in this book. They include my father-in-law, Arie Tabak, for his simple but excellent Israeli salad; Susan Webb (who introduced my family to many simple child-friendly dishes) for her apple recipes; Pam Tate, for her yummy hot bean dip; and my son, Evan Tabak. Somewhere about midway through this long project, Evan (seven years old at the time) invented a pear and mango smoothie. Even as I write this, pears and mangoes ripen on my kitchen counter as this smoothie is still a favorite of ours.

My sons Evan and Adam Tabak and my husband Harry Chaim Tabak, as well as our extended family, have been a constant source of sustenance and inspiration. It's a pleasure to cook for such an enthusiastic and appreciative group of people.

The staff at Broadway Books has been most impressive, even at a point when I am just beginning to know them. Many thanks to Rebecca Holland for so ably overseeing the various components of this project,

Pei Loi Koay for the fabulous interior design, Patti Ratchford for the beautiful cover, and Karen Fraley for the final, fine-tooth-comb copyedit. I'd also like to acknowledge editorial assistant Anne Resnik, always helpful and willing to go the extra step with grace and good humor.

Finally, my heartfelt thanks to my editor, Jennifer Josephy. Though we've worked on several projects together, her bringing this one to Broadway Books has truly been a gift. I feel fortunate to have an editor who has been such a steadfast supporter and role model, and so, this book is dedicated to her.

Introduction

Ask any time-crunched cook what they look for in a meal, and the words "fast" and "easy" will likely come up. I'd like to add one more word to the busy cook's vocabulary: "Simple." It's a relaxing concept that goes beyond ease—after all, a soup can have 25 ingredients that need merely to be tossed into the pot and so would be considered easy. Simple implies a paring down, getting to the essentials.

To my mind, simplicity does not by any means imply mindlessness; rather, I'd go along with Walt Whitman's view that "simplicity is the glory of expression." By focusing on a few high-quality, well-chosen ingredients, I can enjoy a simple meal as much as a more elaborate one.

My website, *In a Vegetarian Kitchen* (www.vegkitchen.com—please visit!), has been a wonderful forum through which to communicate with readers. My core readership seems to be busy, conscientious people who want to eat well despite feeling time-crunched. They appreciate varied, low-fat meals that don't take a lot of time to prepare. *Vegetarian Express* is the book that visitors write to me about most frequently. Many readers, especially working parents, tell me that this book of quick and easy menus has been a lifesaver for them. I co-wrote it when my two sons were toddlers. At that time, I was certain that when they got a little older, I could return to the more elaborate meal preparation I enjoyed in the years B.C. (Before Children).

This never happened; life continued busier than ever. Between caring for a home, meeting my work deadlines, parenting two curious and active boys (with endless activities that bump right up against dinnertime), and finding the odd moments to spend with my husband, extended family, and friends, I found myself craving simpler meals more than ever.

Being a devotee of good, healthful meals, I began developing recipes that are pared down to their very essence, but remain splendid. And while cooking this way most often results in quick meals, the more important criterion is simplicity. I did not want to leave out favorite ingredients because they aren't "fast foods." There are those rare days, like stormy Sundays, when dinner doesn't have to be on the table in a half hour; on days like those, I don't mind baking a butternut squash or a casserole, cooking barley, or simmering a pot of beans for several hours, if I'm free to do other things while they cook. In fact, the heady aromas of long-cooking foods are among my favorite comforts. While I wouldn't be so foolhardy as to suggest this kind of cooking for weeknights at 6 P.M., having these ingredients cooked and ready for weekday meals is quite enjoyable. Precooked foods like these, though, are not a requisite for the recipes in this book. Simple but longer-cooking recipes are included for a sense of balance.

Keeping things simple takes the frantic quality—and pressure—out of preparing a meal. Simplifying helps you to slow down and enjoy the process of cooking. Permit yourself to make these recipes at whatever pace pleases you. Sometimes, I'll opt for a simple main dish even though I'm not in a rush, allowing me to devote time and energy to another part of the meal—a special salad, several different kinds of vegetables for my family to sample, or a homemade dessert.

When I opted to limit the recipes to five or fewer ingredients, I decided the only things that would not "count" were water, salt, and pepper. When recipes are this basic, some shortcuts are inevitable. One of the best routes to maximum flavor are complex sauces—ones that someone else has made. Stock your pantry with good-quality salsas, stir-fry sauces, pasta sauces, and such, and splendidly simple meals will always be at the ready.

The recipes here focus on whole foods and fresh produce in combination with high-quality convenience foods (such as canned beans, quick-cooking grains, ready-to-use soy foods, pizza crust, the aforementioned prepared sauces, and the like). Nearly all the ingredients used are available in well-stocked supermarkets. Menu suggestions following the recipes show how to round out a meal. And I encourage you to serve lots of fresh vegetables and salads requiring no special recipes.

The simple approach has yielded one more delightful benefit—my young sons are more likely to try new foods if they are uncomplicated. When it comes to getting children to eat a variety of healthy foods, the simpler they are, the better. I have come away from this project with many new meals we can enjoy as a family. Still, I include a wide range of recipes with flavors that appeal to adult tastes. For instance, a meal of Leek and Red Pepper Hash Brown Potatoes (page 183), with recipe-free accompaniments of sautéed soy "sausage" links and a simple salad of mixed baby greens, tomatoes, and carrots is a meal that nourishes both body and soul—with a dash of sophistication.

I hope that *The Vegetarian 5-Ingredient Gourmet* will inspire anyone who believes they don't have the time to eat well to add more healthful meals to their repertoire. I also hope that this collection will give aspiring vegetarians an incentive to have meatless meals more frequently. Eating well, along with regular exercise, are the two most important lifestyle choices you can make in maintaining good health. An abundance of delicious food, simply prepared, enhances the quality of daily life like few other things can.

Stocking the Pantry for Simple Meals

Don't you hate walking into the kitchen at the end of a long, busy day, having no clue what to make, let alone the ingredients for a decent meal? A well-stocked pantry and an easy meal plan will help beat the "I-don't-know-what-to make" blues. I'll tackle both subjects, but first, let's deal with the pantry. Use this list as a guideline to stocking up on key ingredients. This way, no matter how time-crunched life gets, you can be sure that a healthful, nearly effortless meal awaits at the end of the day!

BASIC PANTRY STAPLES

Nonperishable Dry Goods

Beans, canned: Look for good-quality beans, without additives, or better yet, organic canned or jarred beans from natural foods stores or co-ops, including your favorites from the following:

- Black beans
- Black-eyed peas
- Chickpeas (garbanzos)
- Great Northern beans (cannellini)
- Pink beans
- Pinto beans
- Red or kidney beans

Beans, dried: If you're inclined to cook beans from scratch, I don't object! Black beans, adzuki beans, and navy beans are particularly good cooked from scratch; there are also pink, kidney, red, and large white beans; brown and red lentils; and split peas. Look for lots of tips on cooking beans from scratch on pages 110 to 111.

Chilies, green, in 4- or 7-ounce cans, chopped, mild or hot, as preferred

Grains: If you are going to store whole grains at room temperature, don't buy more than what you will use up in about three months. During hot summer months, refrigerate them.

- Barley
- Bulgur
- Couscous
- Rice (long-grain brown, basmati, Arborio, quick-cooking, etc.)
- Quinoa
- Wild rice

Herbs and spices, dried: Keep a good range of commonly used varieties on hand; seasoning blends, especially an all-purpose salt-free herb-and-spice blend, a good-quality curry powder, as well as an Italian herb seasoning blend, are especially useful.

Oils:

Dark sesame oil
Extra-virgin olive oil
Light olive oil

Pastas and noodles: Keep a good supply of different sizes and shapes of pasta in your pantry. Some useful shapes to have on hand include angel hair, thin spaghetti, spirals (rotini), ziti or penne, fettuccine, and linguine. A few Asian noodles, such as udon, soba, and rice vermicelli, are available in natural foods stores and are nice to have on hand, too.

Soy sauce: Sometimes marketed under the name tamari or shoyu; buy a good natural brand for best flavor.

Tomato products, canned:

Diced, in 14- to 16-ounce cans
Crushed or pureed, in 14-, 16-, and 28-ounce cans
Tomato sauce

Vinegars:

Balsamic (dark and/or white)
Red wine or white wine vinegar
Rice vinegar (for Asian-style cooking)

Prepared Condiments, Sauces, and Such

These items are what I call "simplicity's little helpers." Packing abundant flavor, they can have you eating great-tasting meals in no time. Though most of these are available in supermarkets, try their natural foods counterparts; they're usually all-natural and sometimes even organic.

- Barbecue sauce (great for broiling or stir-frying tofu, tempeh, or seitan)
- Pasta or marinara sauce (this comes in many natural and flavorful varieties)
- Pizza sauce
- Salad dressings (natural, low-fat varieties; I find red wine vinaigrette, balsamic vinaigrette, and ranch most useful)

- Salsa, tomato-based, mild to hot as you prefer
- Salsa, tomatillo (salsa verde)
- Thai peanut sauce
- Stir-fry sauce

Pantry Vegetables

- Garlic
- Onions (yellow, red, or both)
- Potatoes, white (red-skinned are an excellent all-purpose potato)
- Potatoes, sweet (for fall and winter)

Refrigerator Staples

Refrigerator staples are more subjective to define than pantry staples. That being the case, this is a fairly short list, concentrating on the ingredients that I feel are essential to have on hand to ensure flexibility in meal preparation.

- Butter or margarine (both to be used sparingly; look for a natural brand that is free of hydrogenated oils and trans-fatty acids)
- Cheeses, shredded (low-fat if preferred, or soy cheese)
- Parmesan cheese, freshly grated (or if you prefer, try Parmesan-style soy cheese)
- Ketchup
- Lemons
- Mayonnaise (preferably commercially prepared soy mayonnaise)
- Milk, 1% low-fat or soy
- Mustard, prepared (Dijon is excellent)
- Tofu (in various forms including silken, soft, firm, or extra-firm, and baked. See more detailed description of the various forms of tofu on page 136)
- Yogurts, plain and flavored

Freezer Staples

- Burger and hot dog rolls
- Hero or sub rolls
- Pastas, frozen (ravioli, tortellini, cavatelli, or gnocchi)
- Pita bread
- Pizza crusts

- Soy bacon
- Soy hot dogs
- Tortillas, corn and flour
- Vegetables of your choice (corn kernels, green beans, green peas, and chopped spinach are useful)
- Veggie burgers

Fresh Fruits and Vegetables

Though fresh produce is undoubtedly a staple in this book's recipes and menus, it would be cumbersome to list all those used. Produce is the food I shop for most frequently, since I like to have it as fresh as possible. Though the seasonality of produce has been stretched by imports, I like to stick with what is truly seasonal—as well as local—as much as possible. Please support family farms by shopping at local farm stands and farmers' markets if you have access to them. Cast a vote for organic produce (as well as organic eggs and dairy products) by buying them as often as you can; they are more expensive, to be sure, but if there is more of a demand, prices will come down.

Planning Weekly Menus

Now that your pantry is brimming with useful staples, you can plan your meals more readily, with fewer last-minute shopping trips. Even when you haven't planned ahead, there will be something great to fall back on, like easy homemade pizzas or burritos, or a veggie burger accompanied by a coleslaw that takes you minutes to prepare.

I have to admit that despite all my years of cooking (and writing about it), until recently I often decided what to make for dinner in the morning, then scavenged for ingredients at some point during the day. While this is fun to do on occasion, nearly daily decision-making has lost its charm.

I was amazed (and a little abashed) to discover how much time is saved by a mere 15-minute weekly meal-planning and shopping list–making session. Basically, I need only three menus for the week, for our family of four moderate eaters. If I make the right quantities, I can count on leftovers for another three nights. I might also include a special menu for the kids on a night when my husband and I want to have something too spicy or exotic for their tastes. One night a week, we might eat out or have company at home, which I deal with separately.

Meal-planning and most of the shopping is usually done every Sunday (consistency helps). Often, my husband or I will shop for produce separately at a local farm stand or produce market. Once every month or two, I stock up on bulk items such as grains at a natural foods market.

A great deal of mixing and matching can be done with the recipes in this book. If you're comfortable with doing so, you can combine and recombine them to create a myriad of meals. Many people just starting to make more frequent meatless meals appreciate guidance in menu-planning, so the menu suggestions can be useful starting points in discovering what goes well with what. As for the recipes themselves, feel free to add and adjust ingredients to your personal taste. Nothing is set in stone; you can follow the basic formulas just as they are, or you can improvise as you see fit.

Use the handy forms that follow to create your menus and shopping list. First, list the dinners you wish to make for the week, complete with side dishes and fruits or desserts. Then, use the shopping list to fill in everything you'll need for the week, including breakfast and lunch foods and nonfood items. Try to produce one master shopping list so you don't find yourself running back and forth to the store. Use the master list of staples on pages 4 to 7 once or twice a month to help stock up on standard ingredients.

WEEKLY MENU-PLANNING GUIDE

This list allows for five menus, on the premise that you will likely have at least one meal's worth of leftovers during the week, and one where you may eat out, have carry-out, or invite company, for which you will plan separately.

List main dishes and accompaniments:

1. ______________________________

Served with: ______________________________

____

____

2. ______________________________

Served with: ______________________________

____

____

3. ______________________________

Served with: ______________________________

____

____

4. ______________________________

Served with: ______________________________

____

____

5. ______________________________

Served with: ______________________________

____

____

WEEKLY SHOPPING LIST

Pantry and refrigerator staples to be replenished
(includes canned and jarred goods, oils, dry seasonings, pastas, and condiments)

Produce

Soy products

Grains, legumes, and bulk items

Dairy (milk, yogurt, cheeses, eggs, butter or margarine, etc.)

Frozen foods

Breads (pizza crust, breads, pita, tortillas, burger and hot dog rolls, etc.)

Cereal

Baking goods

Snack foods, juices, and other beverages

Other (paper goods, nonfood items, etc.)

Explanation of Nutritional Analysis

All breakdowns are based on one serving, unless specified otherwise. When there's a range in the serving amount, the average number of servings is used (i.e., when a recipe specifies 6 to 8 servings, the analysis is based on 7 servings). When more than one ingredient is listed as an option, the first ingredient is used in the analysis. Usually, the optional ingredient will not change the analysis significantly.

Ingredients listed as optional, most often found at the end of the recipe, are not included in the analysis. When salt is listed as "to taste," its sodium content is not included in the analysis. The analysis of sodium content of canned beans factors in that rinsing them well of their salty brine reduces sodium by about one-third.

With the use of convenience products in tandem with fresh ingredients, it's important to use those that are as high quality as you can find. While the vast majority of ingredients are available in well-stocked supermarkets, you might find, for example, that an organic marinara sauce found in a natural foods market is significantly lower in sodium and sugar than its supermarket counterpart. Similarly, a natural, whole-grain pizza crust purchased in a natural foods market is not only more nutritious, but contains a fraction of the sodium found in certain national brands. While both versions of a convenience product might be good tasting and high quality, the more natural ones rely on inherent flavor. The same is true for many other prepared products.

Certainly the choice of what to buy and where to buy it is ultimately yours, and in most cases, sodium content aside, the products found in supermarkets serve very well. However, I feel it's always good to explore other options.

CHAPTER 1

Simplicity in a Soup Pot

Have you ever noticed that the phrase "soul-satisfying" often accompanies the word "soup"? A good soup does as much for the spirit as it does for the stomach. Whether it's an Asian-style broth or a thick puree, I can think of no other food that gives as much comfort.

Of all the sections in this book, I found this one to be most challenging. For me, making soup is a magical alchemy—cutting up a number of ingredients, adding a pinch of several spices and seasonings, and, after heating long enough, the disparate mixture gradually becomes a cohesive (and very flavorful) whole. And despite (or maybe because of) having written an entire book on vegetarian soups, it was not as easy as I thought to come up with soups that can perform this culinary magic with five or fewer ingredients.

More so than in some of the other categories in this book, I rely on "helpers" as shortcuts to good flavor. Canned vegetable stock or bouillon, seasoning mixes, and often, a single assertive fresh herb helped me ensure flavorful results in very simple soups.

These recipes are for those times when you crave a soup that can be prepared quickly, but not one that comes straight from a can. Many are nearly instant; others take as much time to simmer as a soup made with a multitude of ingredients. But in either case, I hope you will find that phrase, "soul-satisfying," an apt description.

Cold Potato-Barley Buttermilk Soup

6 SERVINGS

4 medium-large potatoes

2 cups fresh green beans, trimmed and cut into 1-inch lengths (or frozen cut green beans, thawed)

1½ cups cooked barley (from ½ cup raw; see Basic Cooked Barley, page 101)

2 cups buttermilk

¼ cup chopped fresh dill

Salt and freshly ground pepper to taste

Calories: 183 • Total fat: 0 g
Protein: 6 g • Carbohydrate: 38 g
Cholesterol: 3 mg • Sodium: 50 mg

Potatoes, barley, and buttermilk are a trio that I find blissfully refreshing in the summer, served cold in a soup.

1 Peel the potatoes and cut into approximately ½-inch dice. Cover with water and bring to a simmer. Cover and cook until the potatoes are about half done, about 10 minutes. Add the green beans and cook until both are tender but not overdone, about 10 minutes longer. Remove from the heat, but do not drain.

2 Let the potato-green bean mixture stand, uncovered, until it is at room temperature, then add the remaining ingredients. Serve at room temperature, or cover and refrigerate until chilled, if desired.

Cold Soups

Mid- to late summer is our brief chance to grab what we can of sun, sand, and—soup. Okay, so soup might not be something that springs immediately to mind when you think of summer pleasures, but I find few things more refreshing on a warm summer day than a bowl of cold soup.

To round out a meal of cold soup, add a substantial salad, a good bread, and if you'd like, some fresh corn on the cob. These cool, flavorful elixirs whet the wilted appetite like nothing else can!

Warm or Cold Tomato and White Bean Soup

Fresh herbal overtones lift the flavor of this instant soup. White beans make a creamy base for soups, dips, and sauces.

6 SERVINGS

Two 16-ounce cans cannellini (large white beans), drained and rinsed

One 28-ounce can stewed low-sodium tomatoes

2 scallions, green parts only, chopped

2 tablespoons minced fresh cilantro, parsley, or dill, or to taste

1 to 2 teaspoons salt-free herb-and-spice seasoning mix, or to taste

Freshly ground pepper to taste

1 Reserve half of the beans and place the rest in a food processor along with the remaining ingredients.

2 Puree until smooth. Transfer to a serving container if serving cold or to a large saucepan if serving hot. Stir in the reserved beans.

3 Serve at once if you'd like this at room temperature, or cover and refrigerate until chilled if desired. If you'd like to serve this warm, heat slowly in a large saucepan, and serve.

Calories: 179 • Total fat: 0 g
Protein: 9 g • Carbohydrate: 34 g
Cholesterol: 0 mg • Sodium: 344 mg

Creamy Pinto Bean Puree

5 TO 6 SERVINGS

Two 16-ounce cans pinto beans, drained and rinsed

One 14- to 16-ounce can low-sodium diced tomatoes or one 14- to 16-ounce can Mexican-style stewed tomatoes

1 cup low-fat plain yogurt or soy yogurt

1/4 cup fresh cilantro or parsley leaves

1 teaspoon chili powder

Salt and freshly ground pepper to taste

Calories: 220 • Total fat: 1 g
Protein: 13 g • Carbohydrate: 39 g
Cholesterol: 3 mg • Sodium: 445 mg

This features a base of canned beans and is best served at room temperature.

For a smooth texture, combine all the ingredients, plus 1 cup water, in a food processor and process until just pureed. For a soup with added texture, reserve ½ cup or so of the pinto beans, then stir into the pureed mixture.

MENU

Creamy Pinto Bean Puree *(this page)*

Mushroom and Bell Pepper Quesadillas or Soft Tacos *(page 172)*

Shredded dark green lettuce and diced tomatoes

Good-quality low-fat tortilla chips

Cold Fresh Tomato Soup

6 SERVINGS

Here's a great way to take advantage of late summer's sublime tomatoes. Use the ripest tomatoes possible.

3 pounds flavorful tomatoes, quartered

1 cup tomato juice, or as needed

¼ cup chopped fresh basil or dill

1 to 2 scallions, minced, optional

Juice of ½ lemon

Salt and freshly ground pepper to taste

1 Place all the ingredients in a food processor and process to a chunky puree.

2 Transfer to a serving container and serve at once, or cover and refrigerate until chilled, if desired.

Calories: 53 • Total fat: 0 g
Protein: 2 g • Carbohydrate: 11 g
Cholesterol: 0 mg • Sodium: 141 mg

MENU

Cold Fresh Tomato Soup *(this page)*

Pasta "Tuna" Salad *(page 60)*

or

Pasta and Broccoli Salad *(page 58)*

Fresh Italian bread

Fresh Tomato and Corn Soup

6 SERVINGS

3 pounds flavorful tomatoes

4 to 6 ears fresh corn, uncooked

1 tablespoon light olive oil

1 large onion, finely chopped

2 to 4 tablespoons minced fresh parsley

Salt and freshly ground pepper to taste

Calories: 123 • Total fat: 3 g
Protein: 3 g • Carbohydrate: 21 g
Cholesterol: 0 mg • Sodium: 22 mg

This soup is simple but labor intensive. If you want to immerse yourself in the summery, sensory experience of peeling fresh tomatoes and scraping kernels off of corn cobs, you won't regret it. This is an appealing accompaniment to a late summer meal of grilled vegetables and veggie burgers.

1 Bring water to a simmer in a soup pot. Add the whole tomatoes, bring to a simmer, and cook for 1 minute. Remove from the heat and drain.

2 When the tomatoes are cool enough to handle, slip off the skins, chop them into bite-size pieces, and set aside.

3 Scrape the corn kernels off of the cobs and set them aside.

4 Heat the oil in the same soup pot. Add the onion and sauté over medium heat until golden, then add the corn kernels and enough fresh water to cover. Bring to a simmer. Cover and simmer gently until the corn is just tender, 5 to 10 minutes.

5 Add the tomatoes and parsley. Return to a simmer and cook for another 5 minutes. Remove from the heat and season with salt and pepper. Let the soup stand until just warm, and serve.

Cold Curried Cucumber Soup

6 SERVINGS

Here's another nearly-instant cold soup. While cucumbers may not be the most nutritious of vegetables, they are undoubtedly one of the most refreshing. On a very hot day, if you want to be as cool as one, serve this lilting cucumber soup.

Combine all the ingredients, plus 2 cups water, in a serving container and stir together well. If time allows, cover and refrigerate for about an hour before serving to allow the flavors to blend.

MENU

Cold Curried Cucumber Soup *(this page)*

Warm pita bread

Curried Potato-Tomato Salad *(page 57)*

Fruited Bulgur Salad *(page 48)*

2 cups low-fat plain yogurt or soy yogurt

1 large cucumber, peeled, seeded, and grated (or ½ large English cucumber)

¼ cup minced fresh cilantro or parsley

2 scallions, thinly sliced

1 to 2 teaspoons good-quality curry powder, or to taste

Salt to taste

Calories: 74 • Total fat: 1 g
Protein: 6 g • Carbohydrate: 9 g
Cholesterol: 6 mg • Sodium: 84 mg

Miso Onion Soup

6 SERVINGS

2 tablespoons light olive oil

6 medium white or red onions, quartered and thinly sliced

3 to 4 garlic cloves, minced

1 teaspoon grated fresh ginger

3 to 4 tablespoons miso (any variety) dissolved in ⅓ cup warm water, or to taste

Salt and freshly ground pepper to taste

Calories: 108 • Total fat: 5 g
Protein: 7 g • Carbohydrate: 13 g
Cholesterol: 0 mg • Sodium: 465 mg

This is a soothing remedy when you are coming down with a cold—though you need not wait for a cold to try it!

1 Heat the oil in a soup pot. Add the onions and sauté over medium-low heat until golden. Add the garlic and continue to sauté slowly until the onions are lightly browned, stirring often, 15 to 20 minutes.

2 Add 5 cups water and the ginger. Bring to a simmer. Cover and simmer gently for 15 minutes.

3 Stir in the dissolved miso, remove from the heat, and season. Allow the soup to stand for 15 minutes, covered, and serve.

Miso Soup with Mushrooms, Snow Peas, and Tofu

4 TO 6 SERVINGS

This nicely flavored miso soup is made more substantial with the addition of tofu. Fresh shiitake mushrooms impart the best flavor to the broth. Follow with an Asian-style noodle dish, such as Asian Sesame-Soy Noodles *(page 85)**.*

1½ to 2 cups mushrooms (shiitake, cremini, or baby bella), cleaned, stemmed, and sliced

4 ounces (about 2 cups) fresh snow peas, trimmed and cut in half crosswise

8 ounces firm tofu, well drained and cut into small dice

2 scallions, sliced

3 to 4 tablespoons miso (any variety) dissolved in ⅓ cup water

Freshly ground pepper to taste

Calories: 105 • Total fat: 2 g
Protein: 7 g • Carbohydrate: 14 g
Cholesterol: 0 mg • Sodium: 561 mg

1 Combine the mushrooms and 5 cups water in a large saucepan and bring to a simmer. Cover and simmer gently for about 10 minutes.

2 Add the snow peas and tofu. Simmer just until the snow peas are tender-crisp, about 3 minutes.

3 Stir in the scallions and dissolved miso, remove from the heat, season, and serve.

Miso Soup

In Japan, miso soup is often eaten for breakfast. For the Western palate though, I think miso soup is more likely to find acceptance as an appetizer, as it does in Japanese restaurants. Miso, a salty, pungent paste made of fermented soybeans, adds a full-bodied flavor to soup broth. You'll have better luck finding it in natural foods stores than in supermarkets. If you're unfamiliar with the flavor of miso, start with 2 tablespoons in these recipes. Taste, then add more dissolved miso to your liking. Please be aware that once miso is stirred into hot water, it should not be boiled; otherwise, its beneficial enzymes will be destroyed.

Miso comes in several varieties, falling under three basic categories: pure soybean, soybean with barley, and soybean with rice. Soybean *(hatcho)* miso is the most pungent and intense; rice varieties, of which there are several, are the mildest; and barley *(mugi)* miso falls somewhere in the middle. Shiro miso is one variety of mild, yellowish miso (sometimes labeled "mellow white") that is popular in our domestic natural foods markets. Any type of rice miso makes tasty dressings and sauces. All varieties of miso work well in soup—which to choose is entirely up to you and your palate.

Asian Noodle Broth

4 SERVINGS

4 ounces bean-thread (cellophane) or rice-stick noodles

Two 15-ounce cans vegetable broth

8 to 10 ounces white or cremini mushrooms, cleaned and sliced (use presliced if desired)

½ to 1 teaspoon grated fresh ginger, or to taste

3 to 4 scallions, thinly sliced

Freshly ground pepper to taste

Calories: 127 • Total fat: 0 g
Protein: 2 g • Carbohydrate: 28 g
Cholesterol: 0 mg • Sodium: 222 mg

A trip to an Asian market to find exotic noodles is no longer necessary. Most well-stocked supermarkets feature an array of imported noodles in the Asian foods section. See the menu with Instant Tofu and Mixed Vegetable Stir-Fry (page 144).

1 Combine the noodles with hot water to cover in a heatproof container. Cover and soak until al dente, 15 to 20 minutes.

2 Meanwhile, combine the broth, mushrooms, and ginger in a large saucepan and bring to a simmer. Cover and simmer until the mushrooms are done, about 10 minutes.

3 Drain the noodles well. Transfer them to a cutting board and chop in several directions to shorten.

4 Stir the noodles and scallions into the broth and season with pepper. Add a bit more water if the soup is too thick. Serve at once.

Asian-Style Soups

Asian-style soups are ideal to make when you want a good soup quickly, with little forethought. With a burst of inspiration and a few choice ingredients, a tasty soup is a few minutes away. While most soups benefit from being made ahead of time to develop flavor, these are best eaten as soon as they are made.

Rice, Lettuce, and Mushroom Broth

4 TO 6 SERVINGS

8 to 10 ounces white or cremini mushrooms, cleaned and sliced (use presliced if desired)

2 vegetable bouillon cubes

2 cups cooked rice

2 cups finely shredded dark green lettuce

2 scallions, thinly sliced

Salt and freshly ground pepper to taste

Calories: 113 • Total fat: 0 g
Protein: 3 g • Carbohydrate: 23 g
Cholesterol: 0 mg • Sodium: 62 mg

If you find yourself with too much lettuce and some leftover rice, here's a great way to use both.

1 Combine the mushrooms, bouillon cubes, and 4 cups water in a large saucepan and bring to a simmer. Cover and simmer gently until the mushrooms are tender, about 10 minutes.

2 Add the remaining ingredients and cook until everything is heated through, about 5 minutes, and serve.

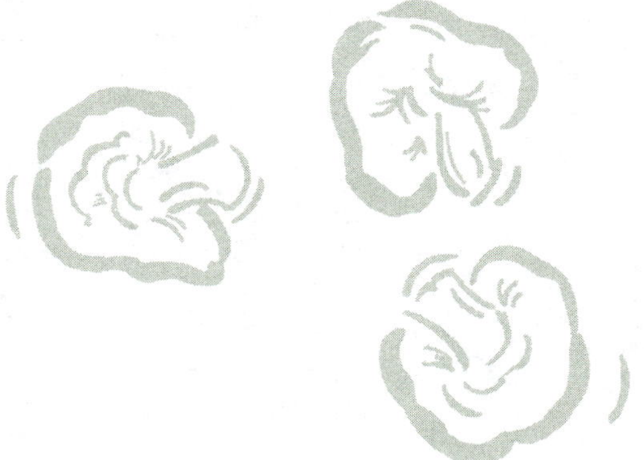

MENU

Rice, Lettuce, and Mushroom Broth *(this page)*

Broccoli and Tofu in Thai Peanut Sauce *(page 143)*

Simple tossed salad (include dark green lettuce, tomatoes, and carrot)

Bok Choy, Tofu, and Baby Corn Soup

6 SERVINGS

Two 15-ounce cans vegetable broth

One 15-ounce can baby corn, with liquid

3 to 4 stalks bok choy, leaves included, thinly sliced

1 pound firm tofu, well drained and diced

2 to 3 scallions, sliced

Freshly ground pepper to taste

Calories: 135 • Total fat: 3 g
Protein: 8 g • Carbohydrate: 17 g
Cholesterol: 0 mg • Sodium: 245 mg

With a generous portion of tofu, this soup is perfect to team with a light noodle dish.

1 Bring the broth to a simmer in a soup pot. Cut the baby corn in half and add it along with its liquid.

2 Add the remaining ingredients and cook just until everything is heated through, no more than 5 minutes. Add a bit more water if the soup is too thick. Serve at once.

MENU

Bok Choy, Tofu, and Baby Corn Soup *(this page)*

Asian Sesame-Soy Noodles *(page 85)*

Steamed broccoli

Fresh fruit or any fruity dessert from Chapter Eleven

Split Pea and Barley Soup

8 OR MORE SERVINGS

This comforting classic thickens considerably as it stands, resulting in a generous quantity of soup. Each time you reheat it, thin it with additional water, and adjust the seasonings. Or, once your original batch cools, consider freezing half of it for later use. This soup is a meal in itself. All you need is a good bread and a salad—simple or bountiful, as you prefer.

One 16-ounce package green or yellow split peas

½ cup pearl barley

1 large onion, finely chopped

3 medium carrots, thinly sliced

2 teaspoons salt-free herb-and-spice seasoning mix

Salt and freshly ground pepper to taste

1 Combine the first 5 ingredients in a large soup pot with 8 cups water. Bring to a simmer. Cover and simmer gently for an hour.

2 Stir in 2 cups water, and simmer until the peas are completely mushy, about 30 minutes. Season with salt and pepper and serve, or cover and let stand off the heat for an hour or so before serving. Thin with water and correct seasonings as needed.

Calories: 117 • Total fat: 0 g
Protein: 5 g • Carbohydrate: 23 g
Cholesterol: 0 mg • Sodium: 12 mg

Split Peas

Green split peas are easily digestible and high in protein. So are yellow peas, which are somewhat milder in flavor, though they can be used interchangeably. These peas are best known for their role in thick hearty soups.

- Try coming up with your own simple split pea soup combinations. These little legumes have a special affinity for tomatoes, garlic, curry, spices, and fresh dill.

- They're a delectable addition to winter stews, especially when combined with potatoes and eggplant.

Curried Red Lentil and Spinach Soup

6 SERVINGS

1 tablespoon light olive oil

1 large onion, finely chopped

1½ cups red lentils, rinsed

1 to 2 teaspoons good-quality curry powder

One 10-ounce package frozen chopped spinach, thawed

Salt to taste

Calories: 100 • Total fat: 2 g
Protein: 5 g • Carbohydrate: 14 g
Cholesterol: 0 mg • Sodium: 43 mg

This warming soup freezes nicely. After eating it for a night or two, freeze some for a rainy day—it's a treat that is both spicy and soothing.

1 Heat the oil in a soup pot. Add the onion and sauté over medium heat until golden.

2 Add the lentils and 6 cups water and bring to a simmer. Stir in 1 teaspoon curry powder, cover, and simmer very gently for 35 to 40 minutes.

3 When the lentils are mushy, stir in the spinach and check the consistency. If the soup is too thick, add about ½ cup water. Season with salt and additional curry powder, if desired.

4 Simmer for another 5 minutes. If time allows, let the soup stand off the heat for an hour or so to develop flavor. Heat through as needed before serving.

MENU

Curried Red Lentil and Spinach Soup *(this page)*

Fresh pita bread

Cranberry Slaw *(page 37)*

or

Red Cabbage, Carrot, and Apricot Salad *(page 37)*

Baked or microwaved potatoes

Leek and Potato Soup

6 SERVINGS

Leeks and potatoes are a classic soup duo. It's a match that's always mild and soothing. For an easy meal, serve this with veggie burgers on whole grain buns and a tomato salad. For maximum flavor, try this with Yukon gold potatoes.

2 tablespoons nonhydrogenated margarine

3 to 4 medium-large leeks, white and palest green parts only, chopped and very well rinsed

6 large potatoes, peeled and diced

2 vegetable bouillon cubes

1 to 1½ cups 1% low-fat milk or soymilk, or as needed

Salt and freshly ground pepper to taste

1 Heat the margarine in a soup pot. Add the leeks and sauté over low heat, stirring often, until they are wilted, 8 to 10 minutes.

2 Add the potatoes, enough water to cover, and the bouillon cubes. Bring to a simmer. Cover and simmer gently until the potatoes are very tender, 25 to 30 minutes.

3 Remove 2 cups of the potatoes with a slotted spoon and mash coarsely. Return to the soup pot and stir in enough milk to achieve a medium-thick consistency. Season with salt and pepper. If time allows, let the soup stand off the heat for an hour or two to develop flavor. Heat through as needed, and serve.

Calories: 218 • Total fat: 5 g
Protein: 4 g • Carbohydrate: 40 g
Cholesterol: 2 mg • Sodium: 140 mg

6 SERVINGS

Creamy Zucchini Soup

2 tablespoons nonhydrogenated margarine or whipped butter

1 medium onion, finely chopped

2 pounds zucchini (about 6 medium-small), grated

2 tablespoons minced fresh dill

1 cup reduced-fat sour cream or plain soy yogurt

Salt and freshly ground pepper to taste

Calories: 120 • Total fat: 9 g
Protein: 3 g • Carbohydrate: 7 g
Cholesterol: 3 mg • Sodium: 66 mg

A food processor with a grating attachment makes this delicious soup easy to prepare. Use smaller zucchini, as they are more flavorful than large ones.

1 Heat the margarine in a soup pot. Add the onion and sauté over medium heat, stirring frequently, until golden.

2 Add the zucchini and continue to sauté, stirring occasionally, 5 to 7 minutes. Add 4 cups water and bring to a simmer. Cover and simmer gently until the zucchini is tender, about 10 minutes.

3 Add additional water if the soup is too thick, and heat through. Remove from the heat and stir in the dill and sour cream. Season with salt and pepper and serve, or cover and let stand off the heat for an hour or so before serving. Heat through as needed. When reheating, heat very slowly without boiling.

Sweet Potato Soup

4 TO 6 SERVINGS

Nutritious sweet potatoes need little embellishment to make a flavorful soup. This one is made extra easy by microwaving the sweet potatoes ahead of time, sparing the cook from having to scrape and dice them. Just scoop, mash, and heat for a comforting, nearly-instant soup.

4 large sweet potatoes

2 cups 1% low-fat milk or soymilk

1 teaspoon salt-free herb-and-spice seasoning mix, or to taste

½ teaspoon ground cinnamon

Pinch of nutmeg

Salt to taste

Calories: 230 • Total fat: 1 g
Protein: 5 g • Carbohydrate: 50 g
Cholesterol: 4 mg • Sodium: 64 mg

1 Microwave the sweet potatoes until very easily pierced with a knife. Depending on your unit, this will take from 16 to 24 minutes to bake them all at once.

2 When the sweet potatoes are cool enough to handle, cut each in half, scoop them out of the skins, and transfer to a bowl. Mash well.

3 Combine the mashed sweet potatoes in a soup pot or large saucepan with the remaining ingredients. Stir together, then heat slowly until the mixture comes to a simmer. Cover and simmer gently for 5 minutes. Serve at once.

MENU

Sweet Potato Soup *(this page)*

Fresh bread of your choice (delicious with corn bread)

Marinated Beans *(page 40)*

Steamed green beans or other green vegetable of your choice

Diced fresh tomatoes and bell pepper strips

6 SERVINGS

Puree of Carrot Soup

2 tablespoons nonhydrogenated margarine

1 large onion, chopped

1 pound carrots, peeled and sliced or coarsely chopped in a food processor

2 medium russet or Yukon gold potatoes, peeled and diced

1 vegetable bouillon cube

Salt and freshly ground pepper to taste

Calories: 136 • Total fat: 5 g
Protein: 2 g • Carbohydrate: 23 g
Cholesterol: 0 mg • Sodium: 124 mg

Mild and light, this is a good introduction to nearly any kind of meal. Use sweet, fresh carrots that aren't the least bitter. Organically grown carrots are a good bet for optimal flavor.

1 Heat the margarine in a soup pot. Add the onion and carrots and sauté over medium heat, stirring frequently, until golden, 10 to 15 minutes.

2 Add the potatoes, 3 cups water, and the bouillon and bring to a simmer. Cover and simmer gently until the vegetables are quite tender, 20 to 25 minutes.

3 With a slotted spoon, scoop out all the solid ingredients and transfer them to a food processor. Process until very smoothly pureed, transfer back to the pot, and stir back into the liquid.

4 Add additional water if the puree is too thick. Season with salt and pepper, and serve, or cover and let stand off the heat for an hour or so before serving.

"Creamy" Mushroom Soup

6 SERVINGS

What luscious flavor from such basic ingredients! Pureed soft tofu or white beans make a deceptively rich base for a soup sure to please mushroom enthusiasts. Serve this soup as an introduction to light pasta or potato dishes.

1 tablespoon nonhydrogenated margarine

1 large onion, chopped

1 pound soft or silken tofu, drained, or one 16-ounce can cannellini (large white beans), drained and rinsed

One 15-ounce can vegetable broth

8 ounces small white or cremini mushrooms, sliced

Salt and freshly ground pepper to taste

1 Heat the margarine in a soup pot, and add the onion. Sauté over medium heat until the onion is golden and soft.

2 Transfer the onion to a food processor along with the tofu or cannellini beans. Process until smoothly pureed, add the vegetable broth, and process again briefly.

3 In the same soup pot, combine the mushrooms with enough water to keep the bottom of the pot moist. Cover and steam the mushrooms until tender, 8 to 10 minutes.

4 Transfer the mixture from the food processor back to the soup pot and stir to combine with the mushrooms. Add a little more water if too thick and heat slowly until heated through. Season with salt and pepper and serve. Or, if time allows, let the soup stand off the heat for an hour or so, then heat through as needed.

Calories: 87 • Total fat: 4 g
Protein: 6 g • Carbohydrate: 6 g
Cholesterol: 0 mg • Sodium: 157 mg

MENU

"Creamy" Mushroom Soup *(this page)*

Colcannon *(page 186)*

or

Roasted Potatoes with Bell Peppers and Onions *(page 184)*

Bountiful tossed salad

Steamed broccoli

CHAPTER 2

Streamlined Salads

Making salads is an enjoyable exercise in creativity, whether you like to improvise with eclectic ingredients or stick with tried-and-true harmonies. Nineteenth-century writer Charles Dudley Warner wrote that "you can put everything . . . into a salad . . . but everything depends on the skill of mixing." I agree. When you consider that salad can be defined not only by greens and tomatoes, but also grains, beans, potatoes, pasta, corn, and almost any vegetable, the possibilities are nearly endless, even when the limit is five ingredients!

My single greatest shortcut to five-ingredient salads is the use of robust, prepared salad dressings. The humblest of ingredients can be transformed when they are dressed in, for instance, a balsamic or raspberry vinaigrette. With so many good, natural salad dressings to choose from, I rarely make them from scratch as I once did.

Salads add color, texture, and a variety of nourishing elements to a meal. Make salads an important part of your evening meal, or make an enticing one for lunch to serve with good bread.

6 TO 8 SERVINGS

Corn Slaw

One 8-ounce bag shredded coleslaw cabbage

2 cups cooked fresh or frozen corn kernels, thawed

2 scallions, green parts only, thinly sliced

½ medium green or red bell pepper, finely diced

½ cup natural low-fat vinaigrette

Salt and freshly ground pepper to taste

Calories: 76 • Total fat: 2 g
Protein: 1 g • Carbohydrate: 11 g
Cholesterol: 0 mg • Sodium: 159 mg

Cabbage and corn kernels are a salad marriage made in heaven.

Combine all of the ingredients in a serving bowl and mix thoroughly. Serve at once or cover and refrigerate until needed.

Simple Slaws

While I appreciate convenient ingredients to simplify meal preparation, I'm not usually drawn to buying precut vegetables. However, shredded coleslaw cabbage captured my fancy ever since it came on the market. I enjoy a variety of coleslaws as simple side salads, but I don't like the mess of shredding a large quantity of cabbage. Shredded cabbage is also handy to use in stir-fries and other dishes (such as Colcannon, page 186).

When buying a bag of coleslaw cabbage, trust your eyes to determine quality. If it looks fresh, it probably is. Avoid any package with a pool of liquid in it. The cabbage should look crisp and dry (but not dried out). Green cabbage mixed with a little red cabbage and some grated carrot is my top choice when buying preshredded coleslaw.

Here are three favorite simple slaws. They are compatible with most any kind of meal (except, of course, those in which cabbage or some other cruciferous vegetable figures prominently) and have become mainstays in my menu-planning.

Creamy Coleslaw

8 SERVINGS

As close to "classic" coleslaw as any of the slaws here, this is especially good with sandwich meals and veggie burgers. See the super-easy menu below. It's a quick and nourishing meal you can make even if dinnertime finds you exhausted.

One 16-ounce bag shredded coleslaw cabbage

1 medium green or red bell pepper, sliced into short, thin strips

¾ cup natural low-fat ranch dressing

2 tablespoons white balsamic or white wine vinegar

Freshly ground pepper to taste

Combine all of the ingredients in a serving bowl and mix thoroughly. Cover and let stand for 15 to 30 minutes before serving, stir again, and serve.

Calories: 53 • Total fat: 5 g
Protein: 0 g • Carbohydrate: 10 g
Cholesterol: 0 mg • Sodium: 208 mg

MENU

Veggie burgers on whole grain buns with your favorite fixings

***Corn Slaw** (page 34), or*

***Creamy Coleslaw** (this page), or*

***Cranberry Slaw** (page 37)*

Microwaved potatoes or sweet potatoes

Stretching the Definition of Salad

Green salads: Even the most common type of salad need not be boring. Turn an ordinary lettuce and tomato salad into a Greek salad by adding crumbled feta cheese, cured black olives, and a sharp vinaigrette. Or try combining lettuces with fruit (avocado, orange wedges, pears, or apples) and nuts.

Grain salads: Any sort of grain that remains firm and separate when cooked makes a substantial, nutty-tasting base for a cold salad. Long-grain brown rice is excellent, as are barley and bulgur. Combine cold grains with beans and vegetables and dress with a vinaigrette.

Pasta salads: Nearly guaranteed crowd-pleasers, pasta salads are quite easy to prepare. They make great summer meals, though they can be served any time of year.

Bean salads: Filling, high-protein bean salads benefit greatly from fresh herbs and strong vinaigrettes. Combining beans with cold grains or pasta is not only delicious, but also results in salads substantial enough to be entrées.

Cooked salads: The most popular cooked salad is potato salad. What would a picnic be without it? Cooked corn kernels also make a great base for a lively salad. Broccoli and cauliflower florets, steamed tender-crisp then cooled and marinated, make a welcome addition to most any meal.

Slaws: All-American slaws complement spicy or grilled foods as well as sandwich meals and veggie burgers. Most slaws are, of course, cabbage-based, but similar grated salads may be made from crisp turnips, carrots, peeled broccoli stems or exotic daikon radishes.

Fruit salads: During warm weather, many people prefer light desserts, and many cooks avoid baking, so fruit salads make refreshing finales to summer meals. When combining fresh fruit, anything goes, but there's no excuse for not making them as pleasing to look at as they are to eat. For a number of ideas, see Simple Summer Fruit Medleys (pages 252 to 253).

Cranberry Slaw

6 TO 8 SERVINGS

This slaw is a delightful companion to spicy dishes, veggie burgers, and bean dishes. It's festive enough to serve with more elaborate meals and at holiday celebrations.

Combine all of the ingredients in a serving bowl and mix thoroughly. Serve at once or cover and refrigerate until needed

One 16-ounce bag shredded coleslaw cabbage (preferably including carrots)

⅔ cup dried cranberries

¼ cup toasted slivered almonds

⅔ cup soy mayonnaise

1 tablespoon fresh lemon juice, optional

Calories: 107 • Total fat: 7 g
Protein: 1 g • Carbohydrate: 8 g
Cholesterol: 0 mg • Sodium: 155 mg

Red Cabbage, Carrot, and Apricot Salad

6 SERVINGS

Here's a nice change of pace from "white" coleslaw. It adds a refreshing note to spicy meals and adds vibrant color to the plate.

1 Grate the cabbage and carrots with a coarse grating attachment in a food processor or slice the cabbage into short thin shreds by hand and grate the carrots with a hand grater, or, if you'd prefer, slice them into thin rounds.

2 Combine the cabbage and carrots in a serving bowl with the remaining ingredients and mix well. Let the salad stand, covered, for about 30 minutes before serving.

½ small head red cabbage

3 to 4 medium or 2 large carrots

½ cup dried apricots, sliced

Juice of ½ lemon

½ cup low-fat vanilla yogurt

Calories: 79 • Total fat: 0 g
Protein: 2 g • Carbohydrate: 16 g
Cholesterol: 1 mg • Sodium: 38 mg

Summer Tomatoes with Fresh Herbs

4 SERVINGS

1½ to 2 pounds flavorful tomatoes, diced

¼ cup minced fresh herbs (basil, dill, or parsley, or any two herbs of your choice)

1 tablespoon extra-virgin olive oil

1 tablespoon fresh lemon juice

Calories: 70 • Total fat: 2 g
Protein: 1 g • Carbohydrate: 8 g
Cholesterol: 0 mg • Sodium: 16 mg

It goes without saying that this is best made with fresh, just-off-the-vine tomatoes!

Combine all of the ingredients in a serving container. Toss gently and serve.

Tomato, Mozzarella, and Bread Salad

4 SERVINGS

2 cups diced day-old Italian bread

1½ to 2 pounds flavorful tomatoes, diced

4 ounces fresh mozzarella cheese, finely diced

4 to 6 fresh basil leaves, thinly sliced

2 tablespoons extra-virgin olive oil

Salt to taste

Calories: 264 • Total fat: 13 g
Protein: 10 g • Carbohydrate: 25 g
Cholesterol: 22 mg • Sodium: 300 mg

A rich, delicious vehicle for showcasing summer's wonderful tomatoes, this salad is an enticing partner for light pasta dishes or pasta salads. See the menu accompanying Farfalle with Mushrooms (page 76).

1 Preheat the oven or toaster oven to 300°F.

2 Arrange the diced bread in a single layer on a baking sheet and bake until dry and crisp, stirring occasionally, 15 or 20 minutes.

3 Combine the remaining ingredients in a serving bowl and toss together. Just before serving, toss in the bread.

Cucumbers and Tomatoes in Yogurt

6 SERVINGS

This is a good palate-cooler to serve with curries and other spicy dishes. Use a creamy-textured yogurt.

Combine all of the ingredients in a serving container. Mix thoroughly and serve

1 large cucumber, peeled, seeded, and diced

2 to 3 medium flavorful tomatoes, diced

One 8-ounce container low-fat plain yogurt or soy yogurt, stirred until creamy

2 to 4 tablespoons chopped fresh dill, parsley, basil, or cilantro, optional

Salt and freshly ground pepper to taste

Calories: 43 • Total fat: 0 g
Protein: 3 g • Carbohydrate: 6 g
Cholesterol: 3 mg • Sodium: 35 mg

Israeli Salad

4 TO 6 SERVINGS

Sometimes Israeli salad is embellished with fresh herbs, olives, or radishes, which you can add if you're so inclined. But here it is in its essential form, the way my father-in-law, Arie Tabak, makes it. He also serves fresh rye bread with it, to soak up the delicious liquid that forms as it stands.

Combine the ingredients in a serving container and toss well. If time allows, let the salad stand at room temperature for 30 minutes or so before serving.

2 medium cucumbers, peeled, seeded, and finely diced

4 medium flavorful tomatoes, finely diced

1 medium green bell pepper, finely diced

1 tablespoon light olive oil

Juice of ½ to 1 lemon, or to taste

Salt and freshly ground pepper to taste

Calories: 64 • Total fat: 3 g
Protein: 1 g • Carbohydrate: 8 g
Cholesterol: 0 mg • Sodium: 11 mg

Marinated Beans

6 SERVINGS

Two 16-ounce cans black, pinto, or pink beans, or black-eyed peas (or a combination of two kinds), drained and rinsed

¼ to ½ cup finely chopped fresh parsley, or to taste

2 to 3 scallions, thinly sliced

½ cup natural low-fat vinaigrette

Freshly ground pepper to taste

Calories: 191 • Total fat: 3 g
Protein: 8 g • Carbohydrate: 31 g
Cholesterol: 0 mg • Sodium: 537 mg

Here's one of my favorites. Most any sort of bean takes well to embellishment with fresh herbs and a good vinaigrette. See the menu suggestion with Sweet Potato Soup (page 29).

Combine the ingredients in a serving container and toss well. Cover and marinate at least 2 hours in the refrigerator, and serve.

Super Flavor-Boosters for Salads

In many of the menus given in this book, I suggest serving a bountiful salad. Including some of the following ingredients with an array of fresh vegetables will help create salads that are abundant, flavorful, and colorful.

- Balsamic vinegar, dark or white
- Dried cranberries
- Chickpeas
- Cured olives (a few go a long way)
- Extra-virgin olive oil
- Feta cheese
- Flavored vinaigrettes (raspberry vinaigrette and balsamic vinaigrette are my favorites)
- Fresh herbs (especially dill)
- Fresh lemons (for juicing)
- Goat cheese (a crumbly type such as Montrachet)
- Pickled beets
- Roasted red peppers
- Toasted sunflower seeds
- Toasted almonds

Lentil and Feta Cheese Salad

6 SERVINGS

There's something appropriate about pairing feta cheese and lentils—perhaps it's the mingling of the salty and peppery flavors.

1 cup green or brown lentils

3 medium firm, flavorful tomatoes, or 5 to 6 plum tomatoes, diced

4 to 6 ounces feta cheese, crumbled

2 to 3 scallions, minced

½ cup natural low-fat vinaigrette

Salt and freshly ground pepper to taste

1 Rinse the lentils and check them for small stones. Combine in a saucepan with 3 cups water and bring to a simmer. Cover and simmer gently until done but still firm, about 30 minutes. Check frequently toward the end of cooking time to make sure the lentils don't become overcooked. Drain any excess water from the lentils, and rinse until cooled.

2 Combine the lentils with the remaining ingredients in a serving bowl and toss together. Serve at once or cover and refrigerate until needed.

Calories: 260 • Total fat: 9 g
Protein: 14 g • Carbohydrate: 31 g
Cholesterol: 21 mg • Sodium: 447 mg

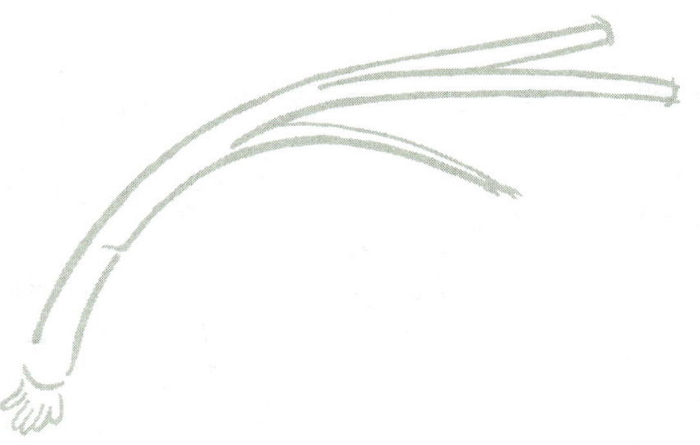

MENU

Lentil and Feta Cheese Salad *(this page)*

Warm pita bread

Spinach Rice *(page 92)*

Cured black olives and sliced green bell peppers

Chickpea Salad with Roasted Peppers

4 SERVINGS

One 20-ounce can chickpeas, drained and rinsed

One 12-ounce jar roasted red peppers, drained and cut into strips

Juice of ½ to 1 lemon, or to taste

1 tablespoon extra-virgin olive oil

Freshly ground pepper to taste

Dark green lettuce leaves

Calories: 211 • Total fat: 4 g
Protein: 6 g • Carbohydrate: 35 g
Cholesterol: 0 mg • Sodium: 307 mg

I often make this to serve with a light pasta dish such as Pasta with Asparagus (page 67).

1 Combine the chickpeas, red peppers, lemon juice, and olive oil in a mixing bowl and toss together. Season with pepper and toss again.

2 Line individual plates or shallow bowls with a few lettuce leaves and divide the salad among them.

Chickpea and Tomato Salad

4 TO 6 SERVINGS

One 20-ounce can chickpeas, drained and rinsed

1½ pounds flavorful ripe tomatoes, diced

Juice of ½ to 1 lemon, or to taste

1 tablespoon extra-virgin olive oil

Thinly shredded lettuce, as desired

Freshly ground pepper to taste

Calories: 188 • Total fat: 4 g
Protein: 7 g • Carbohydrate: 29 g
Cholesterol: 0 mg • Sodium: 282 mg

The shape, texture, and unique flavor of chickpeas make them a perfect salad ingredient. I will often add chickpeas to a salad when the meal's main dish is on the lighter side. See the menu accompanying Pasta with Asparagus (page 67).

Combine the ingredients in a serving container and toss well. Serve at once or refrigerate until needed.

Black Bean Salad with Feta and Red Peppers

6 SERVINGS

A hefty salad like this one can easily share center stage with a grain or pasta dish as shown in the menus for Bulgur with Cabbage and Green Beans (page 109) and Summer Pasta with Fresh Tomatoes (page 64).

Two 16-ounce cans black beans, drained and rinsed

2 medium red bell peppers, cut into short thin strips

½ cup natural low-fat vinaigrette (try balsamic vinaigrette)

½ cup chopped fresh parsley

½ to ⅔ cup crumbled feta or goat cheese (such as Montrachet)

1 Combine the beans, red bell peppers, vinaigrette, and parsley in a mixing bowl and toss well.

2 Divide the salad among individual plates or shallow bowls. Top each serving with some of the feta cheese.

Calories: 253 • Total fat: 8 g
Protein: 12 g • Carbohydrate: 33 g
Cholesterol: 19 mg • Sodium: 776 mg

Black Bean and Corn Salad

6 SERVINGS

One 16- to 20-ounce can black beans, drained and rinsed

3 to 3½ cups cooked fresh or frozen corn kernels, thawed

One 6-ounce jar roasted red peppers, drained and cut into strips

2 medium celery stalks, diced

⅓ cup natural low-fat vinaigrette (try a raspberry vinaigrette for a nice flavor twist)

Calories: 190 • Total fat: 2 g
Protein: 6 g • Carbohydrate: 35 g
Cholesterol: 0 mg • Sodium: 329 mg

Black beans and corn team up to create a substantial salad that's a great potluck or party dish.

Combine the ingredients in a serving container and toss well. Serve at once or refrigerate until needed.

A BUFFET OF HEARTY COLD DISHES FOR COMPANY

Black Bean and Corn Salad *(this page)*

Cranberry Slaw *(page 37)*

Greek-Flavored Potato Salad *(page 56)*

Fruited Bulgur Salad *(page 48)*

Pasta and Broccoli Salad *(page 58)*

Tropical Fruit Medley *(page 244)*

Avocado and Pinto Bean Salad

6 SERVINGS

Avocado is one of the most sensuous foods I know. Don't be afraid of its fat content—it's the kind of fat that's good for you. See the menu with Tomato and Green Chili Quesadillas or Soft Tacos (page 173).

Two 16-ounce cans pinto beans, drained and rinsed

3 medium tomatoes, diced

2 to 3 tablespoons minced fresh cilantro

⅓ to ½ cup natural low-fat vinaigrette, or as needed

Freshly ground pepper to taste

1 large avocado, pitted, peeled, and diced

Combine the beans, tomatoes, cilantro, vinaigrette, and pepper in a serving bowl and toss well. Just before serving, stir in the diced avocado.

Calories: 282 • Total fat: 10 g
Protein: 10 g • Carbohydrate: 39 g
Cholesterol: 0 mg • Sodium: 512 mg

Corn Relish Salad

6 SERVINGS

Like slaws, this salad is nifty served with sandwiches and veggie burgers. It's a great choice for taking on picnics as well.

One 16-ounce package frozen corn kernels, thawed

1 small red bell pepper, finely diced

2 large celery stalks, finely diced

2 scallions, green parts only, thinly sliced

½ cup natural low-fat vinaigrette, or to taste

Salt and freshly ground pepper to taste

Combine the ingredients in a serving container and toss well. Serve at once or refrigerate until needed.

Calories: 140 • Total fat: 2 g
Protein: 2 g • Carbohydrate: 24 g
Cholesterol: 0 mg • Sodium: 194 mg

6 SERVINGS

Barley or Rice and Corn Salad

1 cup pearl barley or brown rice, rinsed

2 cups cooked fresh corn kernels (from 3 medium ears) or one 10-ounce package frozen corn kernels, thawed

1 pint cherry tomatoes, halved

½ cup chopped fresh parsley or ¼ cup chopped fresh dill

½ to ⅔ cup natural low-fat vinaigrette, or as needed (try balsamic vinaigrette)

Salt and freshly ground pepper to taste

Calories: 162 • Total fat: 5 g
Protein: 3 g • Carbohydrate: 28 g
Cholesterol: 0 mg • Sodium: 209 mg

While this is good with either grain suggested, I prefer making it with barley. Its texture contrasted with that of the corn is quite pleasant. Like corn relish, this is a sturdy picnic dish and is also a good accompaniment to grilled or roasted vegetables.

1 Bring 3 cups water to a rapid simmer in a saucepan and stir in the barley or rice. Cover and simmer gently until the water has been absorbed, about 35 minutes. Remove from the heat and set aside, uncovered, until room temperature.

2 Combine the cooled barley or rice with the remaining ingredients in a serving bowl and toss well. Serve at once or cover and refrigerate until needed.

Dilled Barley and Green Bean Salad

6 SERVINGS

In almost any barley dish I make, whether soup, salad, or pilaf, my flavoring of choice is nearly always dill. This duo seems to have a natural affinity for each other.

1 cup pearl barley, rinsed

8 to 10 ounces fresh green beans or one 10-ounce package frozen cut green beans, thawed

2 medium carrots, thinly sliced

¼ cup minced fresh dill

½ cup natural low-fat vinaigrette

Salt and freshly ground pepper to taste

1 Bring 3 cups water to a rapid simmer in a saucepan and stir in the barley. Cover and simmer gently until the water has been absorbed, about 35 minutes. Remove from the heat and set aside, uncovered, until room temperature.

2 Meanwhile, if using fresh green beans, trim them and cut in half. Steam or microwave the fresh or frozen green beans until done to your liking. In either case, make sure the green beans are still bright and green, and rinse under cool water until they are cool.

3 Combine the cooled barley and green beans with the remaining ingredients in a serving bowl and toss well. Serve at once or cover and refrigerate until needed.

Calories: 141 • Total fat: 2 g
Protein: 3 g • Carbohydrate: 24 g
Cholesterol: 0 mg • Sodium: 190 mg

Fruited Bulgur Salad

4 TO 6 SERVINGS

1 cup bulgur

1 cup mixed dried fruit bits (see note)

2 medium celery stalks, finely diced

½ cup natural low-fat honey-mustard dressing

⅓ cup toasted sliced or slivered almonds

Calories: 297 • Total fat: 9 g
Protein: 7 g • Carbohydrate: 48 g
Cholesterol: 0 mg • Sodium: 237 mg

This makes a splendid companion to curried vegetable dishes, as in the menu suggested here.

1 Boil 2 cups water. Pour the water over the bulgur in a heatproof container and cover. Let stand for 30 minutes, then fluff with a fork. Allow the bulgur to cool, uncovered, until it is at room temperature.

2 Transfer the bulgur to a serving container. Add the remaining ingredients, stir to combine, and serve. If making ahead of time, add the almonds just before serving.

Note: Dried fruit bits are shelved with other packaged dried fruits in supermarkets or natural foods stores.

MENU

Fruited Bulgur Salad *(this page)*

Curried Sweet Potatoes with Green Peas *(page 195)*

Steamed cauliflower

Diced fresh tomatoes

Couscous Salad

6 TO 8 SERVINGS

Here's a light grain salad using versatile, quick-cooking couscous.

1 cup couscous

1 medium green bell pepper, cut into short, thin strips

4 to 6 radishes, thinly sliced

2 cups diced flavorful tomatoes

⅓ to ½ cup natural low-fat vinaigrette dressing, or as needed

Salt and freshly ground pepper to taste

1 Boil 2 cups water. Pour the boiling water over the couscous in a heat-proof container. Cover and let stand for 15 minutes, fluff with a fork, and allow to cool to room temperature.

2 Combine the couscous with the remaining ingredients in a serving container and toss well. Serve at once or cover and refrigerate until needed.

Calories: 111 • Total fat: 2 g
Protein: 3 g • Carbohydrate: 19 g
Cholesterol: 0 mg • Sodium: 130 mg

Long-Grain and Wild Rice Salad

6 TO 8 SERVINGS

1½ cups long-grain and wild rice mix

2 large celery stalks, diced

2 large carrots, finely diced

One 12-ounce jar marinated artichokes, chopped, with liquid

¼ cup minced parsley or sliced scallion

Salt and freshly ground pepper to taste

Calories: 129 • Total fat: 0 g
Protein: 3 g • Carbohydrate: 27 g
Cholesterol: 0 mg • Sodium: 84 mg

Wild rice adds a nutty crunch and elegance to salads. This is a wonderful companion to squash dishes such as Stewed Spaghetti Squash, page 220. It's also one of the first things I would consider packing for a fall hike or picnic. Look for long-grain and wild rice mix shelved near rice in well-stocked supermarkets.

1 Bring 4 cups water to a simmer in a saucepan. Stir in the rice mixture, cover, and simmer gently until the water is absorbed, about 35 minutes. If the rice isn't done to your liking, add another ½ cup water and continue to simmer until absorbed. Remove the saucepan from the heat and allow to cool, uncovered, to room temperature.

2 Combine the rice with the remaining ingredients in a serving container and toss well. Serve at once or cover and refrigerate until needed.

Mixed Greens with Beets and Walnuts

4 SERVINGS

4 to 6 ounces mixed baby greens (mesclun), or more as desired

One 12-ounce jar pickled beets, drained

¼ cup finely chopped walnuts

1 tablespoon light olive oil

1 tablespoon lemon juice or white balsamic vinegar, or to taste

Calories: 142 • Total fat: 7 g
Protein: 1 g • Carbohydrate: 16 g
Cholesterol: 0 mg • Sodium: 229 mg

Pickled beets are an appetizing addition to a salad of mixed greens.

Combine the ingredients in a serving bowl, toss well, and serve.

Mixed Greens with Tomatoes, Feta, and Olives

4 TO 6 SERVINGS

This is a modified version of Greek salad. I like to serve it with spinach dishes, as suggested in the menu with Spinach Rice (page 92). Or serve it with Hummus (page 229) and warm pita bread if you are expecting company for lunch.

4 to 6 ounces mixed baby greens (mesclun) or dark green lettuce leaves, or more as desired

3 to 4 medium flavorful tomatoes, diced

4 ounces crumbled feta cheese

⅓ to ½ cup black olives, preferably cured

1 tablespoon extra-virgin olive oil

Combine the ingredients in a serving bowl, toss well, and serve.

Calories: 120 • Total fat: 10 g
Protein: 4 g • Carbohydrate: 4 g
Cholesterol: 20 mg • Sodium: 343 mg

Mixed Greens

Fresh mixed greens, once the exclusive domain of upscale restaurants, are now readily available in almost every supermarket's produce section. Often called mesclun, it's also sold as "spring mix" or "baby greens." This melange of exotic lettuces can dress up a simple meal in a big way.

Mixed greens show up often in my salads. I enjoy the brisk flavors and variety of textures and colors. You need not dilute their appeal with a lot of extra ingredients. Honestly, a splash of olive oil and balsamic vinegar is enough to do them justice. But if you'd like a little more embellishment, the next few recipes are my favorite ways to dress up these lively greens.

What might you find in these mixes? There's nearly always frisée, a lacy, light-green relative of endive, as well as radicchio, a red chicory well loved in Italian cuisine. Other greens that may show up are arugula, mâche (also called "corn salad"), amaranth, and sorrel. Often an Asian green such as mizuna or tat-soi is added as well.

The per-pound price of mixed greens is high, but unless you're making a party-sized salad, you will be purchasing only a few ounces at a time. When buying them, let your eyes be a guide to their freshness. It's easy to tell when they've had it—they lose their springy shapes and go limp. Note that the amounts given in the following recipes are meant as guidelines; no need for measuring.

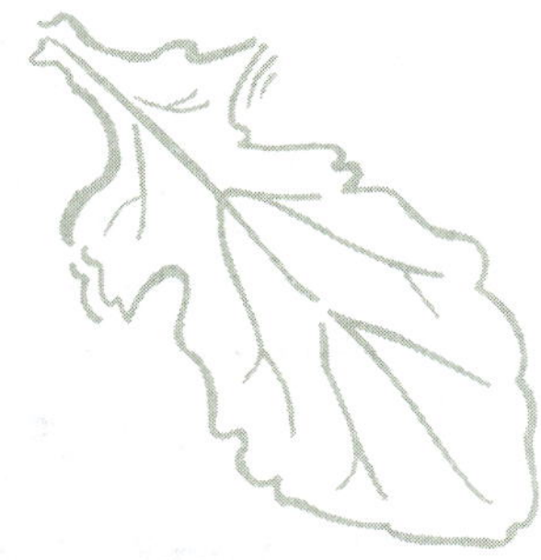

Mixed Greens with Oranges and Almonds

4 SERVINGS

4 to 6 ounces mixed baby greens (mesclun), or more as desired

3 to 4 clementines or small seedless oranges, peeled and sectioned

¼ cup toasted slivered almonds

Natural low-fat honey-mustard or raspberry vinaigrette dressing, to taste

Several thinly sliced rings of red onion, optional

Calories: 153 • Total fat: 5 g
Protein: 5 g • Carbohydrate: 19 g
Cholesterol: 25 mg • Sodium: 320 mg

Here's a salad sure to brighten a winter meal, when clementines are in season.

Combine the ingredients in a serving bowl, toss well, and serve.

Mixed Greens with Pears, Cranberries, and Goat Cheese

4 SERVINGS

4 to 6 ounces mixed baby greens (mesclun), or more as desired

2 firm pears (preferably Bosc), cored and diced

¼ cup dried cranberries

4 ounces crumbled goat cheese

Natural low-fat balsamic vinaigrette or raspberry vinaigrette dressing to taste

Calories: 168 • Total fat: 8 g
Protein: 5 g • Carbohydrate: 17 g
Cholesterol: 25 mg • Sodium: 452 mg

I'm not one to eat pears out of hand, but I like them—slightly underripe—in salads. Contrasted with the pleasant bite of goat cheese and the sweetness of dried cranberries, this salad is a party for the palate.

Combine the ingredients in a serving bowl, toss well, and serve.

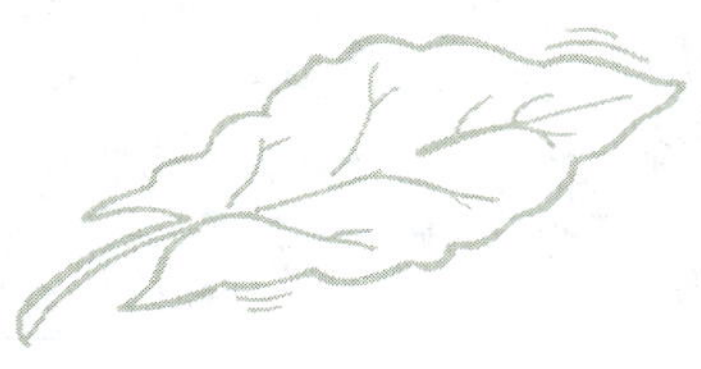

Mixed Greens with Wild Mushrooms

This salad makes an earthy companion to light pasta dishes. Look for packages of fresh mixed wild mushrooms in the produce section of well-stocked supermarkets. They contain a melange of three or four varieties, which may include cremini, shiitake, oyster, or others.

4 TO 6 SERVINGS

One 6- to 8-ounce package fresh mixed wild mushrooms

1 tablespoon extra-virgin olive oil

1 tablespoon balsamic vinegar, plus more for salad

4 to 6 ounces mixed baby greens (mesclun), or more as desired

1 cup halved cherry tomatoes or diced flavorful tomatoes

1 Clean the mushrooms, remove and discard any tough or withered stems, and slice the caps.

2 Heat 1 teaspoon of the oil along with the vinegar slowly in a skillet. Add the mushrooms, and stir to coat. Cover and cook over medium heat until the mushrooms are just wilted, about 5 minutes. Transfer the mushrooms to a serving container and allow them to cool.

3 Once the mushrooms have cooled, combine them (along with the liquid) with the greens and tomatoes. Add the remaining 2 teaspoons oil and additional vinegar to taste, toss well, and serve.

Calories: 31 • Total fat: 3 g
Protein: 1 g • Carbohydrate: 4 g
Cholesterol: 0 mg • Sodium: 7 mg

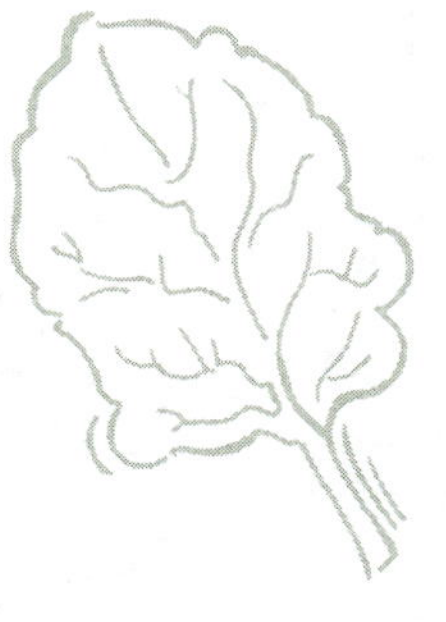

Simple Potato Salad

6 SERVINGS

6 medium-large red-skinned potatoes

½ cup soy mayonnaise

2 teaspoons Dijon mustard

2 celery stalks, diced

2 scallions, thinly sliced

Salt and freshly ground pepper to taste

Calories: 168 • Total fat: 4 g
Protein: 2 g • Carbohydrate: 29 g
Cholesterol: 0 mg • Sodium: 199 mg

Going on a picnic? Don't leave home without this salad, which pares potato salad down to its marvelous essence. This is also excellent with grilled or broiled soyfoods or seitan, as in the menu accompanying Baked Barbecue Tofu and Peppers (page 141).

1 If you'd like to keep the skins on the potatoes, scrub them well. Microwave or bake the potatoes in their skins until done but still firm. Let the potatoes cool to room temperature.

2 If you prefer to use peeled potatoes in the salad, slip their skins off when they have cooled. Dice the potatoes into approximately ¾-inch chunks, and place them in a serving container.

3 Combine the mayonnaise and mustard in a small bowl and stir together. Pour over the potatoes, add the remaining ingredients, and mix well. Cover and refrigerate until needed or serve at once.

AN ABUNDANT PICNIC

Simple Potato Salad *(this page)*

Corn Relish Salad *(page 45)*

Fresh bread

Chickpea Spread *(page 239)*

Baby carrots and cherry tomatoes

Simple Summer Fruit Medley *of your choice (pages 252 to 253)*

Warm Potato Salad with Goat Cheese

4 SERVINGS

A few choice ingredients contribute to this elegant potato salad. If you like goat cheese, you'll love this one.

2 to 2½ pounds tiny new potatoes or 6 medium red-skinned potatoes, scrubbed

½ cup natural low-fat vinaigrette, preferably balsamic

4 to 6 ounces mixed baby greens (mesclun)

4 ounces crumbled goat cheese (such as Montrachet)

1 Bake or microwave the potatoes until done but still firm. When cool enough to handle, cut the new potatoes in half, or cut the regular potatoes into large dice.

2 Combine the potatoes with the vinaigrette in a mixing bowl and stir gently. Let stand for about 10 minutes.

3 Divide the greens among 4 salad plates or shallow bowls. Drain off any excess vinaigrette from the potatoes in a small container and drizzle it over the greens.

4 Divide the potatoes among the salad plates, placing them atop the greens. Top each serving with goat cheese and serve.

Calories: 352 • Total fat: 11 g
Protein: 7 g • Carbohydrate: 56 g
Cholesterol: 25 mg • Sodium: 597 mg

Greek-Flavored Potato Salad

6 SERVINGS

5 to 6 medium-large red-skinned potatoes, scrubbed

10 to 12 ounces fresh green beans (or one 10-ounce package frozen cut green beans, thawed)

½ cup chopped pitted black olives, preferably cured

4 ounces feta or crumbled goat cheese (such as Montrachet)

½ cup natural low-fat vinaigrette, preferably balsamic vinaigrette

Freshly ground pepper to taste

Calories: 236 • Total fat: 10 g
Protein: 5 g • Carbohydrate: 32 g
Cholesterol: 17 mg • Sodium: 481 mg

An exercise in elegant simplicity, this salad makes a delicious contribution to a buffet of room-temperature dishes for company.

1 Bake or microwave the potatoes until done but still firm. When cool enough to handle, but warm, cut into large dice.

2 If using fresh green beans, trim them and cut them in half crosswise. Steam the fresh or frozen green beans with a little water in a covered saucepan, or in a covered container in the microwave, until tender-crisp, about 5 minutes. Refresh under cool water until just warm, then drain thoroughly.

3 Combine the potatoes and green beans in a serving container with the remaining ingredients and toss well. This is best served just warm or at room temperature.

Curried Potato-Tomato Salad

6 SERVINGS

Potatoes and tomatoes in a curry-flavored yogurt make a luscious summertime treat.

5 to 6 medium-large red-skinned potatoes

⅔ cup low-fat plain yogurt or soy yogurt, or as needed

1 to 2 teaspoons good-quality curry powder, or to taste

3 medium flavorful ripe tomatoes, or 4 to 5 plum tomatoes, diced

¼ cup chopped fresh cilantro

Salt and freshly ground pepper to taste

1 If you'd like to keep the skins on the potatoes, scrub them well. Microwave or bake the potatoes in their skins until done but still firm. Let the potatoes cool to room temperature.

2 If you prefer to use peeled potatoes in the salad, slip their skins off when they have cooled. Dice the potatoes into approximately ¾-inch chunks, and place them in a serving container.

3 Combine the yogurt and curry powder in a small bowl and stir together. Pour over the potatoes, add the remaining ingredients, and mix well. Cover and refrigerate until needed or serve at once.

Calories: 146 • Total fat: 0 g
Protein: 3 g • Carbohydrate: 32 g
Cholesterol: 2 mg • Sodium: 32 mg

Pasta and Broccoli Salad

6 SERVINGS

8 ounces pasta, any small shape (rotini, gemelli, or medium shells work well)

2 medium or large broccoli crowns, cut into bite-size pieces, steamed until tender-crisp, and rinsed until cool

½ cup pitted black olives, halved

1 medium red bell pepper, cut into short thin strips

⅓ cup natural low-fat vinaigrette, or as needed

Salt and freshly ground pepper to taste

Calories: 94 • Total fat: 5 g
Protein: 2 g • Carbohydrate: 11 g
Cholesterol: 0 mg • Sodium: 203 mg

Broccoli is one of the most harmonious additions to pasta salad. Try this in the menu with Pizza Margherita (page 154).

1 Cook the pasta according to package directions until al dente. Rinse under cold running water until the pasta cools. Drain and transfer to a serving container.

2 Combine the pasta with the remaining ingredients and toss well. Cover and refrigerate until needed or serve at once.

Cold Angel Hair Pasta with Fresh Corn and Tomatoes

6 SERVINGS

A lovely cold dish to be enjoyed in late summer, this is a great vehicle for the season's ripe tomatoes. This is delicious with Creamy Pinto Bean Puree (page 16) for a satisfying summer meal.

8 to 10 ounces angel hair pasta (capellini)

2 cups cooked fresh corn kernels (from 3 medium ears)

2 pounds flavorful tomatoes, diced

½ cup natural low-fat vinaigrette (try balsamic vinaigrette)

6 to 8 fresh basil leaves, thinly sliced

Salt and freshly ground pepper to taste

1 Cook the pasta according to package directions until al dente. Rinse under cold running water until the pasta cools. Drain and transfer to a serving container.

2 Combine the pasta with the remaining ingredients and toss well. Cover and refrigerate until needed or serve at once.

Calories: 170 • Total fat: 4 g
Protein: 4 g • Carbohydrate: 29 g
Cholesterol: 0 mg • Sodium: 191 mg

Pasta "Tuna" Salad

6 SERVINGS

8 ounces pasta, any small shape (twists or small shells work well)

One 8-ounce package baked tofu, finely diced (see headnote)

2 large celery stalks, finely diced

⅓ cup chopped black olives

½ cup soy mayonnaise

Salt and freshly ground pepper to taste

Calories: 187 • Total fat: 9 g
Protein: 10 g • Carbohydrate: 14 g
Cholesterol: 0 mg • Sodium: 381 mg

For more information on baked tofu, see page 136. I'd like to see this superb product go mainstream! See the menu with Cold Fresh Tomato Soup (page 17). This would also be just as good served with Fresh Tomato and Corn Soup (page 18).

1 Cook the pasta according to package directions until al dente. Rinse under cold running water until the pasta cools. Drain and transfer to a serving container.

2 Combine the pasta with the remaining ingredients and toss well. Cover and refrigerate until needed or serve at once.

Pasta, Presently

CHAPTER 3

Pasta is like an easygoing friend who is always there for you. Goodness knows, pasta has always been there for me, from the noodle soups of my childhood, to the endless pasta meals during college, to my early days of parenting two babies. During those times, I would often rush frantically into the kitchen to cook up a pot of noodles, knowing it was the one thing everyone would eat. My sons are now school-aged, but still, not a week goes by when pasta doesn't figure into the menu at least once or twice. Even if I'm preparing a sauce the kids may not care for, I can set aside some of the pasta to serve it warm and buttered; they'll never turn it down.

The beauty of pasta is that, with dozens of shapes and sauces to mix and match, it can never get boring. It cooks quickly, it's nourishing, and yes, it's low in fat. In the time it takes to bring water to a boil and cook the pasta, a sauce with a compatible cooking time can be prepared. More often than not, a pasta meal can be completed with some good bread and a salad. The late James Beard summed it up best when he said that "the only true and classical way to eat pasta is with gusto."

Easy Vegetable Lasagna

6 TO 8 SERVINGS

One 28-ounce jar natural, good-quality pasta sauce

One 8-ounce package no-boil lasagna noodles

One 15-ounce container part-skim ricotta cheese

About 3 cups lightly steamed vegetables of your choice (broccoli florets, zucchini, or fresh spinach)

One 8-ounce package part-skim grated mozzarella cheese

Calories: 282 • Total fat: 11 g
Protein: 20 g • Carbohydrate: 23 g
Cholesterol: 37 mg • Sodium: 536 mg

I used to think of lasagna as quite labor-intensive until no-boil noodles came to the rescue. It's always a great company or potluck favorite. Now that lasagna is so easy to assemble, you might consider it everyday fare (remember, though, it does take time to bake). This is hearty enough to complete with fresh bread and a big salad.

1 Preheat the oven to 350°F.

2 Use a 9 by 13-inch casserole dish. Spread a thin layer of pasta sauce on the bottom, and line the bottom of the casserole with 1 layer of lasagna noodles. Use as many as needed to line the pan; 3 or 4 should do.

3 In a mixing bowl, thin the ricotta cheese with about ¼ cup water. Stir until well blended, then gently and carefully spread one-third of it over the noodles with a cake spatula.

4 Spoon an even layer of about one-third of the remaining pasta sauce over the ricotta. Sprinkle about one-third of the vegetables over the sauce. Follow with about one-third of the mozzarella cheese, then start the layers over again with the noodles. Repeat twice, ending with the mozzarella cheese.

5 Cover and bake until the noodles are tender (test by piercing through all of the layers with a fork), 35 to 40 minutes. If you like, bake uncovered until the cheese begins to turn golden, about 5 minutes more. Remove from the oven and let stand for 5 minutes. Cut into squares to serve.

Variation: Substitute 1 pound soft tofu, drained and well mashed, for the ricotta cheese.

Pasta Cooking Tips

In most pasta recipes, few cooking instructions are given aside from cooking in plenty of rapidly simmering water, then draining. And honestly, there isn't much more to it than just that. Still, I do have a few general tips for cooking pasta that may come in handy:

- Though a precise amount is not necessary, use plenty of cooking water to prevent a gummy texture. There is a rule of thumb: 2½ quarts of water per 8 ounces of pasta. Salting the cooking water is optional (I don't).

- After bringing water to a rolling boil in a large cooking pot, add the pasta, and stir several times while the water returns to a boil to prevent clumping. Keep the water going at a very rapid simmer (it need not be an angry boil!) until the pasta is cooked al dente—that is, done, but with a good resistance to the bite.

- Pasta often seems to take somewhat more (or less) time to cook than package directions indicate. So refer to the package as a guideline only. Toward the end of cooking time, test frequently for al dente texture.

- Drain the pasta immediately once it is done. Rinse it only if it's going into a cold salad. Have the sauce or additional ingredients ready by the time the pasta is cooked and toss together immediately to prevent the pasta from sticking together.

Summer Pasta with Fresh Tomatoes

4 SERVINGS

8 to 10 ounces rotini (pasta twists) or other short chunky shape

2 to 2½ pounds flavorful juicy tomatoes, diced

2 tablespoons extra-virgin olive oil

Juice of ½ lemon or lime

6 to 8 fresh basil leaves, thinly sliced, or to taste

Salt and freshly ground pepper to taste

Calories: 182 • Total fat: 7 g
Protein: 4 g • Carbohydrate: 25 g
Cholesterol: 0 mg • Sodium: 21 mg

One of my favorite ways to use summer's heavenly ripe tomatoes is to toss them, uncooked, with warm pasta.

1 Cook the pasta according to package directions and drain.

2 Combine the pasta with the remaining ingredients, including the juices from the chopped tomatoes and toss well. Serve at once or let stand until room temperature before serving.

MENU

A COOL MENU FOR A WARM SUMMER NIGHT

Summer Pasta with Fresh Tomatoes *(this page)*

Black Bean Salad with Feta and Red Peppers *(page 43)*

Fresh focaccia

Simple Summer Fruit Medley *of your choice (pages 252 to 253)*

Southwestern Salsa Pasta

4 TO 6 SERVINGS

Salsa is an easy way to dress up pasta, resulting in an offbeat, festive dish.

8 ounces rotini (pasta twists)

One 16-ounce can black beans, drained and rinsed

1 cup cooked fresh corn (from 1 to 2 ears) or frozen corn kernels, thawed

One 16-ounce jar tomato salsa, mild or medium-hot, or to taste

2 to 3 scallions, thinly sliced

1 Cook the pasta according to package directions and drain.

2 Meanwhile, combine the beans, corn, salsa, and scallions in a saucepan and bring to a simmer.

3 Combine the pasta and sauce, toss well, and serve.

Calories: 187 • Total fat: 0 g
Protein: 8 g • Carbohydrate: 37 g
Cholesterol: 0 mg • Sodium: 442 mg

MENU

Southwestern Salsa Pasta *(this page)*

Avocado and Ricotta Soft Tacos *(page 174)*

Coleslaw cabbage, dressed with vinaigrette

Whatever Shape You Fancy

With literally hundreds of pasta shapes to choose from, how do you decide which to use with what sauce? There are no rules set in stone, but here are a few tips to help you decide:

- Long, thin pasta or noodles are compatible with lighter or smoother sauces.
- Large pasta shapes, including penne, mostaccioli, or rigatoni, are perfect with chunkier sauces.
- Spiral pastas (such as rotini or fusilli) are probably the most versatile. They're perfect for highly textured sauces that would slide off most any other shape. They're small enough to be used in soups and substantial enough for cold pasta salads.
- Smooth-surfaced pastas, including ziti, gemelli, or farfalle (bowties), are just right for creamy and smooth sauces.
- Kids like small pasta shapes (elbow macaroni, tiny shells, tiny tubes), thin noodles (angel hair pasta, fine egg noodles), and fun shapes (wagon wheels, stars, alphabet noodles).

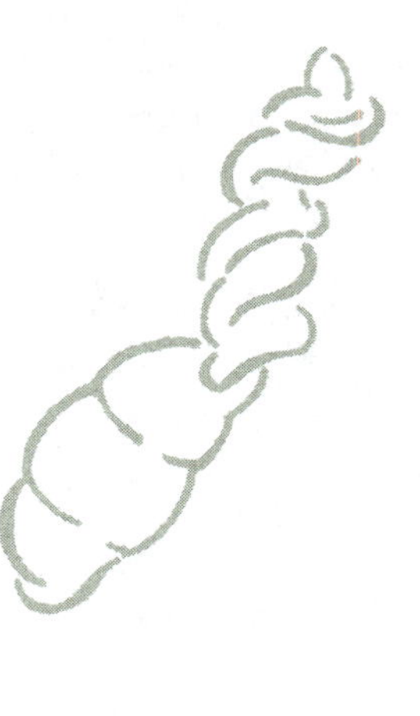

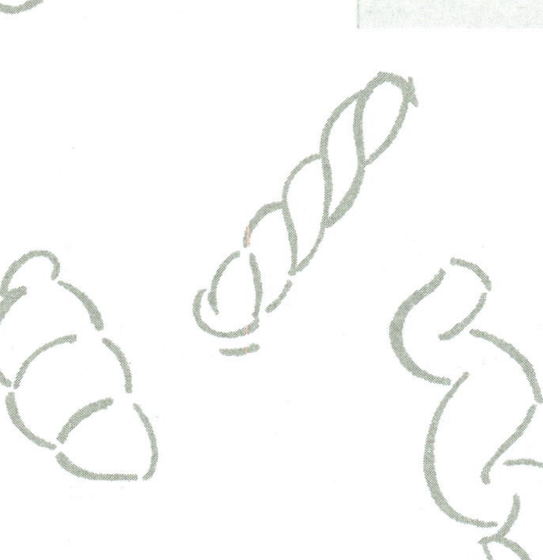

Pasta with Asparagus

4 SERVINGS

Here's a simple way to say "happy spring." Do try this with goat cheese—the contrast of its slight bite and the mild flavor of asparagus is tantalizing.

1 Cook the pasta according to package directions and drain.

2 Meanwhile, trim the woody ends from the asparagus spears and scrape any tough skin with a vegetable peeler (fresh slender spring asparagus usually needs no scraping). Cut the spears into 1- to 2-inch-long pieces.

3 Heat the oil in a large skillet and add the garlic. Sauté over low heat until golden, about 1 minute. Add the asparagus and a small amount of water. Cover and steam until the asparagus is done to your liking but still bright green.

4 Combine the pasta, asparagus mixture, and cheese in a serving container and toss well. Season with salt and pepper, and serve at once.

10 to 12 ounces pasta, any short shape

12 to 16 ounces asparagus, preferably slender

2 tablespoons extra-virgin olive oil

3 to 4 garlic cloves, minced

½ cup crumbled goat cheese (such as Montrachet), grated fresh Parmesan cheese, or crumbled feta cheese

Salt and freshly ground pepper to taste

Calories: 244 • Total fat: 12 g
Protein: 9 g • Carbohydrate: 23 g
Cholesterol: 25 mg • Sodium: 321 mg

MENU

Pasta with Asparagus *(this page)*

Chickpea and Tomato Salad *(page 42)*

or

Chickpea Salad with Roasted Peppers *(page 42)*

Fresh Italian bread

Baby carrots and sliced red peppers

Hungarian Cabbage Noodles

6 SERVINGS

2 tablespoons light olive oil

1 large onion, quartered and thinly sliced

One 16-ounce bag shredded coleslaw cabbage

12 ounces wide egg noodles, preferably yolk-free

1 tablespoon poppy seeds, or as needed

Salt and freshly ground pepper to taste

Calories: 144 • Total fat: 6 g
Protein: 4 g • Carbohydrate: 19 g
Cholesterol: 18 mg • Sodium: 15 mg

This tasty Slavic dish can be made in a snap with shredded coleslaw cabbage. For a complete meal, accompany each serving with a couple of links of sautéed soy "sausages" and a salad of dark green lettuce and tomatoes.

1 Heat the oil in an extra-wide skillet or stir-fry pan. Add the onion and sauté over medium heat until golden. Add the cabbage and a small amount of water; cover and cook, stirring occasionally, until the cabbage is limp and just beginning to brown lightly, 10 to 12 minutes.

2 Meanwhile, cook the noodles according to package directions and drain. Transfer to a large serving container.

3 Add the cabbage mixture and poppy seeds to the noodles and toss gently but thoroughly. Season to taste with salt and lots of pepper, and serve.

Pasta with Red Pepper Sauce

4 TO 6 SERVINGS

The secret ingredient in this smooth sauce is silken tofu. Blended silken tofu makes a great base for sauces that seem creamy, but are actually pure soy goodness. Look for it in your supermarket's produce section (as well as in natural foods stores). Complete this meal with some fresh bread and a bountiful tossed salad. Or serve it with any of the mixed greens salads on pages 50 to 53.

12 ounces pasta, any short chunky shape

1 cup frozen green peas, thawed

2 tablespoons nonhydrogenated margarine

One 12-ounce jar roasted red peppers, drained

One 12.3-ounce package firm silken tofu

1 teaspoon salt, or to taste

Freshly ground pepper to taste

1 Cook the pasta according to package directions. Plunge the peas into the pasta cooking water to heat them. Drain the pasta and return to the pot. Stir in the margarine to melt.

2 Meanwhile, combine the peppers and tofu in a food processor and process until smoothly pureed.

3 Combine the sauce with the pasta and peas in the pot and stir together. Cook just until the sauce is heated through. Season with salt and pepper, and serve.

Calories: 168 • Total fat: 6 g
Protein: 8 g • Carbohydrate: 21 g
Cholesterol: 0 mg • Sodium: 67 mg

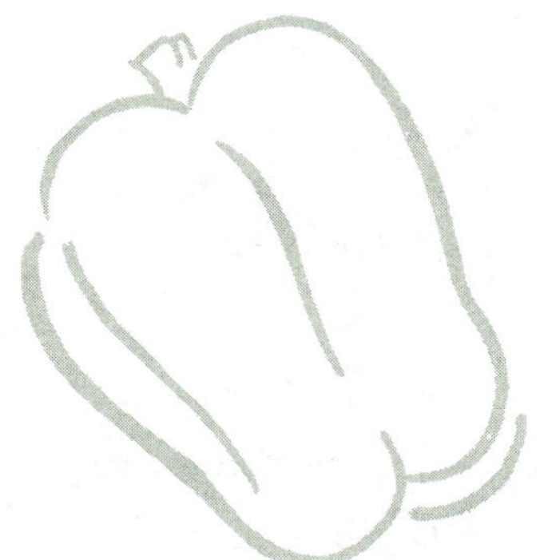

Pasta with Creamed Spinach

4 TO 6 SERVINGS

12 ounces pasta, any short shape

One recipe Contemporary Creamed Spinach (page 212)

Calories: 181 • Total fat: 5 g
Protein: 9 g • Carbohydrate: 23 g
Cholesterol: 0 mg • Sodium: 162 mg

Spinach fans, this pasta dish is for you. This nourishing green, enveloped in silken tofu and tossed with pasta, will comfort your taste buds and make you feel virtuous at the same time.

1 Cook the pasta according to package directions, drain, and return to the pot.

2 Meanwhile, prepare the creamed spinach recipe. Combine it with the pasta in the pot and stir together. Cook just until the sauce is heated through. Serve at once.

MENU

Pasta with Creamed Spinach *(this page)*

or

Ricotta Pasta with Fresh Spinach *(page 71)*

Red Cabbage, Carrot, and Apricot Salad *(page 37)*

Broiled Portabella Mushrooms *(page 203)*

Ricotta Pasta with Fresh Spinach

In my family, we like the unembellished flavor of fresh spinach. I often serve it briefly steamed, with just a touch of nonhydrogenated margarine, which makes a great topping for grains as well as mild pasta dishes like this one.

4 SERVINGS

12 ounces pasta (see note)

2 tablespoons nonhydrogenated margarine

1 cup part-skim ricotta cheese

⅓ cup grated fresh Parmesan cheese

Salt and freshly ground pepper to taste

One 10- to 12-ounce package fresh spinach, well washed and stemmed

Calories: 276 • Total fat: 12 g
Protein: 15 g • Carbohydrate: 25 g
Cholesterol: 24 mg • Sodium: 322 mg

1 Cook the pasta according to package directions and drain, reserving ½ cup of the hot pasta cooking water. Transfer the pasta to a serving container, toss with 1½ tablespoons of the margarine, and cover.

2 In a mixing bowl, combine the ricotta with the reserved pasta cooking water and stir until well blended. Stir into the pasta along with the Parmesan, and season with salt and pepper.

3 Cover and steam the spinach using just the water clinging to the leaves in the same pot used to cook the pasta. This should take only a minute or two. Drain the spinach well and chop coarsely. Transfer to a small serving bowl and toss with the remaining ½ tablespoon margarine. Serve at once, topping each serving with some of the steamed spinach.

Note: This works well with a variety of pastas; try spinach fettuccine, medium shells, or a tri-colored pasta.

Ravioli or Tortellini with Sweet Potato Sauce

4 TO 6 SERVINGS

1 large sweet potato

One 16-ounce package frozen ricotta, tofu, or spinach ravioli or tortellini

1 tablespoon nonhydrogenated margarine

2 to 3 garlic cloves, minced

1 cup 1% low-fat milk or soymilk, or as needed

Salt and freshly ground pepper to taste

Calories: 356 • Total fat: 9 g
Protein: 15 g • Carbohydrate: 54 g
Cholesterol: 29 mg • Sodium: 353 mg

Sweet potato sauce for pasta? It's offbeat, I'll admit, but a surprisingly good match. This is wonderful with a quick sauté of bell peppers and squashes; or serve it as suggested in the accompanying menu.

1 Bake or microwave the sweet potato in its skin until tender. Plunge into a bowl of cold water.

2 Cook the pasta according to package directions, drain, and return to the pot.

3 Meanwhile, heat the margarine in a small skillet. Add the garlic and sauté over low heat until golden, about 1 minute, and remove from the heat.

4 Drain the sweet potato, peel, and mash it well in a small mixing bowl. Add the sautéed garlic and enough milk to make a thick sauce. Season.

5 Combine the sauce with the pasta in the pot. Cook just until the sauce is heated through. Serve at once.

MENU

Ravioli or Tortellini with Sweet Potato Sauce *(this page)*

Asparagus, Squash, and Red Pepper Sauté *(page 210)*

or

Roasted Italian Vegetables *(page 205)*

Black olives and diced tomatoes

Zucchini Tortellini

4 TO 6 SERVINGS

Combine one filled pasta with one mild vegetable, and if you are lucky as I am, your kids might actually like this as much as you do! Serve this with fresh bread or focaccia and a platter of raw vegetables. Or, to make this a more sophisticated meal, serve with any of the mixed greens salads on pages 50 to 53, and some good wine.

One 16-ounce package ricotta or tofu tortellini

2½ tablespoons extra-virgin olive oil

3 to 4 garlic cloves, minced

4 small zucchini, sliced

⅓ cup grated fresh Parmesan cheese or Parmesan-style soy cheese

Salt and freshly ground pepper to taste

1 Cook the tortellini according to package directions, drain, and return to the pot.

2 Meanwhile, heat 1½ tablespoons of the oil in a large skillet. Add the garlic and zucchini and sauté over medium heat until the zucchini is tender-crisp to your liking.

3 Combine the cooked pasta and zucchini mixture in a serving container. Add the remaining tablespoon of olive oil along with the Parmesan cheese and toss together. Season with salt and pepper, toss again, and serve.

Calories: 342 • Total fat: 15 g
Protein: 15 g • Carbohydrate: 39 g
Cholesterol: 31 mg • Sodium: 392 mg

4 SERVINGS

Pasta with Triple Red Sauce

½ cup sliced sun-dried tomatoes (not oil-cured)

12 ounces pasta, any long or short shape

One 28-ounce jar natural, good-quality pasta sauce

One 12-ounce jar roasted red peppers, drained and sliced into strips

Grated fresh Parmesan cheese or Parmesan-style soy cheese for topping, optional

Calories: 218 • Total fat: 5 g
Protein: 8 g • Carbohydrate: 37 g
Cholesterol: 0 mg • Sodium: 620 mg

Start with a well-flavored prepared pasta sauce, perhaps one made with chunky vegetables, mushrooms, or bell peppers. With the addition of roasted peppers and dried tomatoes, a special pasta meal can be yours in a flash.

1 If the dried tomatoes you are using aren't moist, soak them in hot water for about 10 minutes and drain.

2 Cook the pasta according to package directions and drain.

3 In a large saucepan, combine the pasta sauce, dried tomatoes, and red peppers. Cook slowly, covered, until heated through.

4 Combine the cooked pasta and sauce in a serving container and toss well. Serve, passing around the Parmesan cheese for topping, if desired.

Pasta with Olive Sauce

6 SERVINGS

Here's another great way to embellish a good prepared pasta sauce.

16 ounces pasta, any long or short shape

One 28-ounce jar natural good-quality pasta sauce

One 14- to 16-ounce can low-sodium diced tomatoes, with liquid

½ cup chopped pitted green olives, preferably cured

¼ cup minced fresh basil or parsley, optional

Freshly ground pepper to taste

1 Cook the pasta according to package directions and drain.

2 Meanwhile, combine the pasta sauce, tomatoes, and olives in a saucepan. Cook gently until heated through.

3 Combine the cooked pasta with the sauce in a serving container. Add the optional basil and toss together. Season with pepper, and serve.

Calories: 162 • Total fat: 3 g
Protein: 6 g • Carbohydrate: 27 g
Cholesterol: 0 mg • Sodium: 519 mg

MENU

A NEARLY INSTANT PASTA FEAST

Pasta with Olive Sauce *(this page)*

or

Pasta with Triple Red Sauce *(page 74)*

Fresh mozzarella cheese and sliced tomatoes

Fresh focaccia

Italian pickled vegetable mix (from the deli counter)

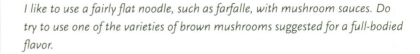

Farfalle with Mushrooms

4 SERVINGS

10 to 12 ounces farfalle (bowtie pasta)

2 tablespoons extra-virgin olive oil

2 to 3 garlic cloves, minced

10 to 12 ounces cremini, baby bella, or white mushrooms, cleaned and sliced

½ cup grated fresh Parmesan cheese or Parmesan-style soy cheese, plus more for topping, optional

Salt and freshly ground pepper to taste

Calories: 214 • Total fat: 10 g
Protein: 8 g • Carbohydrate: 22 g
Cholesterol: 8 mg • Sodium: 191 mg

I like to use a fairly flat noodle, such as farfalle, with mushroom sauces. Do try to use one of the varieties of brown mushrooms suggested for a full-bodied flavor.

1 Cook the pasta according to package directions and drain.

2 Meanwhile, heat the oil in a skillet. Add the garlic and sauté over low heat, just until the garlic begins to turn golden, about 1 minute.

3 Add the mushrooms. Cover and cook, stirring occasionally, until they are tender and have released some liquid, about 10 minutes.

4 Combine the pasta with the mushroom mixture in a serving container. Add the Parmesan cheese and toss together. Season with salt and pepper and serve, passing around additional Parmesan cheese for topping, if desired.

MENU

Farfalle with Mushrooms *(this page)*

Chickpea and Tomato Salad *(page 42)*

Roasted Italian Vegetables *(page 205)*

or

Steamed broccoli or sautéed broccoli rabe

Pasta and Cauliflower Curry

4 SERVINGS

Pasta isn't customarily seasoned with curry, but I've long enjoyed this combination.

10 to 12 ounces pasta, any short chunky shape

1 small head cauliflower, cut into bite-size pieces

One 28-ounce can low-sodium diced tomatoes, with liquid

1 cup frozen green peas, thawed

2 teaspoons good-quality curry powder, or to taste

Salt to taste

Calories: 165 • Total fat: 0 g
Protein: 7 g • Carbohydrate: 33 g
Cholesterol: 0 mg • Sodium: 25 mg

1 Cook the pasta according to package directions and drain.

2 Meanwhile, steam the cauliflower in a large saucepan until tender-crisp to your liking. Add the tomatoes, peas, and curry powder and bring to a simmer. Cook gently over medium-low heat, just until the mixture is heated through.

3 Combine the pasta and cauliflower mixture in a serving container and toss together. Season with salt and serve.

MENU

Pasta and Cauliflower Curry *(this page)*

Cucumbers and Tomatoes in Yogurt *(page 39)*

Steamed asparagus, broccoli, or green beans

Fresh pita or other flatbread

Pasta with Broccoli and Dried Tomatoes

4 SERVINGS

½ to ⅔ cup sliced sun-dried tomatoes (not oil-cured)

10 to 12 ounces pasta, any short chunky shape (see variation)

2 to 3 good-size broccoli crowns, cut into bite-size pieces

2½ tablespoons extra-virgin olive oil

½ cup grated fresh Parmesan cheese or Parmesan-style soy cheese

Salt and freshly ground pepper to taste

Calories: 238 • Total fat: 11 g
Protein: 9 g • Carbohydrate: 24 g
Cholesterol: 8 mg • Sodium: 207 mg

Here's a simple dish that borders on the sublime. In my family, we are all fans of broccoli, so this combination never fails to please. Serve with Mixed Greens with Oranges and Almonds (page 52).

1 If the dried tomatoes you are using aren't moist, soak them in hot water for about 10 minutes and drain.

2 Cook the pasta according to package directions and drain.

3 Meanwhile, steam the broccoli in a covered saucepan on the stovetop or in a covered microwave-safe container in the microwave, using a small quantity of water, until just a little beyond tender-crisp, and drain.

4 Combine the cooked pasta with the broccoli in a serving container. Add the oil, dried tomatoes, and Parmesan cheese and toss together. Season with salt and pepper and serve.

Variation: For a heartier dish, use a 16-ounce package of frozen ricotta cavatelli.

Spinach Fettuccine with Summer Squash

4 SERVINGS

This quick and colorful pasta dish will give you a summery feeling any time of year.

One 12-ounce package spinach fettuccine

2 tablespoons extra-virgin olive oil

2 medium yellow summer squashes, halved lengthwise and sliced

One pint cherry tomatoes, halved

½ cup grated fresh Parmesan cheese or Parmesan-style soy cheese

Salt and freshly ground pepper to taste

1 Cook the pasta according to package directions and drain.

2 Meanwhile, heat the oil in a skillet. Add the squash and sauté over medium heat, stirring often, until tender-crisp to your liking. Add the tomatoes and continue to cook until they are just heated through.

3 Combine the pasta with the squash mixture in a serving container. Add the Parmesan cheese and toss together. If a little more moisture is needed, add a small amount of water and toss again. Season with salt and pepper, and serve.

Calories: 248 • Total fat: 10 g
Protein: 10 g • Carbohydrate: 29 g
Cholesterol: 8 mg • Sodium: 203 mg

MENU

Spinach Fettuccine with Summer Squash *(this page)*

Corn Frittata Parmesan *(page 224)*

or

Contemporary Creamed Spinach *(page 212)*

Simple tossed salad

6 SERVINGS

Hearty Pasta and Pink Beans

One 16-ounce bag frozen cheese ravioli, ricotta cavatelli, or gnocchi

One 16-ounce can pink beans, drained and rinsed

One 28-ounce jar good-quality chunky pasta sauce

Grated fresh Parmesan cheese for topping, optional

Calories: 228 • Total fat: 7 g
Protein: 12 g • Carbohydrate: 31 g
Cholesterol: 15 mg • Sodium: 766 mg

Use hearty pasta from the frozen foods section for this filling dish. All you need to complete this meal is a bountiful salad and some fresh bread. If you'd like, add a steamed green vegetable as well.

1 Cook the gnocchi according to package directions. Just before draining, add the beans to the water and cook briefly to heat them. Drain the mixture well and transfer to a serving container.

2 Stir in the pasta sauce and serve, passing around some Parmesan cheese for topping, if desired.

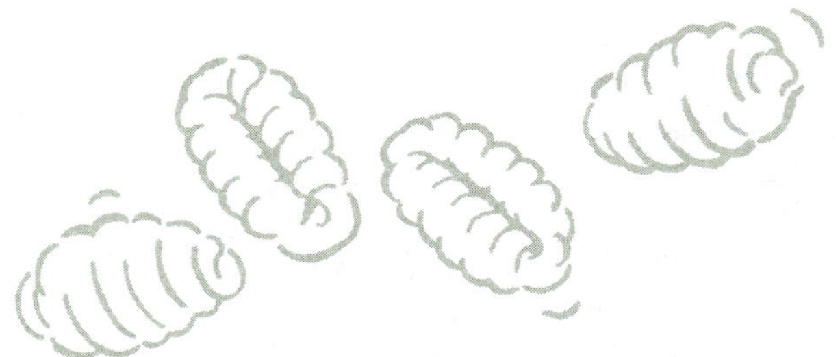

Gnocchi with Fresh Greens

4 TO 6 SERVINGS

Gnocchi are hearty dumplings made with potato flour and semolina. You'll find them in the frozen foods section of most any supermarket, shelved near ravioli and other frozen pastas. Have the spinach or chard washed and chopped before starting so this dish can come together quickly.

One 16-ounce bag frozen gnocchi

2 tablespoons extra-virgin olive oil

3 to 4 garlic cloves, minced

10 to 12 ounces fresh spinach or Swiss chard, well washed, stemmed, and coarsely chopped

One 14- to 16-ounce can low-sodium diced tomatoes (Italian-style, if desired)

Salt and freshly ground pepper to taste

1 Cook the gnocchi according to package directions and drain.

2 Meanwhile, heat the oil in a large pot or steep-sided stir-fry pan. Sauté the garlic over low heat until golden, about 2 minutes.

3 Add the greens and cover. Steam, using only the water clinging to the leaves, until just wilted, 1 to 2 minutes. Add the tomatoes and cook just until everything is heated through.

4 Combine the gnocchi with the greens mixture in a serving container and toss well. Season with salt and pepper, and serve.

Calories: 274 • Total fat: 7 g
Protein: 7 g • Carbohydrate: 45 g
Cholesterol: 0 mg • Sodium: 68 mg

MENU

Gnocchi with Fresh Greens *(this page)*

Broiled Portabella Mushrooms *(page 203)*

Bountiful tossed salad, including pink beans or chickpeas

Breadsticks

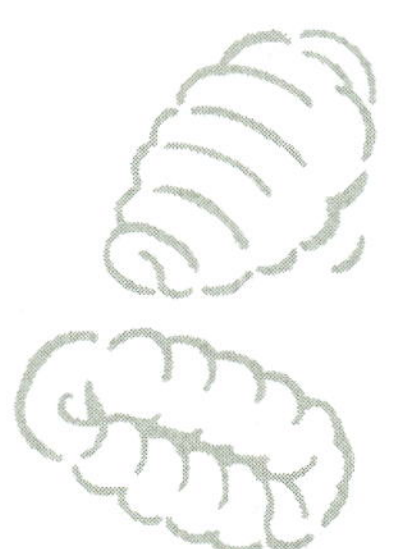

Noodles with Stir-Fried Tofu and Broccoli

4 SERVINGS

1 pound firm tofu

8 ounces udon, soba, Chinese wheat noodles, or linguine

1 tablespoon peanut oil

2 large broccoli crowns, cut into bite-size pieces

⅓ cup good-quality stir-fry sauce or ½ cup Thai peanut sauce, or to taste

Calories: 393 • Total fat: 13 g
Protein: 16 g • Carbohydrate: 52 g
Cholesterol: 0 mg • Sodium: 375 mg

Look for Asian noodles in natural foods stores as well as in the Asian foods section of well-stocked supermarkets.

1 Cut the tofu into ½-inch-thick slices. Blot well between several layers of paper towel or clean tea-towels, then cut into ½-inch dice.

2 Cook the noodles according to package directions and drain.

3 Meanwhile, heat the oil in a stir-fry pan, wok, or extra-large skillet. Add the tofu and stir-fry over medium-high heat until golden on most sides; transfer to a plate.

4 Combine the broccoli and about ¼ cup of water in the stir-fry pan. Cover and steam until the broccoli is tender-crisp.

5 Add the tofu and cooked noodles to the pan along with the stir-fry sauce. Toss gently and thoroughly. Continue to cook just until everything is heated through, and serve.

MENU

Noodles with Stir-Fried Tofu and Broccoli *(this page)*

Maple-Roasted Carrots *(page 207)*

or

Broiled Japanese Eggplant *(page 214)*

Corn Slaw *(page 34)*

Instant Vegetable Lo Mein

4 SERVINGS

This nearly-instant dish is fun to eat with chopsticks. In China and Japan, long noodles in broth are "slurped" (yes, this is considered proper table manners); then, the broth is eaten with a spoon. Look for Japanese-style frozen vegetables where other frozen vegetable medleys are shelved in well-stocked supermarkets.

One 8- to 10-ounce package fresh lo mein noodles or one 9-ounce package refrigerated fresh linguine

One 16-ounce package Japanese-style frozen mixed vegetables, thawed

Two 15-ounce cans vegetable broth

½ teaspoon grated fresh ginger or ¼ teaspoon ground ginger

Teriyaki sauce or light soy sauce to taste

1 Cook the noodles according to package directions (fresh noodles cook very quickly, usually in 2 to 3 minutes) and drain.

2 While the water is coming to a simmer for the noodles, steam the vegetables in a small amount of water in a wok or stir-fry pan, covered, until done to your liking, then drain and return to the wok.

3 Add the cooked noodles, broth, and ginger to the wok and stir together. Cook over medium-high heat just until heated through.

4 Serve in shallow bowls, including some broth in each serving. Pass around teriyaki sauce to season the noodles as desired.

Calories: 267 • Total fat: 3 g
Protein: 13 g • Carbohydrate: 47 g
Cholesterol: 0 mg • Sodium: 385 mg

MENU

Instant Vegetable Lo Mein *(this page)*

Sweet and Savory Sautéed or Baked Tofu *(page 135)**

Crisp raw vegetables of your choice

*Use the baked option with this menu so you can concentrate on the stovetop activities. Prepare the tofu dish first and bake it while preparing the lo mein recipe.

Asian Noodles

In the following three recipes, I recommend using either soba (buckwheat noodles), udon, or Chinese wheat noodles. Not long ago, a trip to an Asian grocery or natural foods store would be necessary to find these noodles, but now they're available in the Asian foods section of well-stocked supermarkets. There are other varieties you might like to explore, such as bean thread and rice-stick noodles. Most come in 8-ounce packages, and all cook quickly.

Chinese wheat noodles (lo mein): These long, flat noodles are about ¼ inch wide and have a consistency that is a cross between linguine and delicate egg noodles.

Soba (buckwheat noodles): Spaghetti-shaped soba noodles are made of hearty-tasting buckwheat flour combined with wheat, or whole wheat flour. They cook to a warm brown shade that contrasts nicely with green vegetables.

Udon: Long and flat, udon noodles are closest in shape to linguine. They also come in a whole wheat variety which you are more likely to find in natural foods stores. Imported from Japan, they have a smoother texture and milder flavor than domestic whole wheat pastas.

Asian Sesame-Soy Noodles

4 SERVINGS

This simply flavored noodle dish is good served with Asian-style tofu dishes. See the menu suggested on page 135 with Sweet and Savory Sautéed or Baked Tofu as well as the one given here. If you can't find Asian noodles, substitute linguine.

8 ounces udon, soba, Chinese wheat noodles, or linguine

2 tablespoons dark sesame oil

2 to 3 tablespoons soy sauce, or to taste

1 teaspoon honey or maple syrup

1 to 2 scallions, thinly sliced

1 Cook the noodles according to package directions and drain.

2 Meanwhile, combine the oil, soy sauce, and honey in a small bowl and stir to blend.

3 Combine the noodles and sauce in a serving container and toss well. Sprinkle the scallions on top and serve.

Calories: 276 • Total fat: 8 g
Protein: 7 g • Carbohydrate: 44 g
Cholesterol: 0 mg • Sodium: 628 mg

MENU

Asian Sesame-Soy Noodles *(this page)*

Broccoli and Tofu in Thai Peanut Sauce *(page 143)*

or

Instant Tofu and Mixed Vegetable Stir-Fry *(page 144)*

Crisp raw carrot and celery sticks

Peanut Butter Noodles

4 TO 6 CHILD-SIZE SERVINGS

8 ounces pasta, any short fun shape (spirals, wagon wheels, or small shells)

½ cup creamy peanut butter

1 tablespoon honey or maple syrup

1 to 2 tablespoons teriyaki sauce, or to taste

¼ teaspoon ground ginger

Calories: 220 • Total fat: 12 g
Protein: 9 g • Carbohydrate: 20 g
Cholesterol: 0 mg • Sodium: 216 mg

This chapter ends with two child-friendly recipes, hence the smaller portions. If you think your kids would share some with their parents, you can increase the proportions of the recipes.

1 Cook the pasta according to package directions and drain.

2 Combine the remaining ingredients with ½ cup warm water in a small mixing bowl and whisk together until smooth. Combine with the pasta in a serving container and toss until the sauce coats the pasta evenly. Serve warm or at room temperature.

MENU

A CHILD-FRIENDLY MEAL

Peanut Butter Noodles *(this page)*

or

Macaroni and Cheese *(page 87)*

Chunky Applesauce *(page 250) or store-bought applesauce*

Light Cheese Dip *(page 234)*

Crisp raw vegetables

Macaroni and Cheese

6 TO 8 CHILD-SIZE SERVINGS

This basic macaroni and cheese is on the rich side (it just doesn't work with reduced-fat cheese), but it is so comforting. Even if you don't have kids, you can make this when you're in the mood for "nursery food."

10 to 12 ounces elbow macaroni or other short pasta shape

3 tablespoons unbleached white flour

1½ cups 1% low-fat milk or plain soy milk

2 tablespoons nonhydrogenated margarine

2 cups grated cheddar or cheddar-style soy cheese

Salt to taste

Calories: 241 • Total fat: 13 g
Protein: 12 g • Carbohydrate: 15 g
Cholesterol: 36 mg • Sodium: 265 mg

1 Cook the macaroni according to package directions and drain.

2 Meanwhile, dissolve the flour in ½ cup of the milk, and combine with the remaining 1 cup milk, the margarine, and cheese in a saucepan. Slowly bring to a gentle simmer, stirring often. Cook over low heat until the sauce is smooth and thick, 4 to 5 minutes.

3 Combine the cooked macaroni and sauce in a serving container and stir together. Season with salt and serve.

Variation: Bake in a casserole dish at 400° until the top is golden and crusty, 20 to 30 minutes.

CHAPTER 4

The Zen of Grains and Beans

Grains and beans are the very heart of a healthful, plant-based diet. And what better cornerstone for a vegetarian repertoire than two of the most venerable and nourishing foods known?

More than half of the world's cultivated land is used to produce grain crops, and for most of the world's people, grains are indeed the proverbial "staff of life." This has been less true in the United States and other Western cultures, but with the popularization of ethnic and natural cookery, the use of whole grains is on the increase. In addition, there has been a growing recognition that complex carbohydrates and high-fiber foods are vital to a healthy lifestyle. Whole grains are among the best foods to fill those needs.

As for beans, they have finally shaken off their stigma as a fattening, "poor man's" food. Available in a rainbow of earthy hues, they've emerged as lean and tasty, even gourmet, fare. Like whole grains, they are an excellent source of complex carbohydrates and fiber. In a vegetarian diet, they can be a primary source of protein, too.

The notion that the complementary proteins of grains and beans must be combined in the same meal to be fully usable has been downplayed. Current wisdom tells us that in a varied diet, these plant-based proteins can join forces throughout the day. Still, there's no argument that they complement one another superbly on the dinner plate, so it makes sense to pair them in the same meal (and quite often, in the same dish). Satisfying and versatile, grains and beans deserve a prominent place in your repertoire, whether you are a full-time vegetarian or not.

Rice

Rice, the staple grain for nearly half the world's population is a symbol of daily sustenance as well as fertility and abundance. I'm not such a purist that white rice never touches my lips; it makes a comforting risotto (using white Arborio rice), a smooth rice pudding, and it can be a delicate counterpoint to hearty or spicy dishes. Still, you should know that refined white rice, even enriched, doesn't compare with the nutritional profile of brown rice. With the bran and germ gone, white rice contains only a fraction of the vitamin, mineral, and fiber content of brown.

Few grains are as versatile as rice. In many Asian countries, hardly a meal is served without it. Rice pilafs, fragrant with spices, herbs, and nuts, are well known in the cuisines of India and the Near and Middle East. In Mexico and the southwestern states, rice frequently accompanies tortilla specialties. In the American South, rice is a cherished staple from the Carolinas to Louisiana, where it is teamed with beans (as in the New Orleans classic red beans and rice), used in baking and desserts, and often served as a side dish.

BASIC COOKED BROWN RICE

The amount of water recommended for cooking brown rice varies, whether in cookbooks or on the packaging itself. A ratio of 2½ cups water to 1 cup rice has rarely done me wrong (although a 2 to 1 ratio has). If you like a more tender grain, use a 3 to 1 ratio.

Rinse brown rice well in a fine sieve. Then, bring water to a rapid simmer in a medium saucepan, stir in the rice, and return to a gentle simmer. Cover and cook until the water is absorbed, about 35 minutes.

- Use leftover cooked rice in muffin, quick bread, or pancake batter.

- Cold rice makes an excellent base for hearty grain salad. See Barley or Rice and Corn Salad, page 46, or improvise by combining cold rice with some finely diced crisp vegetables and a flavorful vinaigrette.

- Use plain brown rice or Lightly Embellished Brown Rice (page 91) as a bed for stir-fries, bean dishes (such as chili), and curries.

Lightly Embellished Brown Rice

6 SERVINGS

When you're serving cooked brown rice as a side dish or as a bed of grain for beans or vegetables, here's a way to give it a little extra flavor.

1 vegetable bouillon cube

1½ cups brown rice (see note)

2 tablespoons nonhydrogenated margarine

1 Bring 4 cups water to a simmer with the bouillon cube in a medium saucepan. Stir in the rice, cover, and simmer gently until the water is absorbed, about 35 minutes.

2 Stir in the margarine and serve.

Note: If you'd like to use quick-cooking brown rice, follow package directions for a 6-serving portion and adjust the amount of water accordingly.

Calories: 190 • Total fat: 4 g
Protein: 4 g • Carbohydrate: 34 g
Cholesterol: 0 mg • Sodium: 93 mg

Spinach Rice

6 SERVINGS

1 vegetable bouillon cube

1½ cups brown rice (see note)

2 tablespoons nonhydrogenated margarine

One 10-ounce package frozen chopped spinach, thawed

1 to 2 scallions, thinly sliced

Salt and freshly ground pepper to taste

Calories: 203 • Total fat: 5 g
Protein: 4 g • Carbohydrate: 36 g
Cholesterol: 0 mg • Sodium: 134 mg

Frozen chopped spinach dresses up plain brown rice with little extra effort.

1 Bring 4 cups water to a simmer with the bouillon cube in a medium saucepan. Stir in the rice, cover, and simmer gently until the water is absorbed, about 35 minutes.

2 Stir in the remaining ingredients and continue to cook just until everything is heated through. Serve at once.

Note: If you'd like to use quick-cooking brown rice, follow package directions for a 6-serving portion and adjust the amount of water accordingly.

MENU

Spinach Rice *(this page)*

Hummus *(page 229)*

Warm pita wedges

Mixed Greens with Tomatoes, Feta, and Olives *(page 51)*

Brown Rice Varieties

The supermarket is a handy place to buy long-grain brown rice (as well as quick-cooking brown rice), but to explore other varieties, visit a well-stocked natural foods store or food co-op. There you'll more likely find brown basmati, jasmine, wehani, and others (though Texmati, a domestically grown basmati, is available in many supermarkets). These specialty rices are exceptionally aromatic, enhancing their delicate flavors. Follow the same preparation guidelines as for Basic Cooked Brown Rice (page 90).

The Long, Medium, and Short of It

Once you begin to explore the varieties of rice, you'll notice that it comes in various grain types—long, medium, and short. How do you know which to use? This guide will simplify the decision for you:

Long-grain rice: This slender variety is probably the most common. It cooks to a firm, separate texture that's especially suitable for pilafs, cold rice salads, and as a bed of grain for vegetable and bean dishes.

Medium-grain rice: This cooks to a fluffier, more tender texture than long-grain, and so is suitable for use in casseroles, for stuffing vegetables, and for adding texture to baked goods. If you like its consistency, though, there's nothing wrong with using it as a bed of grain as well.

Short-grain rice: This plump grain cooks to a dense texture and has a slightly sweeter taste than long- or medium-grain varieties. Its slight stickiness makes it a good choice for rice puddings, croquettes, casseroles, or savory loaves.

Chinese-Style Vegetable Fried Rice

6 SERVINGS

1½ cups brown rice

2 tablespoons light olive oil

One 16-ounce bag frozen mixed vegetables, thawed

4 to 5 scallions, minced

Soy sauce to taste

Freshly ground pepper to taste

Calories: 235 • Total fat: 5 g
Protein: 5 g • Carbohydrate: 42 g
Cholesterol: 0 mg • Sodium: 48 mg

A simple reproduction of a Chinese restaurant favorite, this is excellent served with tofu dishes.

1 Bring 4 cups water to a simmer in a medium saucepan. Stir in the rice, cover, and simmer gently until the water is absorbed, about 35 minutes.

2 When the rice is nearly done, heat the oil in a stir-fry pan or extra-wide skillet. Add the vegetables and stir-fry over medium-high heat for 5 minutes. Add the scallions and stir-fry for another minute or two.

3 Stir in the rice, and season to taste with soy sauce and pepper. Stir-fry for another 2 to 3 minutes, and serve.

Variation: To make a quick version of this, use quick-cooking brown rice. Follow package directions for a 6-serving portion.

MENU

Chinese-Style Vegetable Fried Rice *(this page)*

Shake-and-Bake Tofu *(page 138)*

Baby carrots, cherry tomatoes, and sliced bell peppers

Ricotta and Green Chili Rice

6 SERVINGS

A lively accompaniment to simple bean dishes or tortilla specialties.

1 to 2 vegetable bouillon cubes

$1\frac{1}{2}$ cups brown rice

One 4-ounce can chopped mild green chilies or 1 to 2 small fresh hot chilies, seeded and minced

1 cup part-skim ricotta cheese

$\frac{1}{4}$ cup minced fresh cilantro or parsley, or 2 to 3 scallions, thinly sliced

Freshly ground pepper to taste

1 Bring 4 cups water to a simmer with the bouillon cubes in a medium saucepan. Stir in the rice, cover, and simmer gently until the water is absorbed, about 35 minutes.

2 Stir in the remaining ingredients and continue to cook until everything is heated through. Serve at once.

Variation: To make a quick version of this, use quick-cooking brown rice. Follow package directions for a 6-serving portion.

Calories: 221 • Total fat: 3 g
Protein: 9 g • Carbohydrate: 37 g
Cholesterol: 13 mg • Sodium: 103 mg

MENU

Ricotta and Green Chili Rice *(this page)*

Slow-Simmered Beans *(page 117)*

or

Marinated Beans *(page 40)*

Simple tossed salad

Gingered Coconut Rice

6 SERVINGS

One 16-ounce can reduced-fat coconut milk

1½ cups brown or brown basmati rice

2 to 3 garlic cloves, very finely minced

1 to 2 teaspoons grated fresh ginger, or to taste

1 to 2 teaspoons good-quality curry powder, or to taste

Salt to taste

Calories: 226 • Total fat: 7 g
Protein: 4 g • Carbohydrate: 35 g
Cholesterol: 0 mg • Sodium: 8 mg

Simple yet gently assertive, serve this with bean dishes and vegetable curries.

1 Combine 2 cups water and the coconut milk in a large saucepan and bring to a simmer.

2 Stir in the rice, garlic, ginger, and curry powder. Cover and simmer gently until the water is absorbed, about 35 minutes. Season and serve.

MENU

Gingered Coconut Rice *(this page)*

Garlicky Black Beans *(page 113)*

Tomato-Mango Salsa *(page 237)*

Sliced red and green bell peppers

Baked Risotto

6 SERVINGS

Risotto is a classic Italian dish made of Arborio rice, a starchy, short-grain variety that cooks to a creamy consistency. Most well-stocked supermarkets carry it, either near other rice products or with specialty grains.

1½ cups Arborio rice

Two 15-ounce cans vegetable stock

2 garlic cloves, very finely minced

About 1½ cups steamed fresh vegetable of your choice (green peas, fresh corn kernels, finely chopped asparagus, or sliced wild mushrooms)

Grated fresh Parmesan cheese or Parmesan-style soy cheese for topping, optional

1 Preheat the oven to 375°F.

2 Combine the rice with the stock, 1 cup water, and the garlic in a 2-quart casserole. Cover and bake for 1 hour, stirring every 15 minutes. At the third stirring, stir in 1 cup water. When done, the rice should have a tender and creamy texture.

3 Stir in the vegetable, and let the risotto stand for 5 minutes before serving. Pass around the Parmesan cheese for topping.

Calories: 144 • Total fat: 0 g
Protein: 4 g • Carbohydrate: 30 g
Cholesterol: 0 mg • Sodium: 100 mg

Risotto

If you're familiar with this dish, you probably think of constant standing and stirring, since that is, in fact, how risotto is traditionally made. Preparing risotto is actually not that difficult, and it's a great exercise in mindful cooking, but this process may not appeal to everyone. If you want to experience this great Italian comfort food, here's an easier way.

In this baked version, you just throw everything into a casserole dish and put it in the oven, stirring once every 15 minutes. The results are terrific, and while you enjoy the aroma permeating from the oven, you can relax and listen to opera with a glass of wine in hand.

MENU

Baked Risotto *(this page)*

White Bean and Dried Tomato Spread *(page 239)*

Fresh Italian bread

Bountiful tossed salad

Rice with Chickpeas and Tomatoes

4 TO 6 SERVINGS

1 cup brown rice

One 16-ounce can chickpeas, drained and rinsed

One 16-ounce can low-sodium diced tomatoes, with liquid

2 to 3 scallions, sliced

1 to 2 teaspoons cumin, or to taste

Salt and freshly ground pepper to taste

Calories: 238 • Total fat: 1 g
Protein: 8 g • Carbohydrate: 47 g
Cholesterol: 0 mg • Sodium: 224 mg

This grain-and-bean duo makes a basic, hearty main dish. Some steamed broccoli or green beans and a colorful salad complete the meal.

1 Bring 3 cups water to a simmer in a large saucepan. Stir in the rice, cover, and simmer gently until the water is absorbed, about 35 minutes.

2 Stir the remaining ingredients into the rice and cook until everything is heated through. Serve at once.

Chickpeas

Even those who aren't keen on beans might make an exception for versatile, tasty chickpeas, a.k.a. garbanzos. Americans have come to appreciate them in popular Middle Eastern, Indian, and Mediterranean dishes (such as hummus). If they have a drawback, it's their long cooking time—up to three hours. In this case, the canned version has a definite advantage.

- Mashed and seasoned, chickpeas make an excellent sandwich spread (see Chickpea Spread, page 239).
- Pureed, they thicken hearty vegetable soups and make a good base for dips (see Hummus, page 229).
- Chickpeas are delicious in green salads, or as the main ingredient in heartier salads (see Chickpea Salad with Roasted Peppers and Chickpea and Tomato Salad, page 42).

Long-Grain and Wild Rice Pilaf

6 SERVINGS

Look for long-grain and wild rice mixes near other rice products on supermarket shelves. Wild rice adds an invigorating, nutty flavor and texture to pilaf.

1½ tablespoons nonhydrogenated margarine

1 medium onion, diced

2 large celery stalks, diced

1 to 2 vegetable bouillon cubes

1½ cups long-grain and wild rice mix

Salt and freshly ground pepper to taste

1 Heat the margarine in a large saucepan. Add the onion and sauté over medium heat until golden.

2 Add 4 cups water, the celery, and bouillon cubes and bring to a simmer. Stir in the rice mix, cover, and simmer gently until the water is absorbed, 35 to 40 minutes. Season with salt and pepper, and serve.

Calories: 168 • Total fat: 4 g
Protein: 4 g • Carbohydrate: 28 g
Cholesterol: 0 mg • Sodium: 338 mg

Wild Rice

Did you know that wild rice is not really a type of rice, nor a grain at all? It is actually the seed of a tall aquatic grass that thrives in freshwater lakes or rivers. Most of the crop is harvested in and around Minnesota and other Great Lakes states by Native American-owned companies. Cultivating wild rice on a larger scale has proven difficult, so its niche remains as a specialty gourmet grain.

- Wild rice dishes help dress up fall harvest meals; they are especially compatible with winter squash dishes.
- Combine brown rice with a small amount of wild rice when cooking for added texture and nutty flavor.
- Add a small amount of cooked wild rice to stuffings and other wintery casseroles.

Fragrant Rice and Cashew Pilaf

6 SERVINGS

1½ cups brown basmati, Texmati, jasmine, wehani, or other specialty rice

2 tablespoons nonhydrogenated margarine or whipped butter

3 scallions, thinly sliced

Juice of ½ lemon

⅓ cup toasted chopped cashew pieces

Salt and freshly ground pepper to taste

Calories: 215 • Total fat: 8 g
Protein: 4 g • Carbohydrate: 33 g
Cholesterol: 0 mg • Sodium: 49 mg

The simplicity of this recipe highlights the aroma and flavor of specialty brown rice. If you don't want to search for one of these more exotic types of rice, long-grain brown rice will do. This tasty side dish can enhance many meals.

1 Bring 4 cups water to a simmer in a large saucepan. Stir in the rice, cover, and simmer gently until the water is absorbed, about 35 minutes.

2 Stir the remaining ingredients into the rice, and serve.

Rice and Peas

4 TO 6 SERVINGS

1½ tablespoons nonhydrogenated margarine or whipped butter

1 large onion, chopped

1 vegetable bouillon cube

1 cup brown rice

2 cups frozen petite green peas, thawed

Salt and freshly ground pepper to taste

Calories: 213 • Total fat: 5 g
Protein: 6 g • Carbohydrate: 38 g
Cholesterol: 0 mg • Sodium: 101 mg

This mild rice dish can be used as a side dish, or, in larger portions, as an entrée, accompanied by a tossed salad and a variety of steamed or stir-fried vegetables.

1 Heat the margarine in a large saucepan. Add the onion and sauté over medium heat until golden.

2 Add 3 cups water and the bouillon and bring to a simmer. Stir in the rice, cover, and simmer gently until the water is absorbed, about 35 minutes. Stir in the peas and cook just until heated through. Season with salt and pepper and serve.

Barley with Mushrooms and Browned Onions

4 TO 6 SERVINGS

The darker mushrooms yield a richer flavor, so give them a try. As always, my favorite seasoning for barley is fresh dill. *See menu on page 206.*

1 cup pearl or pot barley

1½ tablespoons light olive oil

2 large onions, quartered and thinly sliced

8 to 10 ounces cremini, baby bella, or white mushrooms

2 to 3 tablespoons minced fresh dill

Salt and freshly ground pepper to taste

1 Bring water (3 cups if using pearl barley; 3½ cups for pot barley) to a rapid simmer in a medium saucepan and stir in the barley. Cover and simmer gently until the water is absorbed, 35 to 40 minutes. Taste, and if you'd like a little more tender texture, add another ½ cup water and simmer until absorbed.

2 Meanwhile, heat the oil in a wide skillet. Add the onions and sauté slowly over low heat until lightly and evenly browned.

3 Add the mushrooms and about ¼ cup water. Cover and cook over medium heat until the mushrooms are wilted, about 8 minutes.

4 Combine the onion and mushroom mixture with the cooked barley in a serving container. Stir in the dill, season with salt and pepper, and serve.

Calories: 171 • Total fat: 5 g
Protein: 4 g • Carbohydrate: 29 g
Cholesterol: 0 mg • Sodium: 7 mg

Barley

Barley, one of the most ancient of cultivated grains, is most commonly available in the pearl variety, the kind sold in supermarkets. Searching a bit further afield, you might find pot barley in natural foods stores and food co-ops. The latter is less refined, retaining more of the natural fiber and bran. Both kinds are mild tasting, pleasantly chewy, and versatile. Basic cooking directions are above (Step 1).

- Barley is a favorite soup grain. Add uncooked barley to long-simmering winter soups (such as Split Pea and Barley Soup, page 25) for extra heartiness. Add cooked barley to cold summer soups (such as Cold Potato-Barley Buttermilk Soup, page 14) for a wonderful texture.
- Think of barley as a change of pace from rice in pilafs and casseroles.
- Barley is delicious as a base for marinated grain salads (see Barley or Rice and Corn Salad, page 46).

Salsa Grain-and-Bean Pilaf

4 TO 6 SERVINGS

4 cups cooked grain of your choice (quinoa, bulgur, rice, couscous, or other)

2 to 2½ cups cooked or canned beans of your choice (pinto, black, or pink beans, black-eyed peas, chickpeas, or other; ¾ to 1 cup raw or one 16- to 20-ounce can, drained and rinsed)

1 cup prepared salsa, or to taste

2 scallions, minced

Salt and freshly ground pepper to taste

¼ cup chopped fresh parsley or cilantro, optional

Calories: 307 • Total fat: 0 g
Protein: 10 g • Carbohydrate: 64 g
Cholesterol: 0 mg • Sodium: 468 mg

This is a flexible recipe that I frequently rely on when I want an easy, nourishing main dish. I vary the combinations each time I make it. See the cooking notes for specifics on cooking grains in this chapter, and pages 110 to 111 for cooking beans, if you choose to use dried beans.

1 Combine all of the ingredients except the optional parsley in a large saucepan and heat slowly until heated through.

2 Stir in the optional parsley, and serve.

MENU

Salsa Grain-and-Bean Pilaf *(this page)*

Baked or microwaved sweet potatoes

Creamy Coleslaw *(page 35)*

or

Simple tossed salad

Chili Cheese Grits

6 TO 8 SERVINGS

Grits are hulled, dried, and cracked corn kernels. To add variety to your grain repertoire, try them! I do urge you to try using stone-ground grits, which are much more flavorful than those sold in supermarkets. However, the latter can't be beat for convenience, especially the quick-cooking kind.

1 cup grits (preferably stone-ground)

2 tablespoons nonhydrogenated margarine

One 4-ounce can chopped mild green chilies

1 or 2 scallions, thinly sliced, optional

1 cup firmly packed grated sharp cheddar cheese or cheddar-style soy cheese

1 teaspoon salt, or to taste

1 Bring 4¾ cups water to a simmer in a large saucepan. Slowly sprinkle in the grits, stirring constantly to avoid lumping. Cook over very low heat until smooth and thick, about 25 minutes for stone-ground and 5 minutes for quick grits.

2 Stir in the remaining ingredients. Heat until the cheese is smoothly melted into the grits and serve.

Calories: 183 • Total fat: 9 g
Protein: 6 g • Carbohydrate: 19 g
Cholesterol: 17 mg • Sodium: 139 mg

MENU

Chili Cheese Grits *(this page)*

Black-Eyed Peas with Greens *(page 123)*

Cherry tomatoes and baby carrots

Quinoa, Broccoli, and Cheese Casserole

6 SERVINGS

1½ cups quinoa, rinsed in a fine sieve

2 tablespoons light olive oil

1 large onion, chopped

2 medium broccoli crowns, cut into bite-size pieces

1 cup grated sharp cheddar cheese or cheddar-style soy cheese

Salt and freshly ground pepper to taste

Calories: 284 • Total fat: 13 g
Protein: 12 g • Carbohydrate: 30 g
Cholesterol: 20 mg • Sodium: 129 mg

This easy casserole offers maximum nourishment. Serve with microwaved or baked sweet potatoes (start the sweet potatoes in the oven about 45 minutes before starting to bake the casserole) and a salad of dark greens and ripe tomatoes.

1 Preheat the oven to 375°F.

2 Bring 3 cups water to a simmer in a medium saucepan. Stir in the quinoa, cover, and simmer gently until the water is absorbed, about 15 minutes.

3 Meanwhile, heat the oil in a large skillet. Add the onion and sauté until golden. Add the broccoli and about ¼ cup water. Cover and steam until the broccoli is just a little more done than tender-crisp, 5 to 7 minutes.

4 In a mixing bowl, combine the cooked quinoa with the broccoli mixture and half of the cheese. Season with salt and pepper and stir well. Transfer the mixture to a lightly oiled, shallow 2-quart casserole. Sprinkle evenly with the remaining cheese. Bake until the top is golden and crisp, 20 to 25 minutes. Let the casserole stand for 5 minutes, and serve.

MENU

Quinoa, Broccoli, and Cheese Casserole *(this page)*

or

Quinoa and Corn Pilaf *(page 105)*

Avocado and Pinto Bean Salad *(page 45)*

Warm flour tortillas

Sautéed zucchini and/or yellow summer squash

Quinoa and Corn Pilaf

4 TO 6 SERVINGS

Two revered ancient grains in one simple, tasty dish.

1 cup quinoa, rinsed in a fine sieve

1½ tablespoons light olive oil

1 large onion, quartered and thinly sliced

2 cups cooked fresh corn kernels (from 3 medium ears) or one 8-ounce package thawed frozen corn kernels

1 teaspoon cumin

Salt and freshly ground pepper to taste

1 Bring 2 cups water to a simmer in a medium saucepan. Stir in the quinoa, cover, and simmer gently until the water is absorbed, about 15 minutes.

2 Meanwhile, heat the oil in a wide skillet. Add the onion and sauté over medium heat until golden. Stir in the corn kernels and continue to sauté until the onion begins to brown lightly.

3 Stir the cooked quinoa into the corn mixture along with the cumin, and season with salt and pepper. If a little more moisture is needed, stir in a small amount of water, and serve.

Calories: 221 • Total fat: 6 g
Protein: 7 g • Carbohydrate: 36 g
Cholesterol: 0 mg • Sodium: 7 mg

Quinoa

Quinoa is a rediscovered food of ancient South American origin. Once the staple nourishment of the Inca culture, it's technically not a grain but the seed of an herb-like plant. Now grown in the American Rockies (replicating the harsh terrain of the Andes, where it once thrived), quinoa is still considered a specialty grain, thus, it is somewhat expensive. Nutritionally, though, you get a lot for your money—quinoa is considered a "super food" for its superb nutritional profile, which includes high-quality protein. Quinoa cooks to a fluffy texture in about 15 minutes and has a mild yet distinct flavor.

BASIC COOKED QUINOA

Use 2 parts water to 1 part quinoa. For variety, you may want to cook it in stock instead of water, or add a bouillon cube to the water. Rinse the quinoa in a fine sieve (very important, since raw quinoa has the residue of a natural, bitter substance called saponins). Bring water to a rapid simmer, then stir in the quinoa. Simmer gently, covered, until the water is absorbed, about 15 minutes. To use as a plain side dish or as a bed of grain, stir in just a touch of nonhydrogenated margarine and salt into the hot grain.

Fruited Couscous

6 SERVINGS

1½ cups couscous

2 tablespoons nonhydrogenated margarine

One 4-ounce package dried fruit bits

2 scallions, thinly sliced

½ to 1 teaspoon good-quality curry powder, or to taste

Salt and freshly ground pepper to taste

Calories: 211 • Total fat: 5 g
Protein: 4 g • Carbohydrate: 40 g
Cholesterol: 0 mg • Sodium: 55 mg

This is a superb accompaniment to curries and other spicy dishes. See the menu with Tofu and Sweet Potato Curry, page 139.

1 Boil 3 cups water. Pour the water over the couscous in a heatproof container. Cover and let stand for 15 minutes, then fluff with a fork.

2 Add the remaining ingredients, stir well, and serve.

Couscous

Couscous often refers to a spicy, complex Moroccan dish, in which the grain used is traditionally cracked millet. But what we refer to as couscous in our culture is actually closely related to pasta. It's made from the same refined, enriched durum wheat, then shaped to resemble a grain. Natural foods stores often carry whole grain couscous. This mild, fluffy grain is versatile and easy to prepare.

- Use couscous as a bed of grain in place of rice for stir-fried vegetables, curries, and highly flavored stews.
- Because couscous is so light, it offers a nice contrast to hearty bean dishes.
- It makes a pleasant base for light grain salads such as Couscous Salad (page 49).

BASIC COOKED COUSCOUS

Use 2 parts water to 1 part couscous. Place the amount of grain needed in a heatproof bowl or casserole dish. Bring the amount of water needed to a boil, then pour it over the couscous. Cover and let stand for 15 minutes, then fluff with a fork. To use as a simple side dish, stir a touch of nonhydrogenated margarine or whipped butter into the hot cooked grain and season with a little salt. Children seem to like couscous this way; serve it to them in a bowl to make it easier to scoop up (and avoid a mess!).

Couscous with Peas, Cashews, and Raisins

This mild side dish complements vegetable curries as well as recipes made with hearty winter vegetables, as in the accompanying menu.

6 SERVINGS

1½ cups couscous

2 tablespoons nonhydrogenated margarine

1 cup frozen green peas, thawed and steamed

⅓ cup toasted cashew pieces

½ cup dark raisins

Salt and freshly ground pepper to taste

Calories: 258 • Total fat: 7 g
Protein: 7 g • Carbohydrate: 42 g
Cholesterol: 0 mg • Sodium: 55 mg

1 Boil 3 cups water. Pour the water over the couscous in a heatproof container. Cover and let stand for 15 minutes, then fluff with a fork.

2 Add the remaining ingredients and stir well. If the mixture needs more moisture, stir in a small amount of water, and serve.

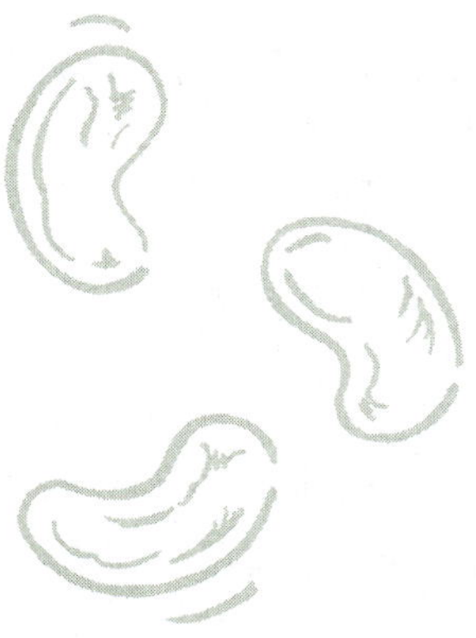

MENU

Couscous with Peas, Cashews, and Raisins *(this page)*

Stewed Spaghetti Squash *(page 220)*

or

Roasted Root Vegetables *(page 206)*

Simple tossed salad

Bulgur with Pasta

6 SERVINGS

1 cup raw bulgur

1 cup tiny seashell or bowtie pasta

2 tablespoons nonhydrogenated margarine

⅓ cup grated fresh Parmesan cheese or Parmesan-style soy cheese

2 scallions, thinly sliced

Salt and freshly ground pepper to taste

Calories: 227 • Total fat: 5 g
Protein: 8 g • Carbohydrate: 36 g
Cholesterol: 3 mg • Sodium: 125 mg

The contrast of whole grain and pasta makes for a very satisfying side dish. You can also make this by substituting whole grain couscous or quinoa for the bulgur. Serve this with Baked Barbecue Tofu and Peppers (page 141) and a tossed salad for an easy, hearty meal.

1 Boil 2 cups water. Pour the water over the bulgur in a heatproof container. Cover and let stand until the water is absorbed, about 30 minutes. Or combine the water and bulgur in a small saucepan and simmer until the water is absorbed, about 15 minutes.

2 Meanwhile, cook the pasta according to package directions and drain.

3 Combine the cooked bulgur and pasta in a serving container. Stir in the margarine to melt. Then stir in the Parmesan cheese and scallions. Season with salt and pepper, and serve.

Bulgur

Bulgur is made from steamed and cracked whole wheat berries. When cooked, it has a chewy texture and a flavor that is reminiscent of brown rice, though somewhat nuttier. A staple in Near and Middle Eastern cuisine, bulgur is perhaps best known as the main ingredient in tabbouleh salad. This easy-to-prepare whole grain is a great addition to a healthy, varied diet. Basic cooking directions are above (Step 1).

- Use bulgur as a bed of grain for hearty bean dishes. It's especially good with chickpeas and black-eyed peas.
- Bulgur pilafs can be made by adding cooked beans or toasted nuts to the cooked grain; dried fruits, chopped scallion, and fresh herbs are good embellishments.
- Like other grains, bulgur makes a tasty base for hearty cold salads such as Fruited Bulgur Salad (page 48).

Bulgur with Cabbage and Green Beans

6 SERVINGS

Bulgur is delicious with lightly browned onion and cabbage. The green beans add a companionable flavor and texture.

1 cup raw bulgur

2 tablespoons light olive oil

1 large red or yellow onion, quartered and thinly sliced

One 8-ounce package shredded coleslaw cabbage

One 10-ounce package frozen French-cut green beans, thawed

Salt and freshly ground pepper to taste

1 Boil 2 cups water. Pour the water over the bulgur in a heatproof container. Cover and let stand until the water is absorbed, about 30 minutes. Or combine the water and bulgur in a small saucepan and simmer until the water is absorbed, about 15 minutes.

2 Heat the oil in a large skillet or stir-fry pan. Add the onion and sauté over medium-low heat until translucent. Layer the cabbage and green beans over the onions, cover, and cook for 5 minutes. Then uncover, turn the heat up to medium-high, and sauté, stirring frequently until all the vegetables are lightly and evenly browned.

3 Transfer the cooked bulgur to the skillet and stir it in. Sauté for another 3 to 4 minutes, stirring often. Season with salt and pepper, and serve.

Calories: 166 • Total fat: 5 g
Protein: 5 g • Carbohydrate: 26 g
Cholesterol: 0 mg • Sodium: 12 mg

MENU

Bulgur with Cabbage and Green Beans *(this page)*

Black Bean Salad with Feta and Red Peppers *(page 43)*

Steamed summer squash

Fresh fruit or any fruity dessert from Chapter Eleven

Beans and Legumes

Beans and legumes are nutritional powerhouses, rich in protein and fiber, and very low in fat. They boast a slew of vitamins (B vitamins in particular) and essential minerals (notably iron).

Preparation time for cooking beans is minimal, though the beans themselves take their sweet time to cook. It's worth cooking your own if you need a large quantity for dishes like black bean soup or red beans and rice. You can also control the amount of salt and seasonings that go in.

There are several ways to cook beans: conventional soaking and cooking, pressure cooking, and by slow cooker cooking. Cooking time is determined by several factors, including simmering temperature, soaking time, the size and freshness of the beans, and even the altitude at which you live. Every cup of dry beans yields about 2½ cups cooked.

CONVENTIONAL SOAK-AND-COOK METHOD

1. Rinse and sort the beans, removing discolored or shriveled ones. Combine them in a large pot with 6 to 8 cups water. Cover and soak overnight (during warm weather, soak in the refrigerator to prevent spoilage).

Or, cut soaking time by using the quick-soak method: Bring 6 to 8 cups water and the beans to a boil, turn off the heat, and let stand, covered, for an hour or so. Note that some legumes, notably lentils and split peas, don't require soaking.

2. To reduce the gas-producing quality of beans, replace soaking water with fresh water before cooking. The fresh water should be about double the volume of the beans. You can add spices at this point, but *don't* add salt yet, nor any other acidic foods such as tomatoes or lemon juice; they harden the skins and lengthen cooking time. Add these only once the beans are tender.

3. Bring the water and beans to a rapid simmer; then lower the heat, cover, and simmer gently. Leave the cover slightly ajar to prevent foaming over. Cooking the beans slowly and thoroughly develops good flavor, prevents the skins from bursting prematurely, and assures better digestibility. Beans are done when they mash easily between thumb and forefinger. Generally, beans take 1 to 2 hours to cook, depending on the variety.

PRESSURE-COOKER METHOD

Pressure cooking greatly reduces cooking time and is not the treacherous appliance once feared. You'll do fine if you follow the manufacturer's instructions and make sure the vents on the cooker aren't clogged by foam. The risk of foaming is greatly reduced if you fill the pressure cooker no more than one third full with water and beans, and add a tablespoon of oil.

Certain legumes—split peas, lima beans, fava beans, and soybeans—aren't always recommended for pressure cooking because they foam excessively. Cookbooks by Lorna Sass deal extensively with pressure cooking beans and other natural foods. Please defer to her expertise if you'd like to learn more on the subject.

SLOW-COOKER METHOD

Beans cooked in a slow cooker (otherwise known as a Crock-Pot) turn out beautifully tender and digestible, with a thick broth. Follow specific instructions provided by the manufacturer. Soak first, then drain. To cook, use four parts water to one part beans. To make a tasty broth, add chopped onions, garlic, a bay leaf or other dried herbs to taste. Bring the water to a boil in the cooker, then set it at high. Cover and cook for 6 to 8 hours.

Canned Beans

If time is an issue (it often is in my life, as I'm sure it is in yours), I'd rather reach for canned beans than forgo the pleasure of using them. The essential difference between canned beans and those you cook yourself is the sodium content in the former, which can be pretty high. Drain and rinse the canned beans well before using them to reduce the sodium, and use caution when adding any extra salt to the dish in which they are used.

For a high-quality alternative, try the organic cooked beans available in natural foods stores. I prefer canned chickpeas to home-cooked, which take an inordinately long time to become tender, and are not as tasty.

6 SERVINGS

Black Bean Nachos Grandes

6 ounces good-quality tortilla chips, preferably low-fat

1 cup canned black beans, drained and rinsed

½ cup frozen corn kernels, thawed

Salsa, as desired

1½ cups grated Monterey Jack or cheddar cheese

Calories: 292 • Total fat: 13 g
Protein: 12 g • Carbohydrate: 29 g
Cholesterol: 25 mg • Sodium: 304 mg

This is terrific as an appetizer, snack, or accompaniment to a simple grain dish. I like using stone-ground tortilla chips, which are generally available from natural foods stores and specialty markets. But do explore the varieties available in supermarkets as well. Look for all-natural ingredients and read the nutrition labels, as they vary greatly in fat content. Not more than 3 grams of fat per 1-ounce serving is ideal. Baked tortilla chips can be a good choice as well.

1 To microwave, spread the chips out in a single layer on a large platter, or divide among two plates. Sprinkle the remaining ingredients evenly over the chips. Microwave each batch until the cheese is bubbly, 1 to 2 minutes, and serve at once.

2 To bake, preheat the oven to 400°. Spread the chips out in a single layer on a baking sheet (line with foil if desired). Sprinkle the remaining ingredients evenly over the chips. Bake until the cheese is bubbly, 5 to 7 minutes, and serve.

Black Beans

These small beans are famous for their role in black bean soup and in Cuban cuisine. They are a flavorful part of Mexican, Southwestern, and Mediterranean cuisines as well. Their pleasantly bold flavor holds up well to strong seasonings such as thyme, oregano, cilantro, and cumin.

- Black beans are wonderfully enhanced by onions, garlic, olive oil, and lemon juice.
- As a salad base, black beans combine well with bell peppers, corn, tomatoes, scallions, and feta cheese. See Black Bean Salad with Feta and Red Peppers, and Black Bean and Corn Salad (pages 43 and 44).
- Black beans are delicious served with simple rice dishes and in tortilla specialties.

Garlicky Black Beans

6 SERVINGS

Black beans are delicious with lots of garlic. This is one of my favorite ways to serve them.

1 tablespoon extra-virgin olive oil

4 garlic cloves, minced

Two 16-ounce cans black beans, drained and rinsed, or 4 cups cooked black beans (from about 1⅔ cups raw)

Juice of ½ to 1 lemon, or to taste

¼ cup minced fresh cilantro or parsley

1 Heat the oil in a large saucepan. Add the garlic and sauté over low heat until golden, 1 or 2 minutes.

2 Add the beans, ½ cup water, and the lemon juice. Cook over medium heat until the mixture comes to a gentle simmer.

3 Remove about ¾ cup of the beans, mash them, and return to the saucepan. Simmer very gently for another 5 minutes. Stir in the cilantro, and serve.

Calories: 178 • Total fat: 3 g
Protein: 8 g • Carbohydrate: 30 g
Cholesterol: 0 mg • Sodium: 361 mg

MENU

Garlicky Black Beans *(this page)*

Cranberry Slaw *(page 37)*

Baked or microwaved sweet potato

or

Stewed Spaghetti Squash *(page 220)*

Green Chili Black Beans

6 SERVINGS

1 tablespoon extra-virgin olive oil

1 medium onion, finely chopped

Two 16-ounce cans black beans, drained and rinsed, or 4 cups cooked black beans (from about 1⅔ cups raw)

One 4- or 7-ounce can chopped mild green chilies

Calories: 194 • Total fat: 3 g
Protein: 9 g • Carbohydrate: 33 g
Cholesterol: 0 mg • Sodium: 362 mg

Serve over rice or wrapped in a tortilla (see Black Bean Burritos, page 167). You can serve them both ways in the same meal, as in the menu here. That way, everyone can decide for themselves how they'd like to enjoy this tasty dish.

1 Heat the oil in a large saucepan. Add the onion and sauté over medium heat until golden.

2 Add the beans and chilies and about ¼ cup water. Cook over medium heat until the mixture comes to a gentle simmer.

3 Remove about ½ cup of the beans, mash them, and return to the saucepan. Simmer gently for another 5 minutes, and serve.

MENU

Green Chili Black Beans *(this page)*

Summer Squash and Corn Sauté *(page 209)*

Hot cooked rice

Warm flour tortillas

Shredded lettuce, diced tomatoes, and black olives

Pinto Beans and Corn

4 TO 6 OR MORE SERVINGS

Here's a hearty stew made entirely of convenient ingredients (unless you opt to cook the beans from scratch). Serve with simple grain dishes or tortilla specialties that don't include beans, such as Mushroom and Bell Pepper Quesadillas or Soft Tacos (page 172).

Two 16-ounce cans pinto or pink beans, drained and rinsed, or 4 cups cooked pinto or pink beans (from about 1⅔ cups raw)

2 cups cooked fresh corn kernels (from 3 medium ears) or frozen corn, thawed

One 14- to 16-ounce can low-sodium or Mexican-style stewed tomatoes, chopped, with liquid

1 jalapeño pepper, seeded and minced, or one 4- to 7-ounce can mild green chilies

1 teaspoon ground cumin

Combine all of the ingredients in a large saucepan or steep-sided stir-fry pan and bring to a simmer. Cover and simmer gently over low heat for 15 minutes. Serve in shallow bowls.

Calories: 263 • Total fat: 1 g
Protein: 12 g • Carbohydrate: 52 g
Cholesterol: 0 mg • Sodium: 444 mg

Pink and Pinto Beans

These related varieties are most widely used in Mexican and Southwestern dishes. Pink beans are slightly smaller and rounder than pintos, which are speckled when raw but turn a warm brown when cooked. Their mellow flavors are similar, so they may be used interchangeably. Both cook to a fine, creamy texture.

- Pink and pinto beans combine nicely with rice or corn, either hot and spiced as a main dish, or cold and marinated as a salad.
- Often used in burritos, enchiladas, and similar tortilla dishes, the flavor of these beans is enhanced by garlic, green chilies, cilantro, cumin, and oregano.

Beer-Stewed Pinto or Pink Beans (*Frijoles Borrachos*)

6 OR MORE SERVINGS

1 cup chopped fresh tomatoes or lightly drained canned diced tomatoes

Two 16-ounce cans pinto or pink beans, drained and rinsed, or 4 cups cooked pinto or pink beans (from about 1⅔ cups raw)

½ cup beer

⅓ cup chopped fresh cilantro

1 jalapeño pepper, seeded and minced, or one 4-ounce can mild green chilies

Salt to taste

Calories: 173 • Total fat: 0 g
Protein: 8 g • Carbohydrate: 32 g
Cholesterol: 0 mg • Sodium: 366 mg

The word borracho *was a nineteenth-century north-of-the-border term for a drunkard, and so the name of this recipe literally means "drunken pinto beans." Simmering the pintos in beer and fresh cilantro gives them a unique flavor.*

1 Combine all of the ingredients in a wide skillet and bring to a simmer. Cover and simmer gently over low heat for 30 minutes.

2 If there is too much liquid in the skillet, cook, uncovered, until it thickens, and serve.

MENU

Beer-Stewed Pinto or Pink Beans *(this page)*

Sweet Potato Quesadillas or Soft Tacos *(page 170)*

or

Tomato and Green Chili Quesadillas or Soft Tacos *(page 173)*

Simple tossed salad

Slow-Simmered Beans

8 OR MORE SERVINGS

There's something enticing about simmering beans for hours until they begin to "melt" into soupiness. This is a superb activity (or nonactivity, more accurately) for a snow-bound day.

1 pound red, kidney, pinto, adzuki, or other raw beans (or try a multi-bean mix)

1 tablespoon light olive oil

2 medium onions, chopped

2 garlic cloves, minced

2 bay leaves

Salt and freshly ground pepper to taste

Calories: 101 • Total fat: 1 g
Protein: 5 g • Carbohydrate: 16 g
Cholesterol: 0 mg • Sodium: 2 mg

1 Follow Step 1 in Beans and Legumes, Conventional Soak-and-Cook Method (page 110).

2 Before cooking, drain the beans, and combine them in a soup pot with plenty of water (about 1½ times their volume). Add the remaining ingredients (except salt and pepper) and bring to a simmer. Cover and simmer over low heat for 1 hour.

3 Check the beans and give them a good stir at this point. There should still be enough water for them to simmer in, at about the same level as the volume of beans. Add more water if necessary.

4 Continue to simmer until some of the beans have burst and have a creamy texture, 1½ to 2 hours over low heat. The simmering liquid should be thick and soupy. Check occasionally and add small amounts of water as needed, just enough to keep the beans simmering. Season with salt and pepper and serve in shallow bowls.

Kidney and Red Beans

These related varieties (red beans are a bit smaller and rounder than kidneys) are among the most widely used beans in North America, but they can be difficult to digest for those just starting to use beans—make sure they're well cooked.

- Kidney and red beans lend themselves well to spicy seasonings—chili powder, cayenne pepper, and paprika—hence their wide use in chili, other Mexican dishes, and the New Orleans classic, red beans and rice.

- Use them in marinated bean salads and pasta salads.

Adzuki Beans with Broccoli and Miso

6 SERVINGS

2 tablespoons light olive oil

2 large onions, quartered and thinly sliced

2 to 3 cups finely chopped broccoli florets

4 cups cooked adzuki or small red beans (from about 1⅔ cups raw), or two 16-ounce cans small red beans, drained and rinsed

2 to 3 tablespoons miso dissolved in ⅓ cup warm water

Freshly ground pepper to taste

Calories: 234 • Total fat: 5 g
Protein: 10 g • Carbohydrate: 36 g
Cholesterol: 0 mg • Sodium: 701 mg

Pungent miso makes an offbeat flavoring for red beans. For more on miso, see page 21.

1 Heat the oil in a large skillet, then add the onions and sauté over medium heat, stirring often, until they just begin to turn light brown.

2 Add the broccoli florets and just enough water to keep the bottom of the skillet moist. Cover and cook until the broccoli is tender-crisp.

3 Add the remaining ingredients, cook over medium-low heat for 10 minutes (don't boil; this destroys the beneficial enzymes in miso), and serve.

Adzuki Beans

A favorite in Japan, these small red beans are now common in American natural foods stores. Adzuki (also spelled aduki) beans are considered among the easiest legumes to digest. They cook faster than most beans, and the taste is comparable to red beans, but more delicate.

- Their Asian origin may inspire cooks to flavor adzuki beans with Asian seasonings such as ginger, tamari, and miso.
- They also can be mixed with grains in pilafs and cold salads. Substitute adzuki beans for red or pinto beans in Mexican dishes; add them to soups and stews.

MENU

Adzuki Beans with Broccoli and Miso *(this page)*

Broiled Japanese Eggplant *(page 214)*

Lightly Embellished Brown Rice *(page 91)*

Sliced red bell peppers

Lima Beans with Tomatoes and Dill

6 SERVINGS

Serve this as a side dish in shallow bowls, or over rice as a main dish.

1 tablespoon light olive oil

1 large onion, quartered and sliced

One 16-ounce bag frozen baby lima beans, thawed

One 28-ounce can low-sodium stewed tomatoes, chopped, with liquid

¼ cup chopped fresh dill, or to taste

Salt and freshly ground pepper to taste

1 Heat the oil in a large skillet. Add the onion and sauté over medium heat until golden. Add the lima beans and tomatoes and bring to a simmer. Cook gently until the lima beans are done to your liking.

2 Stir in the dill, season with salt and pepper, and serve.

Calories: 130 • Total fat: 2 g
Protein: 6 g • Carbohydrate: 21 g
Cholesterol: 0 mg • Sodium: 34 mg

Lima Beans

Lima beans are an essential ingredient in succotash, a Native American dish that has several interesting regional variations. Green baby limas have a delicate flavor that I find more appealing than that of dry limas, which are bland and mealy. Green lima beans are particularly good in highly seasoned tomato-based soups or stews, in sweet-and-sour dishes, and served over rice. Two other varieties are butter beans and fordhooks.

MENU

Lima Beans with Tomatoes and Dill *(this page)*

Lightly Embellished Brown Rice *(page 91)*

Corn on the cob

Bountiful tossed salad

6 SERVINGS

Barbecue-Flavored Baked Beans

1 tablespoon light olive oil

1 large onion, finely chopped

½ cup good-quality natural barbecue sauce

¼ cup maple syrup

Two 16-ounce cans navy beans, drained and rinsed, or 4 cups cooked navy beans (from about 1⅔ cups raw)

Calories: 245 • Total fat: 3 g
Protein: 9 g • Carbohydrate: 46 g
Cholesterol: 0 mg • Sodium: 310 mg

A casserole of beans baking in the oven is one of my favorite cold-weather comforts.

1 Preheat the oven to 325°F.

2 Heat the oil in a small skillet. Add the onion and sauté over low heat until golden.

3 Combine all of the ingredients in a 1½-quart casserole dish and mix well. Cover and bake 45 minutes. Uncover and bake 15 minutes more, and serve.

Navy Beans

Best known for their role in baked beans and soups, navy beans are also known as pea beans, small white beans, or Yankee beans. Whatever you call them, they are much like their larger cousin, the Great Northern bean—creamy and mild but not bland. Navy beans are welcome in grain pilafs or tossed into green salads.

MENU

Barbecue-Flavored Baked Beans *(this page)*

Corn Relish Salad *(page 45)*

Fresh rye bread

Steamed fresh green vegetables of your choice

Cannellini with Fresh and Dried Tomatoes

6 SERVINGS

Here's a zesty bean dish that's practically ready when you are.

1 If the dried tomatoes you are using aren't moist, soak them in hot water for about 10 minutes and drain.

2 Combine all the ingredients in a large saucepan and cook gently until heated through, 6 to 8 minutes. Or, combine the ingredients in a heat-proof container, cover, and microwave until heated through, about 5 minutes, and serve.

¼ to ½ cup sun-dried tomatoes (not oil-cured), cut into strips

Two 16-ounce cans cannellini (large white beans), drained and rinsed, or 4 cups cooked cannellini (from about 1⅔ cups raw)

1 pound fresh flavorful tomatoes, diced

3 to 4 basil leaves, sliced into thin strips, or ¼ cup minced fresh dill

Salt and freshly ground pepper to taste

Calories: 178 • Total fat: 0 g
Protein: 9 g • Carbohydrate: 34 g
Cholesterol: 0 mg • Sodium: 369 mg

Cannellini and Great Northern Beans

The mild flavor and creamy texture of these two very similar beans make them a welcome kitchen staple. Because their taste is neither distinct nor bland, they are equally at home in subtly or boldly seasoned dishes.

- Pureed, they make an excellent base for dips, sauces, or sandwich spreads (see White Bean and Dried Tomato Spread, page 239).
- Pureed cannellini also make a great creamy soup base (see Warm or Cold Tomato and White Bean Soup, page 15).

MENU

Cannellini with Fresh and Dried Tomatoes *(this page)*

Pasta and Broccoli Salad *(page 58)*

Black olives and sliced red bell peppers

Black-Eyed Peas with Bulgur and Tomatoes

6 SERVINGS

½ cup raw bulgur

2 tablespoons light olive oil

3 to 4 garlic cloves, minced

One 28-ounce can low-sodium stewed tomatoes, with liquid

Two 16-ounce cans black-eyed peas, drained and rinsed

Salt and freshly ground pepper to taste

Calories: 234 • Total fat: 5 g
Protein: 9 g • Carbohydrate: 39 g
Cholesterol: 0 mg • Sodium: 194 mg

Black-eyed peas and bulgur create a pleasant synergy in this easy and hearty dish.

1 Boil 1 cup water. Pour the water over the bulgur in a heatproof container. Cover and let stand until the water is absorbed, about 30 minutes. Or combine the water and bulgur in a small saucepan and simmer until the water is absorbed, about 15 minutes.

2 Heat the oil in a stir-fry pan or wide skillet. Add the garlic and sauté over low heat until golden, about 2 minutes.

3 Break up the tomatoes with your hands and add to the pan, followed by the black-eyed peas. Bring to a simmer over medium heat, and stir in the cooked bulgur.

4 Season to taste with salt and pepper. Cook for another 5 minutes, and serve.

MENU

Black-Eyed Peas with Bulgur and Tomatoes *(this page)*

Corn Slaw *(page 34)*

Steamed broccoli or green beans

or

Contemporary Creamed Spinach *(page 212)*

Black-Eyed Peas with Greens

6 SERVINGS

Black-eyed peas and nourishing greens, two foods well-loved in Southern and "soul" cookery, have flavors that team companionably. Serve with baked sweet potatoes, fresh corn bread, and sliced tomatoes.

12 to 16 ounces fresh greens (kale, collards, mustard greens, or Swiss chard)

2 tablespoons light olive oil

1 large onion, quartered and thinly sliced

One 16-ounce can black-eyed peas, drained and rinsed

2 tablespoons balsamic vinegar or apple cider vinegar, or to taste

Salt and freshly ground pepper to taste

1 Wash the greens well. Remove and discard the stems. Trim away thick mid-ribs from the leaves. Discard them or slice thinly and use. Chop the leaves coarsely.

2 Heat the oil in a large soup pot or steep-sided stir-fry pan. Add the onion and sauté over medium heat until golden. Add the greens, cover, and steam until tender. If using Swiss chard, just the water clinging to the leaves is sufficient. For kale and collards, add ¼ to ½ cup of water as needed to keep the mixture moist. Allow 3 to 5 minutes to steam Swiss chard; 10 to 15 minutes to steam the other types of greens.

3 Stir in the black-eyed peas and vinegar. Season to taste with salt and pepper. Cook just until everything is heated through, and serve.

Variation: Use pink, pinto, or black beans instead of black-eyed peas.

Calories: 171 • Total fat: 5 g
Protein: 7 g • Carbohydrate: 24 g
Cholesterol: 0 mg • Sodium: 110 mg

Black-Eyed Peas

As the name suggests, these pale legumes have a black "eye." Their use is prevalent in Africa, where they originated, in the American South, and in Persian cuisine. Black-eyed peas, and their smaller, browner cousin, the field pea, have a distinctive "fresh" flavor.

- Use them in marinated salads (try them in the flexible recipe for Marinated Beans, page 40) and with strong-flavored lettuces.
- Add some to cooked dark leafy greens, as in the recipe for Black-Eyed Peas with Greens (page 123).
- Black-eyed peas combine well with rice and other grains, and their flavor is enhanced by tomatoes, garlic, onions, and thyme.

6 SERVINGS

Lentil and Rice Pilaf

1 vegetable bouillon cube

¾ cup brown rice

¾ cup brown or green lentils, rinsed

3 to 4 scallions, thinly sliced

¼ cup minced fresh parsley or dill

Salt and freshly ground pepper to taste

Calories: 158 • Total fat: 0 g
Protein: 7 g • Carbohydrate: 31 g
Cholesterol: 0 mg • Sodium: 51 mg

Rice and lentils make perfect pilaf partners because they can be cooked together and are done simultaneously.

1 Bring 4 cups water to a simmer in a large saucepan with the bouillon. Stir in the rice and lentils, cover, and simmer gently until the water is absorbed, about 35 minutes.

2 Stir in the remaining ingredients, and serve.

Lentils

These small, peppery legumes cook quickly without soaking. Brown (or green) lentils are widely known in this country, but tiny red lentils, a staple in Indian cookery, are gaining in popularity; they are a bit milder in flavor and cook even faster than larger lentils.

- Lentils are particularly tasty when stewed with curry spices and are highly compatible with spinach (see the following recipe as well as Curried Red Lentil and Spinach Soup, page 26).

- They are wonderful in hearty salads such as Lentil and Feta Cheese Salad (page 41).

MENU

Lentil and Rice Pilaf *(this page)*

Mixed Greens with Tomatoes, Feta, and Olives *(page 51)*

Steamed green beans, asparagus, or broccolini

Curried Lentils with Spinach

4 TO 6 SERVINGS

Lentils and spinach both marry well with curry spices. Each complements the other's flavor, too.

1 cup brown or red lentils, sorted and rinsed

3 to 4 garlic cloves, minced

¼ cup finely chopped onion

1 to 2 teaspoons curry powder, or to taste

Two 10-ounce packages frozen chopped spinach, thawed

Salt to taste

1 Combine 3 cups water, the lentils, garlic, onion, and curry powder in a large saucepan. Bring to a simmer, cover, and simmer very gently until the lentils are tender, 25 to 30 minutes for brown lentils and 20 to 25 minutes for red lentils.

2 Drain the spinach and squeeze out some of the water. Stir into the lentil mixture and season with salt. Cook for another 5 minutes, and serve.

Calories: 173 • Total fat: 0 g
Protein: 11 g • Carbohydrate: 30 g
Cholesterol: 0 mg • Sodium: 101 mg

MENU

Curried Lentils with Spinach *(this page)*

Cucumbers and Tomatoes in Yogurt *(page 39)*

Gingered Baby Carrots and Apricots *(page 208)*

Fresh pita bread

Polenta with Fresh Tomatoes and Mozzarella

3 TO 4 SERVINGS

One 16-ounce tube polenta

1 tablespoon light olive oil

2 medium flavorful firm tomatoes, finely diced

1 cup grated part-skim mozzarella cheese or mozzarella-style soy cheese

3 to 4 fresh basil leaves, thinly sliced, or a sprinkling of dried basil, optional

Calories: 204 • Total fat: 9 g
Protein: 10 g • Carbohydrate: 21 g
Cholesterol: 19 mg • Sodium: 197 mg

These tasty treats resemble miniature pizzas and are an offbeat pairing with light pasta dishes, as in the suggested menu.

1 Cut the polenta into 12 equal slices, each about ½ inch thick. Heat the oil on a nonstick griddle or wide skillet. Arrange the polenta slices on the griddle. Cook both sides over medium heat until golden and crisp, at least 10 minutes per side.

2 Arrange the polenta slices on a large platter. Sprinkle evenly with the tomato, then the mozzarella cheese. Microwave just until the cheese is melted, 2 to 3 minutes. Or, if you prefer, bake the polenta briefly in a preheated 400°F oven in an ovenproof container until the cheese is melted, about 5 minutes. Allow 3 to 4 slices of polenta per serving. Sprinkle each serving with fresh or dried basil, if desired.

MENU

Polenta with Fresh Tomatoes and Mozzarella *(this page)*

Spinach Fettuccine with Summer Squash *(page 79)*

Simple tossed salad

Polenta with Sautéed Bell Peppers

3 TO 4 SERVINGS

The sweet flavor of sautéed peppers contrasts delectably with crisp polenta. Try serving this with Rice and Peas (page 100) and a simple tossed salad.

One 16-ounce tube polenta

2 tablespoons light olive oil

1 large onion, quartered and sliced

2 medium green or red bell peppers or 1 of each, cut into narrow strips

1 teaspoon minced fresh oregano or ¼ teaspoon dried oregano, optional

Salt and freshly ground pepper to taste

1 Cut the polenta into 12 equal slices, each about ½ inch thick. Heat 1 tablespoon of the oil on a nonstick griddle or wide skillet. Arrange the polenta slices on the griddle. Cook both sides over medium heat until golden and crisp, at least 10 minutes per side.

2 Meanwhile, heat the remaining 1 tablespoon oil in a medium skillet. Add the onion and sauté over medium heat until golden. Add the bell pepper strips and continue to sauté, stirring frequently, until tender and just beginning to be touched with brown spots.

3 Stir in the optional oregano, and season with a little salt and pepper. To serve, place 3 to 4 slices of polenta on each plate and spoon some of the peppers mixture over them.

Calories: 172 • Total fat: 8 g
Protein: 2 g • Carbohydrate: 23 g
Cholesterol: 0 mg • Sodium: 2 mg

Polenta

Prepared polenta provides an interesting way to add variety to the daily repertoire. Traditional polenta is simply cooked cornmeal mush, which can be served plain or fancy; the kind you buy in 16- to 24-ounce tubes is cooked cornmeal that's dense enough to slice. Look for polenta with gourmet refrigerated foods (such as fresh pastas) or at the deli counter.

Prepare polenta by slicing it approximately ½ inch thick and cooking on a nonstick griddle or skillet with a little oil or nonhydrogenated margarine (not butter, though; it will burn from such prolonged exposure) over medium heat until golden and slightly crisp on both sides. This takes a bit of time—8 minutes per side seems minimal.

Polenta can be served as a side dish or topped any way you'd like: with warmed leftover vegetable stews and chili or other bean dishes (such as the black bean recipes on pages 112 to 114), or as shown in these recipes.

Seitan, Mushroom, and Onion Stir-Fry

4 TO 6 SERVINGS

2 tablespoons light olive oil

2 large onions, quartered and sliced

10 to 12 ounces white or cremini mushrooms, sliced

1 to 1½ pounds seitan, cut into bite-size chunks

3 to 4 tablespoons natural stir-fry sauce, or to taste

Freshly ground pepper to taste

Calories: 194 • Total fat: 6 g
Protein: 24 g • Carbohydrate: 11 g
Cholesterol: 0 mg • Sodium: 707 mg

A great choice for hearty appetites, this convincingly dispels the notion that vegetarian cuisine is "rabbit food."

1 Heat the oil in a large skillet or stir-fry pan. Add the onions and sauté over medium heat until golden.

2 Add the mushrooms, cover, and cook until they are done to your liking, 5 to 7 minutes.

3 Stir in the seitan and stir-fry sauce. Turn the heat up to medium-high and stir-fry until the seitan chunks are touched by golden-brown spots. Season to taste with pepper, and serve.

MENU

Seitan, Mushroom, and Onion Stir-Fry *(this page)*

or

Seitan Sauté with Bell Peppers *(page 129)*

Lightly Embellished Brown Rice *(page 91)*

or

Fruited Couscous *(page 106)*

Simple tossed salad

Seitan Sauté with Bell Peppers

4 TO 6 SERVINGS

This hearty dish is reminiscent of Chinese restaurant peppersteak.

2 tablespoons light olive oil

1 large onion, chopped

3 medium green or red bell peppers, or a combination, diced

1 to 1½ pounds seitan, ¼ cup of liquid reserved, cut into bite-size chunks

Light soy sauce or teriyaki sauce to taste

Freshly ground pepper to taste

Calories: 252 • Total fat: 6 g
Protein: 39 g • Carbohydrate: 10 g
Cholesterol: 0 mg • Sodium: 242 mg

1 Heat the oil in a large skillet or stir-fry pan. Add the onions and sauté over medium heat until golden.

2 Add the bell peppers and seitan and sauté over medium-high heat, stirring frequently, until the peppers are tender-crisp and the seitan chunks are touched by golden-brown spots. Season to taste with soy sauce and pepper and serve.

Seitan

Seitan is a superb grain product that deserves more attention. Bearing the Japanese name meaning "wheat gluten," it's commonly used in many Asian cuisines. These chewy, moist chunks are often used in Chinese vegetable dishes as a meat imitator.

Seitan is, in fact, sometimes referred to as "wheat meat." It is made by rinsing wheat flour dough of its starchy components, leaving the chewy, high-protein gluten, which is then cooked in a soy sauce and ginger-flavored broth. The medium-brown color and porous surface of the finished product add to its "meatiness." Despite its analogous qualities, seitan doesn't really taste like meat and shouldn't put off anyone who isn't tempted by imitation meats.

Its full-bodied character makes seitan somewhat less versatile than tofu, but still, it lends itself to numerous preparations. The easiest use for it is to simply toss chunks into stir-fries or to grill or broil it using your favorite sauce.

A ready-to-use product, seitan is most often sold in 1- to 1½-pound tubs. As of this writing, I have rarely seen it in supermarkets, so look for it in natural foods stores and food co-ops. If seitan captures your fancy, you may want to try Arrowhead Mill's Seitan Quick Mix so that you can prepare larger quantities. This mix is not *exactly* quick, but certainly more convenient than making seitan from scratch.

Seitan Kebabs

4 SERVINGS

2 medium red bell peppers, cut into 1-inch dice

2 medium zucchini, halved lengthwise, then cut into ½-inch-thick chunks

1 pound seitan, cut into ¾-inch chunks

½ to ⅔ cup natural low-fat barbecue sauce

Calories: 246 • Total fat: 1 g
Protein: 39 g • Carbohydrate: 20 g
Cholesterol: 0 mg • Sodium: 521 mg

These simple kebabs may become a staple for you if you like grilled foods. In the colder months, they turn out well from the broiler. Serve with corn on the cob, diced fresh tomatoes, and a simple slaw made from shredded cabbage and your favorite vinaigrette.

1 Preheat the broiler or grill.

2 Using 8- to 10-inch metal skewers, alternate the bell peppers, zucchini, and seitan, in that order, until all the ingredients are used up. There should be enough for 8 skewers.

3 Brush the barbecue sauce over the kebabs, then place on a foil-lined baking sheet for the broiler or on a piece of foil for the grill. Broil or grill, turning every 3 to 5 minutes (use an oven mitt!) until done to your liking. Allow 2 skewers per serving.

Essential Soy

CHAPTER 5

After a journey of 2,000 years as one of Asia's most revered foods (and perhaps 30 years of making slow inroads into the Western world), soy foods burst into the mainstream media in the mid-1990s. One attention-grabbing headline after another speculated on the benefits of soy, from reducing cholesterol levels in men, to naturally replacing hormones for women, to reducing everyone's risk of osteoporosis.

Studies come and go, but few experts dispute that soy is a remarkable food. Supplying high-quality, easily digestible protein, soy foods are low in fat and rich in essential nutrients as well as medicinal qualities. They deserve a greater role in the way Americans eat and are a boon for anyone moving toward a plant-based diet.

I like soy foods not only because they are good for me, but as a cook, I appreciate their amazing versatility. Tofu alone comes in several forms and consistencies, from chewy to custardy. And soy-based meat analogs—hot dogs, sausages, burger-type crumbles, deli slices, pepperoni, and more—can be helpful to those cutting back on meat. These products also seem to appeal to children; this alone is a great help in expanding family menu options.

It's terrific that so many soy products are now readily available in supermarkets. For anyone still confounded by tofu and its relatives, these simple recipes offer many choices incorporating familiar flavors. And for those of you who are more familiar with soy, these recipes will expand your repertoire of everyday options.

Bell Pepper Scrambled Tofu

4 SERVINGS

1 tablespoon light olive oil

2 medium green or red bell peppers or 1 of each

2 to 3 scallions, sliced

1 pound soft tofu, drained and crumbled

1 teaspoon salt-free herb-and-spice seasoning mix

Salt and freshly ground pepper to taste

Calories: 101 • Total fat: 6 g
Protein: 6 g • Carbohydrate: 5 g
Cholesterol: 0 mg • Sodium: 8 mg

1 Heat the oil in a large skillet. Add the peppers and sauté over medium heat until they are just beginning to be touched with brown spots.

2 Add the remaining ingredients and cook over medium heat, stirring frequently, until everything is heated through, about 5 minutes, and serve.

MENU

A SIMPLE BRUNCH OR LIGHT DINNER

Mushroom Scrambled Tofu *(page 133)*

or

Bell Pepper Scrambled Tofu *(this page)*

Cooked or microwaved tiny new potatoes (allow 3 to 4 per serving)

Whole grain toast

Vegetable juice

Orange sections

Mushroom Scrambled Tofu

Soft tofu is a good choice for dishes in which it is crumbled, as in this and the preceding scramble recipe. Both are good for lunch, a light dinner, or even as part of a casual brunch.

4 SERVINGS

1 tablespoon nonhydrogenated margarine

1 to 1½ cups sliced small white or cremini mushrooms

1 pound soft tofu, drained and crumbled

2 to 3 scallions, sliced

½ to 1 teaspoon mild curry powder

Salt and freshly ground pepper to taste

1 Heat the margarine in a large skillet. Add the mushrooms and cook over medium heat until they are done to your liking. Turn up the heat to cook away any liquid that has formed.

2 Add the remaining ingredients and cook over medium heat, stirring frequently, until everything is heated through, about 5 minutes, and serve.

Calories: 101 • Total fat: 6 g
Protein: 8 g • Carbohydrate: 4 g
Cholesterol: 0 mg • Sodium: 88 mg

Fear of Tofu!

Though tofu is now a household word and quite widely available, it still causes a fair amount of befuddlement. I call this phenomenon "fear of tofu." The most common complaint I hear is that it is just so bland. People have told me they think it tastes like soap or a sponge. I politely refrain from asking them when they last made a meal of soap or sponges, and instead, I point out that tofu's blandness can be its greatest asset. Actually, tofu is sort of like a sponge—and I mean that in the most positive sense. Its absorbent texture helps it soak up the flavors of whatever it is being cooked or seasoned with.

Just as cheese is coagulated from milk, tofu is coagulated from soymilk. A culturing medium is used to solidify it and form it into rectangular blocks. It's those quivering white blocks that seem to send tremors of fear—or at least extreme reluctance—into the hearts of many skeptics.

In Natalie Goldberg's classic book, *Writing Down the Bones,* she relates an amusing saying used by her late Zen teacher, Katagiri Roshi: "Fighting the tofu." This refers to the ego putting up a pointless struggle. "It's fruitless to wrestle with [tofu]," goes her analogy. "You get nowhere."

So don't struggle with tofu—use it in simple preparations that harmonize with its basic bland goodness. But if you honestly can't make peace with it, don't feel bad or guilty. Tofu skeptics who want to put more soy in their diets can do so in other wonderful ways, as you will see in the list on page 147.

MAKES ABOUT 1 DOZEN,
4 TO 6 SERVINGS

Tofu Patties

2 eggs, beaten

1 pound soft tofu, drained well and finely crumbled

¼ cup wheat germ

1 teaspoon salt-free herb-and-spice seasoning mix

Salt to taste

Light olive oil for frying

Calories: 102 • Total fat: 5 g
Protein: 9 g • Carbohydrate: 5 g
Cholesterol: 85 mg • Sodium: 33 mg

These tasty patties can be sandwiched into rolls with lettuce and sliced tomatoes or served on their own as a side dish for grain, potato, or pasta dishes.

1 Combine the eggs, tofu, wheat germ, seasoning mix, and salt in a mixing bowl and stir together until well blended.

2 Heat enough oil to coat a wide nonstick skillet or griddle. Ladle the tofu mixture onto the skillet in ¼-cup portions and flatten. Cook the patties on both sides over medium heat until golden brown. Drain on paper towels. Serve warm or at room temperature.

Sweet and Savory Sautéed or Baked Tofu

4 SERVINGS

1 pound firm or extra-firm tofu

1 tablespoon light olive oil

1 tablespoon honey

2 tablespoons natural soy sauce

Calories: 138 • Total fat: 8 g
Protein: 9 g • Carbohydrate: 7 g
Cholesterol: 0 mg • Sodium: 511 mg

This is a family favorite that I make regularly. It can be sautéed or baked and is a great accompaniment to Asian-style noodle or rice dishes.

1 Cut the tofu into ½-inch-thick slices. Blot well between clean tea towels or several layers of paper towel, and cut into ½-inch dice.

2 To sauté, slowly heat the oil, honey, and soy sauce together in a wide skillet, stirring together as they heat. Add the tofu and stir quickly to coat with the liquid. Sauté over medium-high heat until golden-brown and crisp on most sides, about 10 minutes, and serve.

3 To bake, preheat the oven to 400°F. Combine the oil, honey, and soy sauce in a mixing bowl and stir together. Stir in the tofu to coat with the sauce. Bake in a shallow, foil-lined baking pan, stirring occasionally, until the tofu is golden brown and the liquid has been absorbed, 30 to 40 minutes, and serve.

MENU

Sweet and Savory Sautéed or Baked Tofu *(this page)*

Chinese-Style Vegetable Fried Rice *(page 94)*

or

Asian Sesame-Soy Noodles *(page 85)*

Crisp raw bell pepper strips and carrot and celery sticks

Tofu Varieties

Here's a brief lexicon of the most commonly available tofu varieties and how to best use them.

Silken tofu: Available in 1-pound tubs or 12.3-ounce aseptic packages, this type of tofu is very soft and smooth. It's best when pureed and used as a base for soups, dressings, dips, and sauces. You can even make dessert puddings out of it. For one of my favorite recipes using it, see Soy Scalloped Potatoes (page 182).

Soft tofu: This comes in 1-pound tubs and is good for using crumbled, as in faux scrambled-egg recipes like those on pages 132 and 133; or imitation "egg salad" such as the one on page 238. Finely crumbled, this is also a good substitute for ricotta cheese. Like silken tofu, it can also be pureed and used as a soup or sauce base, though it isn't quite as smooth.

Firm or extra-firm tofu: Again, available in 1-pound tubs and also fresh in chunks or cakes; use this when you want the tofu to hold its shape. Firm tofu is ideal for use in stir-fries, stews, and cutlets.

Baked marinated tofu: I am always lamenting that this product is not more widely available. Look for it in natural foods stores, as I have rarely seen it in supermarkets. It's a chewy, flavorful form of tofu that usually comes in 8-ounce packages. It can be sliced, diced (for this, any brand is fine), or crumbled (the best brand for crumbling is Soy Boy's Tofu Lin, as it is less "crusty" than the others) and used as a chicken or tuna substitute in stir-fries, sandwiches, and casseroles.

Simmered Tofu Teriyaki

4 SERVINGS

This recipe doubles easily for a bigger batch. Accompany with Asian noodles or rice and a simple stir-fry, as suggested in the menu.

1 pound firm tofu, blotted and cut into ¾-inch dice

1 cup canned vegetable stock

2 tablespoons dry white wine

2 tablespoons teriyaki sauce

2 scallions, thinly sliced

1 Combine the first 4 ingredients in a stir-fry pan or medium saucepan. Bring to a simmer, cover, and simmer gently for 10 minutes.

2 Divide the tofu and liquid among 4 shallow bowls. Garnish each serving with some scallions, and serve.

Calories: 114 • Total fat: 5 g
Protein: 8 g • Carbohydrate: 6 g
Cholesterol: 0 mg • Sodium: 292 mg

MENU

Simmered Tofu Teriyaki *(this page)*

Broccoli and Baby Corn Stir-Fry *(page 199)*

Cooked brown rice or Asian noodles

Sliced red bell peppers

Shake-and-Bake Tofu

4 SERVINGS

1 pound firm or extra-firm tofu

¼ cup wheat germ

½ teaspoon salt-free herb-and-spice seasoning mix

½ teaspoon salt

Marinara sauce (warmed), ketchup, salsa, or Yogurt "Tartar Sauce" or Dip (page 231)

Calories: 114 • Total fat: 5 g
Protein: 10 g • Carbohydrate: 5 g
Cholesterol: 0 mg • Sodium: 275 mg

These crispy tofu cutlets are another favorite in our home. Enlist your kids to help with the breading and shaking—they'll have fun with it, and they're more likely to eat anything they've helped make. If you're serving more than four, the recipe doubles easily, but be sure to use two baking sheets as well.

1 Preheat the oven to 425°F.

2 Cut the tofu into ½-inch-thick slices. Blot well between clean tea towels or several layers of paper towel, and cut into ½-inch-wide sticks.

3 Combine the wheat germ, seasoning mix, and salt in a plastic food storage bag; seal and shake lightly to mix. Transfer the cutlets to the bag and shake gently until they are evenly coated with the wheat germ mixture.

4 Arrange the cutlets on a lightly oiled nonstick baking sheet. Bake until golden and firm, 12 to 15 minutes. Serve at once with marinara sauce or other sauce of your choice for dipping or topping.

MENU

A CHILD-FRIENDLY MEAL

Tofu Patties *(page 134)*

or

Shake-and-Bake Tofu *(this page)*

Maple-Roasted Carrots *(page 207)*

Buttered angel hair pasta

Cherry tomatoes and baby carrots

Tofu and Sweet Potato Curry

4 TO 6 SERVINGS

This is as luscious-tasting as it is nourishing.

2 large or 3 medium sweet potatoes

1 pound firm tofu, well drained and diced

One 14- to 16-ounce can low-sodium stewed tomatoes, chopped, with liquid

1 to 2 teaspoons good-quality curry powder, or to taste

4 ounces arugula or baby spinach, well rinsed

Salt to taste

1 Bake or microwave the sweet potatoes in their skins until done but still firm. When cool enough to handle, peel, and cut into large dice.

2 Combine the tofu, tomatoes, and 1 teaspoon of the curry powder in a stir-fry pan or wide skillet. Bring to a simmer, cover, and cook over medium-low heat for 10 minutes.

3 Add the diced sweet potato and continue to cook for another 5 minutes.

4 Add the arugula, cover, and cook very briefly, just until it wilts slightly. Taste and season with more curry if desired. Season with salt and serve.

Calories: 159 • Total fat: 4 g
Protein: 8 g • Carbohydrate: 22 g
Cholesterol: 0 mg • Sodium: 21 mg

MENU

Tofu and Sweet Potato Curry *(this page)*

Cucumbers and Tomatoes in Yogurt *(page 39)*

Fruited Couscous *(page 106)*

Baked Barbecue Tofu and Potato Kebabs

4 SERVINGS

4 medium-large red-skinned potatoes, scrubbed and microwaved until done but still firm

1 pound firm or extra-firm tofu, well drained and cut into ¾-inch chunks

½ cup (or as needed) natural barbecue sauce

Calories: 281 • Total fat: 5 g
Protein: 10 g • Carbohydrate: 48 g
Cholesterol: 0 mg • Sodium: 220 mg

Good Southern corn on the cob (available nearly all year around) served with these tasty kebabs results in a meal recalling outdoor summer barbecues. A sure cure for winter doldrums!

1 Preheat the broiler.

2 When the potatoes are cool enough to handle, cut them into 1-inch chunks. Starting with potato, alternate the potato and tofu chunks on metal skewers. There should be enough for 8 average-length skewers. Place on a foil-lined baking sheet and brush the kebabs generously with barbecue sauce.

3 Broil for 5 minutes, and turn the skewers over carefully, wearing a long oven mitt. Broil for another 5 minutes. If desired, turn once again and broil for an additional 5 minutes. Remove from the oven, and serve.

MENU

Baked Barbecue Tofu and Potato Kebabs *(this page)*

Corn on the cob

Coleslaw (made with shredded coleslaw cabbage and dressing of your choice, or any of the slaw recipes on pages 34 to 37)

Baked Barbecue Tofu and Peppers

4 SERVINGS

So good and very easy, this recipe might just be the ticket to converting tofu skeptics.

1 pound firm or extra-firm tofu

2 green or red bell peppers, or 1 of each, cut into approximately ½ by 2-inch strips

1 large onion, halved and thinly sliced, rings separated

¾ cup natural barbecue sauce, or as needed

1 Preheat the oven to 425°F.

2 Cut the tofu into ½-inch-thick slices, and blot well between clean tea towels or several layers of paper towel. Cut the slices into strips or dice.

3 Stir all the ingredients together in a mixing bowl, and transfer to a foil-lined baking sheet or roasting pan.

4 Bake for 15 minutes, then stir and bake for another 10 minutes, and serve.

Calories: 179 • Total fat: 5 g
Protein: 9 g • Carbohydrate: 24 g
Cholesterol: 0 mg • Sodium: 330 mg

MENU

Baked Barbecue Tofu and Peppers *(this page)*

Simple Potato Salad *(page 54)*

or

Baked or microwaved sweet potato

Bountiful tossed salad

Barbecue-Flavored Tofu and Onion Stir-Fry

4 SERVINGS

1½ tablespoons light olive oil

2 large onions, quartered and thinly sliced (try red or Vidalia onions)

1 pound firm or extra-firm tofu, well drained and diced

½ cup natural barbecue sauce, or as needed (see note)

Hot cooked rice, optional

Calories: 203 • Total fat: 9 g
Protein: 9 g • Carbohydrate: 19 g
Cholesterol: 0 mg • Sodium: 220 mg

As you can see, I really like what barbecue sauce does for tofu. This is excellent over rice.

1 Heat the oil in a stir-fry pan or large skillet. Add the onions and sauté over medium heat until lightly golden.

2 Add the tofu and barbecue sauce and turn the heat up to medium-high. Stir-fry for 6 to 8 minutes, and serve on its own or over rice.

Note: Try honey-teriyaki or mesquite-flavored barbecue sauce. Both are excellent in this preparation.

MENU

Barbecue-Flavored Tofu and Onion Stir-Fry *(this page)*

Hot cooked rice

Steamed vegetables of your choice

Simple tossed salad

Broccoli and Tofu in Thai Peanut Sauce

4 SERVINGS

Spicy Thai peanut sauce is another of my favored shortcuts to great flavor. There are a number of good, natural brands available, some much lower in fat than you might expect. Serve over hot cooked brown rice or Asian noodles such as soba.

2 large broccoli crowns, cut into bite-size florets

1 pound firm or extra-firm tofu, well drained and diced

¾ cup spicy Thai peanut sauce, preferably low-fat, or as needed

Salt to taste

1 Steam the broccoli florets in a covered wok or stir-fry pan with about ½ inch of water, until tender-crisp.

2 Gently stir in the tofu and peanut sauce. Cook over medium heat until heated through. Add salt to taste, and serve at once.

Calories: 176 • Total fat: 9 g
Protein: 9 g • Carbohydrate: 13 g
Cholesterol: 0 mg • Sodium: 106 mg

MENU

Broccoli and Tofu in Thai Peanut Sauce *(this page)*

Hot cooked brown rice or noodles

Mixed Greens with Wild Mushrooms *(page 53)*

Fresh fruit or any fruity dessert from Chapter Eleven

Instant Tofu and Mixed Vegetable Stir-Fry

4 TO 6 SERVINGS

Two 16-ounce packages Asian-style (sometimes labeled Oriental or Japanese) frozen mixed vegetables

¼ cup stir-fry sauce, or to taste

1 pound firm or baked tofu, cut into short, narrow strips

Calories: 134 • Total fat: 4 g
Protein: 10 g • Carbohydrate: 14 g
Cholesterol: 0 mg • Sodium: 400 mg

Look for some of the interesting Asian-style vegetable mélanges in the frozen vegetables section. They're great to have on hand when you crave a quick stir-fry but don't feel like chopping. Serve with hot cooked rice or noodles and raw carrot and celery sticks, or try the accompanying menu.

1 Steam the vegetables in a stir-fry pan or wok, covered, until completely thawed. Drain well and transfer back to the stir-fry pan.

2 Stir in the sauce and stir-fry over medium-high heat until the vegetables are tender-crisp.

3 Add the tofu strips and toss gently. Cook just until heated through, and serve at once.

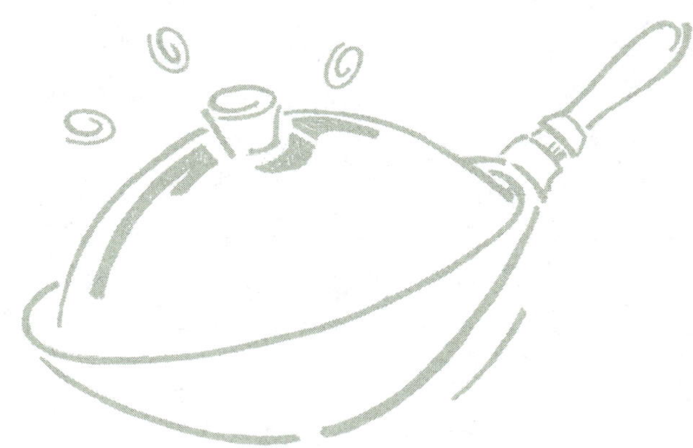

MENU

Instant Tofu and Mixed Vegetable Stir-Fry *(this page)*

Asian Noodle Broth *(page 22)*

Crisp raw vegetable platter

Stir-Fried Tofu and Bok Choy

4 SERVINGS

Bok choy combines crunch and leafiness in one neat package and cooks up quickly in stir-fries.

1 pound firm or extra-firm tofu

1 tablespoon light olive or peanut oil

1 bunch bok choy, with leaves, sliced crosswise and rinsed

3 to 4 tablespoons stir-fry sauce, or to taste

¼ cup coarsely chopped peanuts

1 Cut the tofu into ½-inch-thick slices. Blot well between clean tea towels or several layers of paper towel, and cut into ½-inch dice.

2 Heat the oil in a stir-fry pan or wide skillet. Add the tofu and stir-fry over medium-high heat until golden on most sides, about 10 minutes.

3 Add the bok choy, stir-fry sauce, and about 2 tablespoons of water. Quickly stir together, then stir-fry for another 3 to 4 minutes, just until the bok choy is wilted. Stir in the peanuts, and serve at once.

Calories: 186 • Total fat: 12 g
Protein: 12 g • Carbohydrate: 6 g
Cholesterol: 0 mg • Sodium: 437 mg

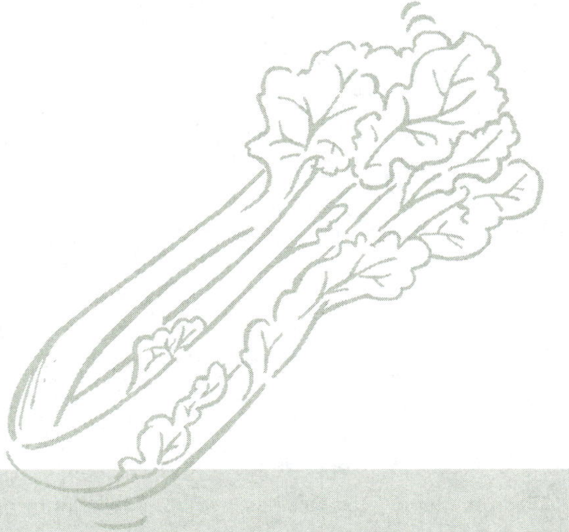

MENU

Stir-Fried Tofu and Bok Choy *(this page)*

Chinese-Style Vegetable Fried Rice *(page 94)*

Sliced red bell peppers

Orange sections (in season)

or fresh fruit of your choice

4 SERVINGS

Sautéed Tempeh Cutlets

One 8-ounce package tempeh

1 tablespoon light olive or peanut oil

2 tablespoons natural soy sauce

Ground coriander, optional

Calories: 148 • Total fat: 7 g
Protein: 10 g • Carbohydrate: 10 g
Cholesterol: 0 mg • Sodium: 460 mg

This is good to serve with meals needing a protein boost or as a sandwich filling. See the menu with Southeast Asian-Style Spicy Mashed Potatoes (page 187).

1 Slice the tempeh in half horizontally, then cut into rectangular pieces approximately 1½ by 2 inches.

2 Heat the oil and soy sauce slowly in a wide skillet. Add the tempeh and sauté over medium heat until golden brown and crisp on both sides, about 10 minutes. Sprinkle with the optional coriander (a traditional seasoning for tempeh) and serve.

Tempeh

Tempeh is a soy food with Indonesian roots. It hasn't gained as much in popularity (or at least in notoriety) as tofu has, perhaps due to an even more offbeat character. Nutritious and chewy, tempeh has a distinct, somewhat fermented flavor. Available in 8-ounce packages, tempeh is available in soy-only or soy-and-grain combinations. Tempeh may not be for everyone, but it's worth a try. You'll find it in natural foods stores and in well-stocked supermarkets, shelved near tofu and other soy products in the produce section. See also Curried Tempeh Spread, page 237.

"Franks" and Beans

6 SERVINGS

I know, I know—this hardly qualifies as a recipe (I can just hear the critics!). Yet this recipe has saved me from take-out more times than I care to admit. Gourmet it's not, but it is low in fat and high in fiber and protein. And since everyone in my family likes this, it ranks among our favorite "emergency" dinners. Serve with Creamy Coleslaw (page 35) and baked sweet potatoes.

Two 16-ounce cans vegetarian baked beans

6 to 8 links soy hot dogs, thinly sliced

1 tablespoon light brown sugar

1½ to 2 teaspoons prepared mustard, or to taste

Combine all of the ingredients in a large saucepan. Bring to a simmer and cook briefly, just until everything is heated through. Serve in shallow bowls.

Calories: 236 • Total fat: 3 g
Protein: 17 g • Carbohydrate: 30 g
Cholesterol: 0 mg • Sodium: 565 mg

Soy Analog Products Worth Exploring

So you've tried tofu and you just can't make peace with it. Before you give up on soy, try some of the products listed below. Some of them are uncanny meat imitators, but without the fat and other detrimental effects. Do note that these soy foods, though almost always made with natural ingredients, are highly processed. Some are high in sodium, and may not give you as much nutritional benefit as plain tofu or tempeh. Still, they may be helpful to those making a transition to a meatless diet as well as anyone looking for more variety in their meals (and who isn't?). All are carried by well-stocked supermarkets. You'll find some in the produce section and others in the frozen foods section.

- Soy "chicken"-style patties, chunks, and nuggets
- Soy "beef"-style chunks
- Soy burgers
- Soy deli slices
- Soy hot dogs
- Soy sausages
- Soy pepperoni
- Soy "ground beef" substitute (sometimes called "crumbles")

"Chili Dogs"

4 TO 6 SERVINGS
(1 OR 2 PER PERSON)

One 16-ounce can spicy fat-free refried beans

One 4- or 7-ounce can chopped mild green chilies

1 teaspoon ground cumin, optional

6 to 8 links soy hot dogs

6 to 8 hot dog rolls or small (6-inch) flour tortillas, warmed

PER EACH:

Calories: 259 • Total fat: 3 g
Protein: 16 g • Carbohydrate: 41 g
Cholesterol: 0 mg • Sodium: 538 mg

This casual concoction may appeal to older kids as well as teens who are beginning to enjoy spicier flavors.

1 Combine the refried beans, chilies, ¼ cup water, and optional cumin in a medium saucepan. Cook gently until heated through.

2 Warm the hot dogs according to package directions. If you'd like, warm the rolls (not necessary if they are fresh).

3 Place a hot dog in each roll and spread plenty of the chili sauce on either side of it (about 2 tablespoons per serving). If using tortillas, place a hot dog toward one edge of the tortilla, spread the rest of the tortilla with chili sauce, and roll up. You will end up with more chili sauce than you will need—save the rest for making simple burritos later in the week or use as a bean dip for tortilla chips.

MENU

"Chili Dogs" *(this page)*

White or Sweet Potato Oven "Fries" *(page 193)*

Simple tossed salad

Steamed broccoli

"Sausage" and Peppers

4 TO 6 SERVINGS

This pairs well with light pasta dishes, as in the suggested menu.

2 tablespoons extra-virgin olive oil

6 to 8 soy "sausage" links

1 large onion, chopped

4 medium green or red bell peppers or 2 of each, cut into narrow strips

2 garlic cloves, minced, optional

Salt and freshly ground pepper to taste

1 Heat ½ tablespoon of the oil in a wide skillet. Add the "sausage" links and sauté, turning on all sides, until golden. Remove to a plate. When cool enough to handle, cut into ½-inch-thick slices.

2 Heat the remaining 1½ tablespoons oil in the same skillet. Add the onion and sauté over medium heat until translucent. Add the bell pepper strips and optional garlic and continue to sauté until the peppers are tender and just beginning to brown.

3 Stir in the "sausage" slices and cook just until heated through. Season with salt and pepper, and serve.

Calories: 115 • Total fat: 7 g
Protein: 6 g • Carbohydrate: 7 g
Cholesterol: 0 mg • Sodium: 240 mg

MENU

"Sausage" and Peppers *(this page)*

Farfalle with Mushrooms *(page 76)*

or

Pasta with Olive Sauce *(page 75)*

Simple tossed salad

"Sausage" and Potatoes

4 TO 6 SERVINGS

6 medium potatoes, preferably red-skinned or Yukon gold

2 tablespoons light olive oil

6 to 8 soy "sausage" links

1 large onion, quartered and sliced

2 cups thinly sliced green or savoy cabbage (for a shortcut, use shredded coleslaw cabbage)

Salt and freshly ground pepper to taste

Calories: 246 • Total fat: 7 g
Protein: 8 g • Carbohydrate: 38 g
Cholesterol: 0 mg • Sodium: 252 mg

If you're feeding "meat-and-potatoes" kind of people, try this out on them. It's quite hearty, but not so "meaty" that it would put off those who aren't fans of meat substitutes.

1 Microwave the potatoes in their skins until done but still firm. When cool enough to handle, peel and slice (plunge them into a bowl of cold water to speed up the cooling, if you'd like).

2 Heat ½ tablespoon of the oil in a wide skillet. Add the "sausage" links and sauté, turning on all sides, until golden. Remove to a plate. When cool enough to handle, cut into ½-inch-thick slices.

3 Heat the remaining 1½ tablespoons oil in the same skillet. Add the onion and sauté over medium heat until translucent. Add the cabbage and about ¼ cup water, and cover. Continue to cook, stirring occasionally, until the onion and cabbage are tender and golden, 8 to 10 minutes.

4 Stir in the "sausage" slices and potatoes and cook just until everything is heated through. If you'd like, turn the heat up to brown the bottom of the mixture, and stir. Season with salt and pepper, and serve.

MENU

A COLORFUL WINTER DINNER

"Sausage" and Potatoes *(this page)*

Mixed Greens with Beets and Walnuts *(page 50)*

Butternut Squash Puree *(page 219)*

Soy Sloppy Joes

4 TO 6 SERVINGS

Soy crumbles were developed to imitate ground beef, but it's not so much their flavor as their texture that does the trick. This is a family-friendly recipe for all to enjoy.

1½ tablespoons light olive oil

1 medium onion, finely chopped

One 12- to 16-ounce package soy "crumbles" (see note)

One 16-ounce can or jar natural pizza sauce

Fresh burger buns (preferably whole-grain) as needed

1 Heat the oil in a large skillet. Add the onion and sauté over medium heat until golden.

2 Add the soy crumbles and sauté over medium-high heat, stirring frequently, until lightly browned, 3 to 4 minutes. Stir in the pizza sauce and cook until heated through, 3 to 4 minutes.

3 Serve at once on buns, open-faced or covered.

Note: Soy crumbles, marketed under two or more brand names including Green Giant and Morningstar Farms, are made of texturized soy protein. Look for this product in the frozen foods section of well-stocked supermarkets, as well as in natural foods stores.

Calories: 508 • Total fat: 7 g
Protein: 51 g • Carbohydrate: 57 g
Cholesterol: 0 mg • Sodium: 432 mg

MENU

Soy Sloppy Joes *(this page)*

Roasted Potatoes with Bell Peppers and Onions *(page 184)*

or

Baked or microwaved sweet potatoes

Corn Slaw *(page 34)*

Cherry tomatoes

6 OR MORE SERVINGS

Nearly Instant "Beefy" Chili

One 12- to 16-ounce package soy "crumbles" (see note, page 151)

One 16-ounce jar tomato salsa, mild or medium-hot, as preferred

Two 16-ounce cans pinto beans, drained and rinsed

1 cup frozen corn kernels, thawed

1 teaspoon ground cumin

Calories: 486 • Total fat: 1 g
Protein: 47 g • Carbohydrate: 70 g
Cholesterol: 0 mg • Sodium: 821 mg

You can make this exceptionally hearty chili even after an exhausting day at work. All of the ingredients get tossed into the pot at once, and while the chili simmers, you can make a simple salad. Serve the meal with stone-ground tortilla chips.

Combine all of the ingredients with ½ cup water in a soup pot or steep-sided stir-fry pan. Bring to a simmer, cover, and simmer gently over medium-low heat for 15 minutes. Serve in shallow bowls.

CHAPTER 6

A Flash in the (Pizza) Pan

Pizza is such a popular food in our culture that it's no longer possible to think of it as an Italian specialty. Each day, Americans supposedly consume the equivalent of 100 acres of pizza (do you ever wonder who comes up with these crazy statistics?). And for the last few decades, pizza has been named as one of the top snack foods in this country.

When pizza is made at home (which doesn't necessarily mean making your own crust), you're in control of the toppings. Pizza can then become a nutritious meal rather than a mere vehicle for cheese. Smothered in vegetables, with cheese as a secondary ingredient (rather than the other way around), pizza provides a fun solution to getting dinner on the table quickly.

Look for good-quality crusts in your supermarket's bread or dairy sections. And by all means, if you're so inclined, making your own whole grain crust can be a fun, occasional treat. Let the recipes here be a jumping-off point. There's nearly no limit to what you can put on a pizza crust. The measurements given in the recipes serve as guidelines; you can make these recipes even easier by layering the ingredients as you see fit.

Pizza Margherita (with Fresh Tomatoes and Basil)

3 TO 4 SERVINGS

One 12- to 14-inch good-quality pizza crust

3 to 4 medium flavorful tomatoes, sliced about ¼ inch thick

¼ cup thinly sliced basil leaves, or to taste

1 to 1½ cups grated part-skim mozzarella cheese or mozzarella-style soy cheese

Freshly ground pepper, optional

Calories: 250 • Total fat: 6 g
Protein: 16 g • Carbohydrate: 30 g
Cholesterol: 23 mg • Sodium: 383 mg

A classic pizza, this is great for cool summer nights, using the season's best tomatoes.

1 Preheat the oven to 425°F.

2 Place the crust on a pan. Arrange the tomatoes on the crust in concentric circles, and sprinkle with the basil and mozzarella. If desired, top with a few grindings of pepper.

3 Bake until the cheese is bubbly, 8 to 10 minutes. Remove from the oven, let stand for 2 to 3 minutes, and cut into 4 or 6 wedges to serve.

MENU

Pizza Margherita *(this page)*

Black Bean and Corn Salad *(page 44)*

or

Pasta and Broccoli Salad *(page 58)*

Tomato and Eggplant Pizza

3 TO 4 SERVINGS

1 medium eggplant, peeled and diced

2 garlic cloves, minced

One 12- to 14-inch good-quality pizza crust

3 to 4 medium tomatoes, sliced about ¼ inch thick, or one 16-ounce can sliced stewed tomatoes, drained

Salt and freshly ground pepper to taste, optional

1 to 1½ cups grated part-skim mozzarella cheese or mozzarella-style soy cheese

Calories: 290 • Total fat: 6 g
Protein: 16 g • Carbohydrate: 40 g
Cholesterol: 23 mg • Sodium: 389 mg

This eggplant-lover's delight is delicious with fresh or canned tomatoes. For a tasty summer meal, serve with a bountiful tossed salad and corn on the cob.

1 Preheat the oven to 425°F.

2 Combine the eggplant and garlic in a medium skillet with a small amount of water. Cover and steam until the eggplant is tender but not mushy, about 8 minutes. Check occasionally to make sure there is enough water to keep the bottom of the skillet moist.

3 Place the crust on a pan. Arrange the tomatoes on the crust, and sprinkle with the eggplant-garlic mixture. If desired, season with a little salt and a few grindings of pepper. Top with the mozzarella.

4 Bake until the cheese is bubbly, 8 to 10 minutes. Remove from the oven, let stand for 2 to 3 minutes, and cut into 4 or 6 wedges to serve.

A note about servings

I base my serving sizes for a 12- to 14-inch pizza on the premise that the pizza will not be the only part of the meal. A 12-inch pizza, if nothing else is being served, may be enough for only two eaters, but with a generous salad plus perhaps another side dish, an amply topped pizza should satisfy 3 to 4 fairly hungry people reasonably well. As I mentioned in the introduction, the ingredient amounts are given here as a guideline; layer ingredients as you see fit.

By all means, try some of these pizza combinations on personal-size crusts, if you'd like. Explore the possibility of using high-quality pizza crusts from a natural foods source; they are far lower in sodium than national brands and sometimes come in whole grain versions. And go easy on cheese, otherwise the purpose of making your own pizza is partially defeated!

3 TO 4 SERVINGS

White Pizza Florentine

10 to 12 ounces fresh spinach, well washed and stemmed

One 12- to 14-inch good-quality pizza crust

1 cup part-skim ricotta cheese

1 cup grated part-skim mozzarella cheese or mozzarella-style soy cheese

1 tablespoon minced fresh oregano or a sprinkling of dried oregano

Calories: 322 • Total fat: 10 g
Protein: 23 g • Carbohydrate: 31 g
Cholesterol: 40 mg • Sodium: 509 mg

I've tried this pizza with frozen and fresh spinach, and while the former isn't bad, fresh spinach makes it a delicacy. Complete the meal with one of the smoothies on pages 245 to 246 and a bountiful tossed salad.

1 Preheat the oven to 425°F.

2 Steam the spinach in a large pot using only the water clinging to the leaves, until just wilted.

3 Place the crust on a pan, spread the ricotta cheese evenly over it, followed by the spinach, mozzarella, and oregano.

4 Bake until the cheese is bubbly, 8 to 10 minutes. Remove from the oven, let stand for 2 to 3 minutes, and cut into 4 or 6 wedges to serve.

Broccoli and Sun-Dried Tomato Pizza (White or Red)

3 TO 4 SERVINGS

Using plenty of broccoli makes this pizza a nourishing meal. Serve with any of the mixed greens salads on pages 51 to 53.

¼ to ½ cup sliced sun-dried tomatoes (not oil-cured)

One 12- to 14-inch good-quality pizza crust

1 cup good-quality marinara or pizza sauce or part-skim ricotta cheese

1 cup grated part-skim mozzarella cheese or mozzarella-style soy cheese

1½ to 2 cups steamed bite-size broccoli florets

1 If the dried tomatoes you are using aren't moist, soak them in hot water for about 10 minutes, and drain.

2 Preheat the oven to 425°F.

3 Place the crust on a pan, spread the sauce or ricotta cheese evenly over it, and sprinkle on the remaining ingredients in the order given.

4 Bake until the cheese is bubbly, 8 to 10 minutes. Remove from the oven, let stand for 2 to 3 minutes, and cut into 4 or 6 wedges to serve.

WITH MARINARA:

Calories: 268 • Total fat: 6 g
Protein: 16 g • Carbohydrate: 28 g
Cholesterol: 19 mg • Sodium: 562 mg

WITH RICOTTA:

Calories: 337 • Total fat: 10 g
Protein: 24 g • Carbohydrate: 35 g
Cholesterol: 40 mg • Sodium: 450 mg

Mixed Olives Pizza (White or Red)

3 TO 4 SERVINGS

One 12- to 14-inch good-quality pizza crust

1 cup good-quality marinara or pizza sauce or part-skim ricotta cheese

1 to 1½ cups grated part-skim mozzarella cheese or mozzarella-style soy cheese

¼ cup chopped green olives

¼ cup chopped black olives

WITH MARINARA:

Calories: 280 • Total fat: 10 g
Protein: 16 g • Carbohydrate: 29 g
Cholesterol: 23 mg • Sodium: 823 mg

WITH RICOTTA:

Calories: 348 • Total fat: 14 g
Protein: 23 g • Carbohydrate: 29 g
Cholesterol: 45 mg • Sodium: 712 mg

Olives add zesty flavor to a traditional pizza.

1 Preheat the oven to 425°F.

2 Place the crust on a pan, spread the sauce or ricotta cheese evenly over it, and sprinkle with the remaining ingredients in the order given.

3 Bake until the cheese is bubbly, 8 to 10 minutes. Remove from the oven, let stand for 2 to 3 minutes, and cut into 6 or 8 wedges to serve.

MENU

Mixed Olives Pizza *(this page)*

Corn Slaw *(page 34)*

Fresh fruit or fruity dessert of your choice from Chapter Eleven

Mushroom and Smoked Mozzarella Pizza (White or Red)

3 TO 4 SERVINGS

Pizza goes gourmet with the use of smoky mozzarella and tasty mushrooms. Like a number of the other pizzas in this chapter, this one makes a complete meal with the addition of a big salad and fresh fruit or a fruity dessert from Chapter Eleven.

1½ cups brown mushrooms (fresh shiitake, cremini, baby bella, or other)

One 12- to 14-inch good-quality pizza crust

1 to 1½ cups good-quality marinara or pizza sauce or part-skim ricotta cheese

¾ cup grated smoked mozzarella cheese

1 to 2 scallions, green parts only, thinly sliced, optional

1 Clean the mushrooms and remove any tough stems (especially on shiitakes). Slice and steam in a small skillet, covered, until done to your liking. Drain off the liquid and set aside.

2 Preheat the oven to 425°F.

3 Place the crust on a pan, spread the sauce or ricotta cheese evenly over it, and sprinkle with the mushrooms, mozzarella, and scallions.

4 Bake until the cheese is bubbly, 8 to 10 minutes. Remove from the oven, let stand for 2 to 3 minutes, and cut into 6 or 8 wedges to serve.

WITH MARINARA:
Calories: 269 • Total fat: 7 g
Protein: 13 g • Carbohydrate: 37 g
Cholesterol: 19 mg • Sodium: 594 mg

WITH RICOTTA:
Calories: 331 • Total fat: 11 g
Protein: 20 g • Carbohydrate: 36 g
Cholesterol: 41 mg • Sodium: 432 mg

"Pepperoni" Pizza

3 TO 4 SERVINGS

One 12- to 14-inch good-quality pizza crust

1 to 1½ cups good-quality marinara or pizza sauce

1 to 1½ cups grated part-skim mozzarella cheese or mozzarella-style soy cheese

4 slices soy "pepperoni" or deli slices, cut into small squares

Hot red pepper flakes, optional

Calories: 339 • Total fat: 9 g
Protein: 26 g • Carbohydrate: 36 g
Cholesterol: 23 mg • Sodium: 803 mg

Soy "pepperoni" has a convincing flavor, but not the greasiness of its meaty counterpart. Predictably, it's low in fat (and sometimes fat-free) and a terrific way to jazz up a homemade pizza. This makes a fun meal for kids and teens with any of the smoothies on pages 245 to 246.

1 Preheat the oven to 425°F.

2 Place the crust on a pan, spread the sauce evenly over it, and sprinkle with the remaining ingredients in the order given.

3 Bake until the cheese is bubbly, 8 to 10 minutes. Remove from the oven, let stand for 2 to 3 minutes, and cut into 4 or 6 wedges to serve.

Two-Onion Pizza

3 TO 4 SERVINGS

1½ tablespoons light olive oil

1 large red onion, quartered and thinly sliced

1 large white or Vidalia onion, quartered and thinly sliced

One 12- to 14-inch good-quality pizza crust

4 ounces smoked mozzarella or sharp cheddar cheese, grated

Calories: 296 • Total fat: 12 g
Protein: 12 g • Carbohydrate: 32 g
Cholesterol: 26 mg • Sodium: 377 mg

With this luscious treat, you'll need only a bountiful tossed salad (and perhaps a steamed green vegetable—broccoli is a nice addition) to make a delightful meal.

1 Preheat the oven to 425°F.

2 Heat the oil in a large skillet. Add the onions and cook slowly, covered, until soft and golden brown, 20 to 25 minutes. Stir occasionally.

3 Place the crust on a pan, arrange the onions on it, and sprinkle with the cheese.

4 Bake until the cheese is bubbly, 8 to 10 minutes. Remove from the oven, let stand for 2 to 3 minutes, and cut into 6 or 8 wedges to serve.

Roasted Red Pepper and Artichoke Pizza (White or Red)

3 TO 4 SERVINGS

Roasted peppers and artichokes give this easy pizza a touch of elegance.

One 12- to 14-inch good-quality pizza crust

1 cup good-quality marinara or pizza sauce or part-skim ricotta cheese

1 to 1½ cups grated part-skim mozzarella cheese or mozzarella-style soy cheese

¾ cup drained thinly sliced roasted red peppers

¾ cup canned artichoke hearts (not marinated), drained and chopped

1 Preheat the oven to 425°F.

2 Place the crust on a pan, spread the sauce or ricotta cheese evenly over it, and sprinkle with the remaining ingredients in the order given.

3 Bake until the cheese is bubbly, 8 to 10 minutes. Remove from the oven, let stand for 2 to 3 minutes, and cut into 6 or 8 wedges to serve.

WITH MARINARA:

Calories: 271 • Total fat: 7 g
Protein: 16 g • Carbohydrate: 33 g
Cholesterol: 23 mg • Sodium: 591 mg

WITH RICOTTA:

Calories: 340 • Total fat: 11 g
Protein: 24 g • Carbohydrate: 33 g
Cholesterol: 45 mg • Sodium: 479 mg

MENU

Roasted Red Pepper and Artichoke Pizza *(this page)*

Marinated Beans *(page 40)*

or

Chickpea and Tomato Salad *(page 42)*

Asparagus and Red Pepper Pizza (White or Red)

3 TO 4 SERVINGS

1 cup fresh asparagus, trimmed and cut into 1-inch lengths

1 medium red bell pepper, cut into short narrow strips

One 12- to 14-inch good-quality pizza crust

1 cup good-quality marinara or pizza sauce or part-skim ricotta cheese

1 cup grated part-skim mozzarella cheese or mozzarella-style soy cheese

WITH MARINARA:

Calories: 250 • Total fat: 6 g
Protein: 15 g • Carbohydrate: 32 g
Cholesterol: 19 mg • Sodium: 553 mg

WITH RICOTTA:

Calories: 320 • Total fat: 10 g
Protein: 22 g • Carbohydrate: 32 g
Cholesterol: 40 gm • Sodium: 441 mg

See the accompanying menu for a pizza meal that celebrates spring.

1 Preheat the oven to 425°F.

2 Steam the asparagus and bell pepper with a small amount of water in a covered saucepan, until tender crisp, and drain.

3 Place the crust on a pan, spread the sauce or ricotta cheese evenly over it. Sprinkle with the cheese, followed by the asparagus-bell pepper mixture.

4 Bake until the cheese is bubbly, 8 to 10 minutes. Remove from the oven, let stand for 2 to 3 minutes, and cut into 6 or 8 wedges to serve.

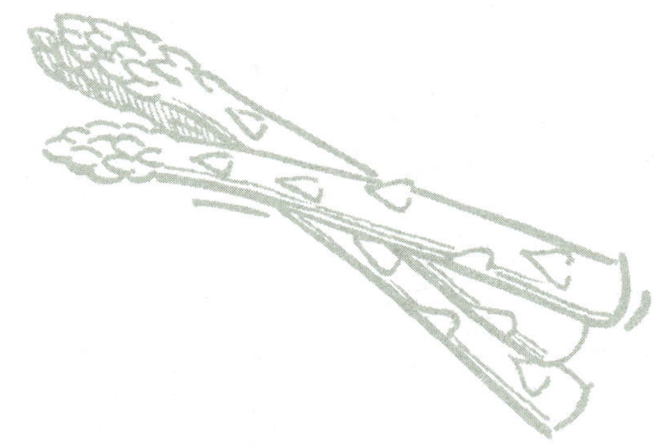

MENU

Asparagus and Red Pepper Pizza *(this page)*

Dilled Barley and Green Bean Salad *(page 47)*

Green Pea and Black Olive Pizza (White or Red)

4 TO 6 SERVINGS

Briny olives and sweet green peas have a pleasant synergy that results in a delicious pizza topping.

1 Preheat the oven to 425°F.

2 Place the crust on a pan, spread the sauce or ricotta cheese evenly over it, and sprinkle with the remaining ingredients in the order given.

3 Bake until the cheese is bubbly, 8 to 10 minutes. Remove from the oven, let stand for 2 to 3 minutes, and cut into 4 or 6 wedges to serve.

MENU

Green Pea and Black Olive Pizza *(this page)*

or

Artichoke, Green Pea, and Cheddar Pizza *(page 164)*

Corn Relish Salad *(page 45)*

Cherry tomatoes

One 12- to 14-inch good-quality pizza crust

1 cup good-quality marinara or pizza sauce or part-skim ricotta cheese

1 to 1½ grated cups part-skim mozzarella cheese or mozzarella-style soy cheese

1 cup frozen green peas, preferably petite peas, thawed

⅓ cup chopped black olives, preferably cured

WITH MARINARA:

Calories: 220 • Total fat: 6 g
Protein: 13 g • Carbohydrate: 26 g
Cholesterol: 16 mg • Sodium: 465 mg

WITH RICOTTA:

Calories: 268 • Total fat: 10 g
Protein: 18 g • Carbohydrate: 26 g
Cholesterol: 31 mg • Sodium: 387 mg

Artichoke, Green Pea, and Cheddar Pizza

3 TO 4 SERVINGS

One 12- to 14-inch good-quality pizza crust

1 cup good-quality marinara or pizza sauce

1 to 1½ cups grated sharp cheddar cheese or cheddar-style soy cheese

One 16-ounce can artichoke hearts, drained and chopped

½ cup frozen green peas (preferably petite), thawed

Calories: 378 • Total fat: 14 g
Protein: 19 g • Carbohydrate: 42 g
Cholesterol: 43 mg • Sodium: 763 mg

Cheddar cheese is a pleasing change of pace from the usual mozzarella.

1 Preheat the oven to 425°F.

2 Place the crust on a pan, and arrange the remaining ingredients on it in the order given.

3 Bake until the cheese is bubbly, 8 to 10 minutes. Remove from the oven, let stand for 2 to 3 minutes, and cut into 4 or 6 wedges to serve.

Mexican Pizza

3 TO 4 SERVINGS

One 12- to 14-inch good-quality pizza crust

1 cup (half of a 16-ounce can) spicy fat-free refried beans, thinned with a small amount of water

1 cup mild or medium-hot salsa

1 to 1½ cups grated cheddar cheese or Monterey Jack cheese, or Jack- or cheddar-style soy cheese

½ cup frozen corn kernels, thawed

Calories: 393 • Total fat: 13 g
Protein: 20 g • Carbohydrate: 47 g
Cholesterol: 43 mg • Sodium: 977 mg

Layer on the Southwestern flavors in this playful pizza variation. Serve with a tossed salad and stone-ground tortilla chips. This tastes best with sharp cheddar or Monterey Jack, but use reduced-fat cheddar if you prefer.

1 Preheat the oven to 425°F.

2 Place the crust on a pan. Spread it with the refried beans, then the salsa. Sprinkle with the cheese and corn kernels.

3 Bake until the cheese is bubbly, 8 to 10 minutes. Remove from the oven, let stand for 2 to 3 minutes, and cut into 4 or 6 wedges to serve.

CHAPTER 7

Rudimentary Wraps

Flour tortillas or lavash wraps with savory fillings make a delightful basis for simple meals. A welcome bonus is the fact that these meals are as quick to prepare as they are delicious to eat. It's fun to involve the entire family—or your guests—in the preparation. Place the ingredients to be wrapped on the table along with the warmed wrappers and let everyone fill and roll their own.

In this section, you will find an enticing array of burritos, quesadillas, soft tacos, and more, all with a Southwestern flair. There are also several wraps with eclectic fillings that make use of either soft lavash bread or large wrappers or flour tortillas. These are as suitable for lunch (especially for guests) as they are for a light dinner.

When you crave something a little different, this just may be the chapter to explore.

Tortilla Flat (Refried Bean Pie)

4 SERVINGS

2 burrito-size (10-inch) flour tortillas

One 16-ounce can spicy fat-free refried beans

1 cup grated cheddar cheese or cheddar-style soy cheese

Regular or green (tomatillo) salsa

Calories: 335 • Total fat: 11 g
Protein: 18 g • Carbohydrate: 40 g
Cholesterol: 30 mg • Sodium: 278 mg

I always keep a can or two of refried beans in the pantry and flour tortillas in the freezer for those nights when I am on the verge of reaching for a take-out menu. Even if you are bone-weary by dinnertime, these two ingredients are the ticket to nearly effortless yet highly satisfying meals such as this one and the following burritos.

1 Place one of the tortillas on a lightly oiled round casserole dish.

2 In a mixing bowl, combine the refried beans with ¼ cup warm water and stir together.

3 Spread the refried beans over the tortilla, sprinkle with the grated cheese, top with the remaining tortilla, and cover.

4 Microwave until piping hot, 2 to 3 minutes. Cut into wedges to serve, topping each with a little salsa.

MENU

Tortilla Flat *(this page)*

Cooked brown rice or microwaved baked potato

Sautéed summer squash or zucchini

Shredded lettuce, diced tomatoes, and bell pepper strips

Easy Bean Burritos

6 SERVINGS

These burritos are easy because you are not so much cooking a meal as putting the ingredients on the table. Everyone then makes his or her own.

6 burrito-size (10-inch) flour tortillas

One 16-ounce can spicy vegetarian refried beans

Finely shredded lettuce

2 to 3 medium finely diced tomatoes

1 cup grated cheddar or Monterey Jack cheese, or cheddar- or Jack-style soy cheese, optional

1 Preheat the oven or toaster oven to 400°F. Wrap the entire batch of tortillas in foil and warm while you prepare the filling.

2 Combine the refried beans with ¼ cup water in a saucepan and heat slowly until hot, stirring occasionally. Transfer to a serving container.

3 Place the lettuce and cheese into separate bowls. Have everyone make his or her own burritos as follows: Spread some of the refried beans down the center of each tortilla, followed by a sprinkling of lettuce, tomatoes, and the optional cheese. Roll up snugly and eat out of hand.

Calories: 244 • Total fat: 4 g
Protein: 10 g • Carbohydrate: 42 g
Cholesterol: 0 mg • Sodium: 209 mg

Black Bean Burritos

6 SERVINGS

A basic burrito with a savory filling. Enjoy this simple meal rounded out by baked or microwaved sweet potatoes or corn on the cob and a bountiful tossed salad.

6 burrito-size (10-inch) flour tortillas

1 recipe Green Chili Black Beans (page 114)

1 Preheat the oven or toaster oven to 400°F. Wrap the entire batch of tortillas in foil and warm while preparing the black bean recipe.

2 Divide the black bean mixture among the tortillas, spreading it down the center of each. Roll up snugly and eat out of hand.

Calories: 320 • Total fat: 7 g
Protein: 13 g • Carbohydrate: 52 g
Cholesterol: 0 mg • Sodium: 208 mg

Mashed Potato Burritos

6 SERVINGS

4 large potatoes, peeled and diced

6 burrito-size (10-inch) flour tortillas

¼ to ⅓ cup 1% low-fat milk or soy milk, as needed

Salt to taste

Red or green (tomatillo) salsa

1 cup grated cheddar or Monterey Jack cheese, or cheddar- or Jack-style soy cheese, optional

Calories: 231 • Total fat: 4 g
Protein: 6 g • Carbohydrate: 43 g
Cholesterol: 0 mg • Sodium: 216 mg

This would be an ideal meal to make of leftover mashed potatoes, but that's one leftover I rarely seem to have on hand. If you find yourself with some, these tasty burritos can be made in a flash. Serve with Beer-Stewed Pinto Beans (page 116) and a bountiful salad.

1 Preheat the oven or toaster oven to 400°F.

2 Cover the potatoes with water in a medium saucepan. Bring to a simmer, cover, and simmer gently until tender, about 15 minutes.

3 Meanwhile, wrap the entire batch of tortillas in foil and warm in the oven.

4 Combine the drained potatoes and milk in a mixing bowl and mash well. Season with salt.

5 Divide the mashed potatoes among the tortillas, spreading some down the center of each. Spread a little bit of salsa over the potatoes, and sprinkle with the optional cheese. Roll up snugly and eat out of hand.

"Chicken"-Style Tofu Fajitas

4 SERVINGS
(2 FAJITAS PER SERVING)

In another super-easy, nearly instant tortilla recipe, chewy baked tofu stands in for chicken. You may not find this wonderful product in the supermarket; look for it in natural foods stores.

8 fajita-size (6- to 7-inch) flour tortillas

One 8- to 10-ounce package baked tofu, cut into strips

Red or green (tomatillo) salsa, to taste

1 cup low-fat plain yogurt, reduced-fat sour cream, or soy yogurt

2 cups finely shredded lettuce

Calories: 351 • Total fat: 12 g
Protein: 24 g • Carbohydrate: 38 g
Cholesterol: 4 mg • Sodium: 564 mg

1 Preheat the oven or toaster oven to 400°F. Wrap the entire batch of tortillas in foil and warm while preparing the filling.

2 Place the tofu strips on a plate and microwave briefly until warmed, 1 to 1½ minutes.

3 Spread a little salsa and yogurt down the center of each tortilla, and arrange a few tofu strips over them. Sprinkle with some lettuce, roll up snugly, and eat out of hand.

MENU

"Chicken"-Style Tofu Fajitas *(this page)*

Spinach Rice *(page 92)*

Cherry tomatoes and bell pepper strips

Sweet Potato Quesadillas or Soft Tacos

4 SERVINGS

2 medium sweet potatoes

One 4- to 7-ounce can chopped mild green chilies

4 soft taco-size (8- to 10-inch) flour tortillas

1 cup grated cheddar or Monterey Jack cheese, or cheddar- or Jack-style soy cheese

Reduced-fat sour cream or soy yogurt for topping, optional

Calories: 378 • Total fat: 12 g
Protein: 13 g • Carbohydrate: 52 g
Cholesterol: 30 mg • Sodium: 391 mg

The combination of sweet potatoes, chilies, and cheese is downright sensuous. Serve with Summer Squash and Corn Sauté (page 209) and a simple tossed salad.

1 Bake or microwave the sweet potatoes in their skins until done but still firm. When cool enough to handle, peel, and slice ¼ inch thick.

2 To make quesadillas, preheat the oven to 400°F. Arrange the sweet potatoes and chilies on the entire surface of 2 tortillas. Sprinkle with the cheese, and cover with the remaining tortillas. Arrange the quesadillas on a nonstick baking sheet and bake until the tortillas become lightly golden and crisp on the outside, 12 to 15 minutes; or grill them on a nonstick griddle on both sides until golden. Cut each quesadilla into 4 equal wedges, allowing 2 wedges per serving, and eat out of hand.

3 To make soft tacos, arrange the sweet potato slices in a single layer on one half of each tortilla, then top with the chilies and the cheese. Arrange on individual plates. Heat each serving briefly in the microwave (about 1 minute) or preheated 400°F oven (about 3 minutes) to melt the cheese, then fold over. Eat at once with a knife and fork (topped with sour cream if desired) or cut into 2 wedges and eat out of hand.

Quesadillas and Soft Tacos

Quesadillas are grilled turnovers made with flour tortillas. They can be cooked on a griddle (that's the traditional way) or baked. If they are chock-full of ingredients, it's easier to bake them. Soft tacos made with flour tortillas are more versatile than the more familiar crisp tacos, since you don't have to worry about everything falling out of a crumbly shell. If you start making a quesadilla, but decide not to grill it, you've got a soft taco instead. That's why I offer the either/or option with the four recipes that follow.

Refried Bean and Corn Quesadillas or Soft Tacos

4 SERVINGS

Here are those handy refried beans again, in a different guise. They help hold this tortilla specialty together.

½ medium red bell pepper, cut into thin strips

1 cup cooked fresh corn kernels (from 1 to 2 medium ears) or frozen corn, thawed

1 cup (half of a 16-ounce can) spicy fat-free refried beans (see note)

4 soft taco-size (8- to 10-inch) flour tortillas

1 cup grated cheddar or Monterey Jack cheese, or cheddar- or Jack-style soy cheese

1 Combine ¼ cup water and the bell pepper strips in a large saucepan and steam, covered, for 2 minutes, then add the corn kernels and refried beans. Cook gently until everything is heated through.

2 To make quesadillas preheat the oven to 400°F. Arrange the bean mixture on the entire surface of 2 tortillas. Sprinkle with the cheese, and cover with the remaining tortillas. Arrange the quesadillas on a nonstick baking sheet and bake until the tortillas become lightly golden and crisp on the outside, 12 to 15 minutes; or grill them on a nonstick griddle on both sides until golden. Cut each quesadilla into 4 equal wedges, allowing 2 wedges per serving, and eat out of hand.

3 To make soft tacos, spread some of the filling on one half of each tortilla, then sprinkle with cheese. Arrange on individual plates. Heat each serving briefly in the microwave (about 1 minute) or preheated 400°F oven (about 3 minutes) to melt the cheese, then fold over. Eat at once with a knife and fork or cut into 2 wedges and eat out of hand.

Note: Use the leftover beans as a dip, to make "Chili Dogs" (page 148); or freeze to use at a later time.

Calories: 338 • Total fat: 12 g
Protein: 15 g • Carbohydrate: 40 g
Cholesterol: 30 mg • Sodium: 382 mg

MENU

Refried Bean and Corn Quesadillas or Soft Tacos *(this page)*

Mixed Greens with Oranges and Almonds *(page 52)*

Sliced tomatoes

Baked or microwaved sweet potatoes

Mushroom and Bell Pepper Quesadillas or Soft Tacos

4 SERVINGS

8 ounces white or cremini mushrooms, cleaned and sliced

1 medium red bell pepper, thinly sliced

4 soft taco-size (8- to 10-inch) flour tortillas

1½ cups grated Monterey Jack or Jack-style soy cheese

Salsa, as desired

Calories: 287 • Total fat: 12 g
Protein: 17 g • Carbohydrate: 25 g
Cholesterol: 30 mg • Sodium: 512 mg

A lighter tortilla dish, this is good served with a hearty grain pilaf or a bean dish.

1 Place the mushrooms in a medium skillet and layer the bell peppers on top of them. Add a small amount of water, cover, and steam until the mushrooms are done and the bell peppers are tender-crisp. Drain.

2 To make quesadillas preheat the oven to 400°F. Arrange the mushrooms and peppers on the entire surface of 2 tortillas. Sprinkle with the cheese, and cover with the remaining tortillas. Arrange the quesadillas on a nonstick baking sheet and bake until the tortillas become lightly golden and crisp on the outside, 12 to 15 minutes; or grill them on a nonstick griddle on both sides until golden. Cut each quesadilla into 4 equal wedges, allowing 2 wedges per serving, and eat out of hand.

3 To make soft tacos, arrange some of the mushroom mixture on one half of each tortilla, then top with the cheese and salsa. Arrange on individual plates. Heat each serving briefly in the microwave (about 1 minute) or preheated 400°F oven (about 3 minutes) to melt the cheese, then fold over. Eat at once with a knife and fork or cut into 2 wedges and eat out of hand.

MENU

Mushroom and Bell Pepper Quesadillas or Soft Tacos

(this page)

Green Chili Black Beans *(page 114)*

Simple tossed salad

Tomato and Green Chili Quesadillas or Soft Tacos

4 SERVINGS

Highlighting the flavor of green chilies and fresh tomatoes, these quesadillas or tacos make a great warm-weather meal.

2 medium-firm flavorful tomatoes, thinly sliced

Two 4-ounce or one 7-ounce can chopped mild green chilies

Minced fresh cilantro to taste, optional

4 soft taco-size (8- to 10-inch) flour tortillas

1 to 1½ cups grated cheddar or cheddar-style soy cheese

1 To make quesadillas, preheat the oven to 400°F. Arrange the tomatoes, chilies, and optional cilantro on the entire surface of 2 tortillas. Sprinkle with the cheese, and cover with the remaining tortillas. Arrange the quesadillas on a nonstick baking sheet and bake until the tortillas become lightly golden and crisp on the outside, 12 to 15 minutes; or grill them on a nonstick griddle on both sides until golden. Cut each quesadilla into 4 equal wedges, allowing 2 wedges per serving, and eat out of hand.

2 To make soft tacos, arrange a single layer of tomato slices over one half of each tortilla, and sprinkle with the chilies, cheese, and optional cilantro. Arrange on individual plates. Heat each serving briefly in the microwave (about 1 minute) or preheated 400°F oven (about 3 minutes) to melt the cheese, then fold over. Eat at once with a knife and fork or cut into 2 wedges and eat out of hand.

Calories: 269 • Total fat: 10 g
Protein: 15 g • Carbohydrate: 26 g
Cholesterol: 25 mg • Sodium: 466 mg

MENU

Tomato and Green Chili Quesadillas or Soft Tacos *(this page)*

Avocado and Pinto Bean Salad *(page 45)*

Stone-ground tortilla chips with salsa

4 SERVINGS

Avocado and Ricotta Soft Tacos

1 medium-large ripe avocado, pitted and thinly sliced

4 soft taco-size (8- to 10-inch) flour tortillas

Salsa or canned green chilies, as desired

1 cup part-skim ricotta cheese

2 scallions, thinly sliced

Calories: 301 • Total fat: 15 g
Protein: 13 g • Carbohydrate: 30 g
Cholesterol: 19 mg • Sodium: 285 mg

I opted to make these only as soft tacos, as the filling is a bit too sensuous (a polite word for "messy") for quesadillas. This is definitely a knife-and-fork dish.

1 Arrange a single layer of avocado slices on one-half of each tortilla, top with salsa and ricotta cheese, and sprinkle with scallions. Arrange on individual plates.

2 Heat each serving briefly in the microwave (about 1 minute) or preheated 400°F oven (about 3 minutes), and fold over. Eat at once with a knife and fork.

MENU

SENSUOUS SOUTHWESTERN

Avocado and Ricotta Soft Tacos *(this page)*

Beer-Stewed Pinto or Pink Beans *(page 116)*

or

Marinated Beans *(page 40)*

Tomato-Mango Salsa *(page 237)*

Mushroom, Spinach, and Cheddar Wraps

4 SERVINGS

Spinach and mushrooms are nicely flavored with sharp cheddar in these delectable wraps.

8 to 10 ounces white, cremini, or baby bella mushrooms, cleaned and sliced

10 ounces fresh spinach, well washed, stemmed, and coarsely chopped

Four 10-inch wraps or burrito-size (10-inch) flour tortillas

1 cup grated sharp cheddar cheese or cheddar-style soy cheese

Salsa, optional

1 Steam the mushrooms in a large skillet with enough water to keep the bottom moist. When they are tender, add the spinach, in batches if necessary, cover, and cook, just until the spinach wilts down. Drain well.

2 Divide the mushroom-spinach mixture among the wraps, arranging it down the center of each. Sprinkle evenly with the cheese. If desired, add a stripe of salsa, then wrap up snugly.

3 Briefly heat each wrap individually on a plate in the microwave or in a preheated 400°F oven, just until heated through, and eat out of hand.

Calories: 277 • Total fat: 11 g
Protein: 14 g • Carbohydrate: 25 g
Cholesterol: 30 mg • Sodium: 438 mg

Wraps

In the food world, wraps are relative "new kids on the block," but they've quickly made an impact. Restaurants devoted to these rolled-up sandwiches are popping up everywhere. It's a fast, healthy way to create a special meal to eat out of hand. To make wraps, you can use burrito-size (8- to 10-inch) flour tortillas, special round wraps (available in various flavors such as spinach, herb, and garlic) of about the same size, or soft lavash bread, whose rectangular shape makes a more squared-off wrap. All are available in well-stocked supermarkets. With a little imagination and a few choice ingredients, you are well on the way to a fabulous lunch or dinner treat.

4 OR MORE SERVINGS

Cool Refried Bean Wraps

One 16-ounce can spicy fat-free refried beans

Four 10-inch round wraps or rectangular lavash wraps, lightly warmed if desired

Soy mayonnaise, as needed

2 to 3 plum tomatoes, very thinly sliced

Finely shredded lettuce, as needed

Calories: 304 • Total fat: 4 g
Protein: 13 g • Carbohydrate: 53 g
Cholesterol: 0 mg • Sodium: 213 mg

Refried beans to the rescue once again—this time in a room-temperature wrap that's a delight to serve to lunchtime company or pack into a brown-bag lunch or picnic.

1 Heat the refried beans in a saucepan with about ¼ cup water, just until they are warm and smooth.

2 Spread the wraps thinly with the mayonnaise, then with the refried beans. Top with a single layer of tomatoes, placed here and there, followed by an even sprinkling of the lettuce.

3 Wrap snugly and cut each in half crosswise. Serve at room temperature and eat out of hand.

MENU

WRAPS FOR A LEISURELY LUNCH AT HOME

Any of the wraps on pages 166 to 180

Cherry tomatoes and baby carrots

Stone-ground tortilla chips

Tropical Fruit Medley *(page 244)*

or

Simple Summer Fruit Medley of your choice *(pages 252 to 253)*

Eggplant Parmigiana Wraps

2 TO 4 SERVINGS

Here's an enjoyable way to serve a modified version of eggplant Parmigiana that's lighter than the more customary eggplant hero sandwich.

Two 10-inch round wraps or rectangular lavash wraps, lightly warmed if desired

Good-quality marinara sauce, as needed

1 recipe Versatile Steamed Eggplant (page 215)

1 cup grated part-skim mozzarella cheese or mozzarella-style soy cheese

1 Spread each wrap with a thin layer of marinara sauce. Spread the steamed eggplant over the sauce, and sprinkle with cheese. Roll up each wrap snugly.

2 Place on a large platter and microwave just until warmed, about 2 minutes. Cut each wrap in half crosswise, and eat out of hand.

Calories: 257 • Total fat: 9 g
Protein: 14 g • Carbohydrate: 29 g
Cholesterol: 22 mg • Sodium: 453 mg

Goat Cheese and Red Pepper Wraps

2 TO 4 SERVINGS

Soft goat cheese is a splendid spread for wraps, with a special affinity for red peppers.

2 lavash wraps, 10-inch round wraps, or burrito-size (10-inch) flour tortillas

2 ounces spreadable goat cheese, or to taste

2 to 3 pieces jarred roasted red pepper, drained and thinly sliced

2 tablespoons minced fresh cilantro, optional

1 Place each wrap on a serving plate. Spread thinly with goat cheese, leaving about a ½-inch edge all around.

2 Scatter the red pepper strips over the goat cheese, and sprinkle with the cilantro if desired. Repeat with the remaining wrap.

3 Roll up and microwave just until warmed, about 40 seconds. Cut in half crosswise and eat out of hand.

Calories: 140 • Total fat: 6 g
Protein: 6 g • Carbohydrate: 15 g
Cholesterol: 17 mg • Sodium: 347 mg

Salsa Verde Goat Cheese Wraps

2 TO 4 SERVINGS

Two 10-inch wraps, rectangular lavash wraps, or burrito-size (10-inch) flour tortillas

2 ounces spreadable goat cheese, or as desired

½ cup salsa verde (tomatillo salsa)

Calories: 150 • Total fat: 6 g
Protein: 6 g • Carbohydrate: 17 g
Cholesterol: 17 mg • Sodium: 747 mg

Look for tomatillo salsa shelved near the standard tomato-based salsas. It's a nice change of pace for serving with tortilla specialties.

1 Spread each wrap thinly with the goat cheese, leaving about a ½-inch edge all around.

2 If the salsa is liquidy, strain some of the liquid out with a fine strainer before using. Spread the salsa over the goat cheese on each tortilla, and roll them up.

3 Place on a large platter and microwave just until warmed, about 3 minutes. Place each wrap on an individual plate, cut in half crosswise, and eat out of hand.

MENU

Salsa Verde Goat Cheese Wraps *(this page)*

or

Goat Cheese and Red Pepper Wraps *(page 177)*

Baked or microwaved sweet potatoes

Mixed baby greens salad with tomatoes and carrots

Tofu and Mixed Vegetable Wraps

4 SERVINGS

Here's a superb use for leftovers of Instant Tofu and Mixed Vegetable Stir-Fry. Or do it the other way around: Make the stir-fry especially for these wraps and serve the remainder over rice or noodles the next day.

½ recipe Instant Tofu and Mixed Vegetable Stir-Fry (page 144)

Four 10-inch wraps or flour tortillas

Calories: 236 • Total fat: 6 g
Protein: 11 g • Carbohydrate: 33 g
Cholesterol: 0 mg • Sodium: 531 mg

1 Divide the tofu and mixed vegetable mixture among the wraps, arranging it down the center of each. Wrap up tightly.

2 Place the wraps on a large platter and microwave just until warmed, about 3 minutes. Place each wrap on an individual plate, cut in half crosswise, and eat out of hand.

MENU

Tofu and Mixed Vegetable Wraps *(this page)*
Asian Sesame-Soy Noodles *(page 85)*
Crisp raw vegetable platter

Tossed Salad Wraps

4 SERVINGS

3 cups thinly shredded lettuce

2 medium firm tomatoes, finely diced

½ medium green or red bell pepper, thinly sliced

¼ cup natural, low-fat dressing of your choice (ranch, French, or Thousand Island are good)

Four 10-inch wraps or burrito-size (10-inch) flour tortillas

Calories: 162 • Total fat: 4 g
Protein: 5 g • Carbohydrate: 26 g
Cholesterol: 0 mg • Sodium: 214 mg

A basic tossed salad is transformed into a crunchy sandwich by wrapping it up. This makes a great side dish for grain, bean, pasta, and soy entrées.

1 Combine the first 4 ingredients in a mixing bowl and toss together.

2 Divide the salad among the 4 wraps, distributing it evenly over the entire surface, leaving approximately 2 inches empty at one side of each wrap. Roll up snugly. Cut each in half and eat out of hand.

CHAPTER 8

Pared-Down Potatoes

This isn't the first time I've devoted an entire chapter to spuds—humble (yet glorious) potatoes inspire too many possibilities to tuck them quietly into a chapter on vegetables. The potato is the vegetable equivalent of pasta—a mild, versatile food that offers ultimate comfort, yet it can dazzle the taste buds when prepared imaginatively.

Sometimes I like my potatoes jazzed up, but often I like them plain. And in between jazzy and plain there is much territory to explore. They can be baked, boiled, microwaved, or roasted; they can be sliced, diced, mashed, or hashed; you can stuff them, scallop them, and put them into soups. A potato salad with your sandwich or as part of a picnic is always a welcome treat. In rare cases, potatoes even pop up in dessert—think of delicious sweet potato pie. Potatoes even turn up in the rare chocolate cake recipe.

Speaking of sweet potatoes, which are more nutritious than their white counterparts, I like to encourage more use of them. In addition to the tasty recipes in this chapter, I suggest them as a side dish simply baked (or microwaved) in a number of menus throughout this book. An Irish proverb says, " 'Tis the potato that's the queen of the garden." It's easy to see why.

Soy Scalloped Potatoes

6 SERVINGS

6 large or 8 medium potatoes, preferably red-skinned or Yukon gold

2 tablespoons nonhydrogenated margarine

2 large onions, quartered and thinly sliced

One 12.3-ounce package silken tofu

½ cup 1% low-fat milk or soymilk

Salt to taste

Calories: 227 • Total fat: 6 g
Protein: 6 g • Carbohydrate: 38 g
Cholesterol: 1 mg • Sodium: 68 mg

Here's a deceptively rich-tasting version of scalloped potatoes. It gives you the benefits of soy, minus the bother of making a flour-thickened white sauce.

1 Bake or microwave the potatoes in their skins until done but still firm. When cool enough to handle, peel, and slice about ¼ inch thick.

2 Preheat the oven to 375°F.

3 Heat the margarine in a medium skillet. Add the onions and sauté over medium heat until soft and golden.

4 Puree the tofu in a food processor until very smooth, and drizzle in the milk with the blade still running.

5 Combine the potato slices, onions, and pureed tofu in a large mixing bowl and stir together thoroughly but gently (don't worry if the potato slices break apart). Season with salt.

6 Transfer the mixture to an oiled large shallow baking dish. Bake until the top is golden and slightly crusty, 40 to 45 minutes. Let the casserole cool for 5 minutes, and serve.

MENU

Soy Scalloped Potatoes *(this page)*

Steamed Broccoli and Cauliflower *(page 199)*

Mixed Greens with Beets and Walnuts *(page 50)*

Leek and Red Pepper Hash Brown Potatoes

4 TO 6 SERVINGS

4 large or 6 medium potatoes

2 large or 3 medium leeks

2 tablespoons light olive oil

1 medium red bell pepper, finely diced

Salt and freshly ground pepper to taste

Calories: 205 • Total fat: 6 g
Protein: 2 g • Carbohydrate: 36 g
Cholesterol: 0 mg • Sodium: 20 mg

If you like leeks, you're sure to enjoy this dressed-up version of hash browns. Use firm-textured potatoes, such as red-skinned or Yukon gold, rather than mealy ones, for best results. Serve with sautéed soy "sausage," allowing 2 links per serving, and a salad of mixed baby greens with tomatoes and carrots.

1 Microwave the potatoes in their skins until they are easily pierced with a knife but still firm. Set aside until cool enough to handle, peel, and slice about ½ inch thick.

2 Trim the tough green leaves and bottoms from the leeks and discard. Slice the leeks in half lengthwise, then into ¼-inch slices crosswise. Place in a colander and rinse well.

3 Heat 1 tablespoon of the oil in an extra-wide skillet. Add the leeks and sauté over medium-low heat, covered, until limp, 6 to 8 minutes. Stir occasionally. Add the red pepper and continue to sauté, covered, stirring occasionally, until the leeks are soft, 5 to 8 minutes.

4 Add the remaining 1 tablespoon oil and the potatoes. Raise the heat to medium-high and cook until the potatoes on the bottom are browned. Stir well and cook, until most of the mixture is nicely browned. Season with salt and pepper, and serve.

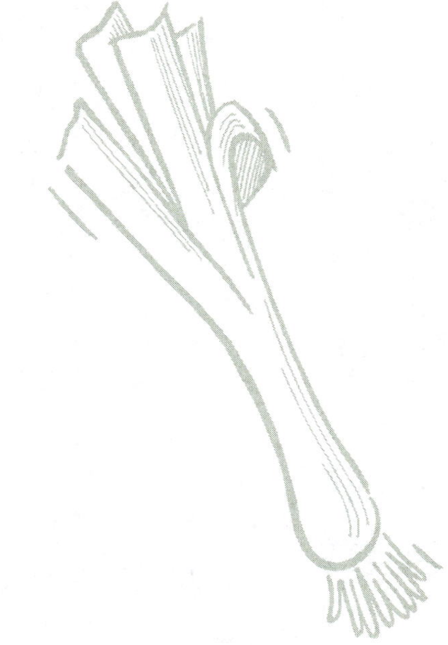

Roasted Potatoes with Bell Peppers and Onions

4 TO 6 SERVINGS

4 to 5 large potatoes, preferably red-skinned or Yukon gold

2 medium red or green bell peppers or 1 of each, cut into thick strips

1 large onion, halved and sliced

2 tablespoons light olive oil

½ teaspoon salt-free herb-and-spice seasoning mix, optional

Salt and freshly ground pepper to taste

Calories: 182 • Total fat: 6 g
Protein: 2 g • Carbohydrate: 31 g
Cholesterol: 0 mg • Sodium: 9 mg

This is a perfect accompaniment to Shake-and-Bake Tofu (page 138), since they both bake at 425°. This needs more time in the oven, so start it first. Complete the meal with a simple salad or coleslaw.

1 Preheat the oven to 425°F.

2 Scrub the potatoes well. Cut them in half lengthwise, then into approximately ¼-inch-thick slices.

3 Combine the potatoes with the remaining ingredients in a large mixing bowl and stir together. Transfer to a roasting pan (foil-lined if you prefer).

4 Bake, stirring gently every 10 minutes, until the potatoes are tender and lightly browned, about 30 minutes, and serve.

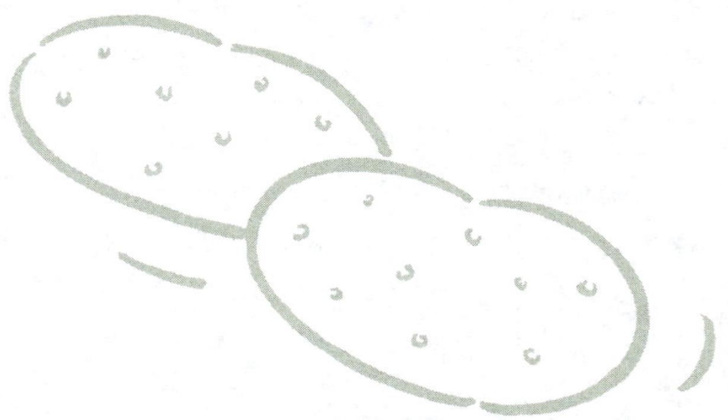

Spanish Potato Frittata

4 SERVINGS

Simplicity is at its best in this hearty egg dish. It's perfect for a cold-weather brunch (see the menu) or as a light dinner dish, served with fresh bread, salad, and orange sections.

3 medium-large potatoes, preferably red-skinned

2 tablespoons light olive oil

1 large onion, chopped

4 eggs, beaten

Salt and freshly ground pepper to taste

Salsa for topping, optional

Calories: 254 • Total fat: 12 g
Protein: 10 g • Carbohydrate: 24 g
Cholesterol: 273 mg • Sodium: 76 mg

1 Microwave or bake the potatoes in their skins until done but still firm. When cool enough to handle, peel, and slice ¼ inch thick.

2 Heat 1 tablespoon of the oil in a large skillet. Add the onion and sauté over medium heat until lightly browned.

3 Combine beaten eggs with the potatoes and onions in a mixing bowl. Season with salt and pepper.

4 Heat the remaining 1 tablespoon oil in the same skillet. Pour in the potato mixture. Cover and cook over medium heat until the bottom is golden brown and the top is fairly set, about 5 minutes.

5 Slide the frittata out onto a plate. Invert the skillet over the plate and quickly flip over so that the frittata goes back into the skillet, uncooked side down. Remove the plate, return the skillet to the heat, and cook the second side, uncovered, until golden brown.

6 Slide the frittata back onto the plate, let cool for a few minutes, cut into 4 wedges and serve at once, passing around some salsa for topping, if desired.

MENU

A HEARTY WINTER BRUNCH

Spanish Potato Frittata *(this page)*

Beer-Stewed Pinto or Pink Beans *(page 116)*

Warm flour tortillas

Sliced tomatoes and bell peppers

Tropical Fruit Medley *(page 244)*

Colcannon (Irish Potato, Cabbage, and Scallion Skillet)

4 TO 6 SERVINGS

4 large potatoes

1½ tablespoons light olive oil

2 cups finely shredded white cabbage (use shredded coleslaw cabbage as a shortcut)

6 scallions, white and green parts, sliced

1 cup 1% low-fat milk or soymilk

Salt and freshly ground pepper to taste

Calories: 158 • Total fat: 4 g
Protein: 3 g • Carbohydrate: 26 g
Cholesterol: 2 mg • Sodium: 35 mg

This tasty Irish classic features potatoes and cabbage browned in a skillet and is embellished with lots of scallions. For a simply delicious meal, serve this with veggie burgers and a tossed salad.

1 Bake or microwave the potatoes in their skins until done. When cool enough to handle, peel, and coarsely mash.

2 Heat the oil in a large skillet. Add the cabbage and sauté, covered, over medium heat, stirring occasionally, until limp. Add the scallions and sauté, uncovered, until the cabbage begins to turn golden. If the skillet becomes dry, add small amounts of water as needed.

3 Add the potatoes and milk, stir everything together, and turn the heat up to medium-high. Cook without stirring until the bottom of the potato mixture gets nicely browned. Fluff with a wooden spoon, season with salt and pepper, and serve.

Southeast Asian-Style Spicy Mashed Potatoes

4 TO 6 SERVINGS

Mashed potatoes are generally comforting, but this version gives your taste buds a wake-up call. Serve with Sautéed Tempeh Cutlets (page 146) and a tossed salad.

5 large potatoes, peeled and diced

1 cup low-fat plain yogurt or soy yogurt

1 tablespoon light olive oil

1 large onion, chopped

1 or 2 small hot fresh chilies, seeded and minced, or one 4-ounce can mild or hot chopped green chilies

Salt to taste

1 Cover the potatoes with water in a large saucepan. Bring to a simmer, cover, and cook gently until the potatoes are quite tender, about 15 minutes. Drain and transfer to a large shallow bowl and mash well, adding the yogurt a little at a time.

2 Heat the oil in a small skillet. Add the onion and sauté until translucent. If using fresh chilies, add them and continue to sauté until the onion is lightly and evenly browned. If using canned chilies, let the onion brown first, then add the chilies and sauté just until heated through.

3 Stir the onion mixture into the mashed potatoes, season with salt, and serve.

Calories: 191 • Total fat: 3 g
Protein: 5 g • Carbohydrate: 35 g
Cholesterol: 3 mg • Sodium: 45 mg

Spinach and Feta-Stuffed Potatoes

4 SERVINGS

4 large baking potatoes

One 10-ounce package frozen chopped spinach, thawed and drained

¼ cup 1% low-fat milk or soymilk

1 scallion, green part only, thinly sliced

½ cup finely crumbled feta cheese

Calories: 218 • Total fat: 5 g
Protein: 8 g • Carbohydrate: 33 g
Cholesterol: 26 mg • Sodium: 392 mg

This recipe gives potatoes a Greek-flavored spin. It's delicious with Warm or Cold Tomato and White Bean Soup (page 15).

1 Bake or microwave the potatoes until done but still firm. When cool enough to handle, cut each in half lengthwise. Scoop out the inside of each potato half, leaving a sturdy shell, about ¼ inch thick all around.

2 Transfer the scooped-out potato to a mixing bowl and mash it coarsely. Add the remaining ingredients and stir well to combine.

3 Stuff the mixture back into the potato shells. Heat as needed in the microwave or in a preheated 400°F oven, and serve.

Stuffed Potatoes

Stuffing potatoes is an enjoyable way to showcase these versatile roots; the following four recipes are hearty enough to serve as entrées. One tip for making stuffed potatoes easier is to bake or microwave the potatoes ahead of time. It's easier to scoop them out when they are at room temperature—they are firmer and less likely to fall apart.

If the potatoes are already cooked when you are ready to stuff them, these tasty treats will be done in a snap, leaving you more time to create an abundant salad and other accompaniments.

Mushroom-Stuffed Potatoes

4 SERVINGS

A small amount of light cream cheese gives these stuffed potatoes a rich flavor. Serve them with a big tossed salad with chickpeas or black-eyed peas, and some steamed green beans or asparagus.

4 large baking potatoes

2 cup Neufchâtel, light cream cheese, or nondairy cream cheese

1 tablespoon light olive oil

1 large onion, chopped

8 ounces white or cremini mushrooms, sliced

Salt and freshly ground pepper to taste

Calories: 214 • Total fat: 6 g
Protein: 4 g • Carbohydrate: 33 g
Cholesterol: 13 mg • Sodium: 67 mg

1 Bake or microwave the potatoes until done but still firm. When cool enough to handle, cut each in half lengthwise. Scoop out the inside of each potato half, leaving a sturdy shell, about ¼ inch thick all around.

2 Transfer the scooped-out potato to a mixing bowl and mash it coarsely. Stir in the Neufchâtel.

3 Heat the oil in a medium skillet. Add the onion and sauté over medium heat until golden. Add the mushrooms, cover, and cook until they are done to your liking, stirring occasionally.

4 Combine the mushroom mixture, including the liquid with the mashed potato in the mixing bowl. Season with salt and pepper and stir well to combine.

5 Stuff the mixture back into the potato shells. Heat as needed in the microwave or in a preheated 400°F oven, and serve.

Broccoli and Cheddar-Stuffed Potatoes

4 SERVINGS

4 large baking potatoes

¼ cup 1% low-fat milk or soymilk

2 cups finely chopped broccoli florets, steamed

1 cup grated cheddar cheese or cheddar-style soy cheese

Salt and freshly ground pepper to taste

Calories: 248 • Total fat: 9 g
Protein: 10 g • Carbohydrate: 30 g
Cholesterol: 31 mg • Sodium: 202 mg

This is a great main dish for kids and teens who have a taste for broccoli. This one's a family favorite, because we all like broccoli so much. For an easy meal, serve with tossed salad and corn on the cob.

1 Bake or microwave the potatoes until done but still firm. When cool enough to handle, cut each in half lengthwise. Scoop out the inside of each potato half, leaving a sturdy shell, about ¼ inch thick all around.

2 Transfer the scooped-out potato to a mixing bowl and mash it coarsely. Add the remaining ingredients and stir well to combine.

3 Stuff the mixture back into the potato shells. Heat as needed in the microwave or in a preheated 400°F oven, and serve.

Zucchini and Goat Cheese-Stuffed Sweet Potatoes

4 SERVINGS

The pleasant bite of goat cheese contrasts deliciously with the smooth sweetness of potatoes.

4 medium-large sweet potatoes

2 tablespoons nonhydrogenated margarine

2 medium-small zucchini, halved lengthwise and thinly sliced

3 to 4 scallions, thinly sliced

⅓ cup creamy goat cheese

Pinch of salt

Calories: 228 • Total fat: 9 g
Protein: 4 g • Carbohydrate: 31 g
Cholesterol: 17 mg • Sodium: 284 mg

1 Bake or microwave the sweet potatoes until done but still firm. When cool enough to handle, cut each in half lengthwise. Scoop out the inside of each potato half, leaving a sturdy shell, about ¼ inch thick all around.

2 Transfer the scooped-out potato to a mixing bowl and mash coarsely.

3 Heat the margarine in a medium skillet. Add the zucchini and sauté, stirring frequently, until it is golden and tender. Add the scallions and sauté for another minute or so.

4 Combine the zucchini mixture with the mashed sweet potato in the mixing bowl. Add the goat cheese and salt, and stir well to combine.

5 Stuff the mixture back into the potato shells. Heat as needed in the microwave or in a preheated 400°F oven, and serve.

MENU

Zucchini and Goat Cheese-Stuffed Sweet Potatoes *(this page)*

Steamed Broccoli and Cauliflower *(page 199)*

Chickpea and Tomato Salad *(page 42)*

Mashed White and Sweet Potatoes

6 SERVINGS

4 medium white potatoes, peeled and diced

2 medium-large sweet potatoes, peeled and diced

2 tablespoons nonhydrogenated margarine

½ to ¾ cup 1% low-fat milk or soymilk

Pinch of nutmeg

Salt to taste

Calories: 201 • Total fat: 5 g
Protein: 3 g • Carbohydrate: 38 g
Cholesterol: 1 mg • Sodium: 68 mg

A traditional side dish is made even better with the addition of sweet potato. The flavors and colors are heightened, and the nutritional quality is enhanced.

1 Cover the potato dice with water in a large saucepan. Bring to a simmer, cover, and simmer gently until the potatoes are quite tender, about 15 minutes.

2 Drain the potatoes and transfer to a mixing bowl. Stir in the margarine until it melts, and add the milk and nutmeg.

3 Mash the potatoes until they are smooth and fluffy. Season with salt. The mashed potatoes will probably need to be heated a bit before serving, so transfer them to a heatproof serving container, cover, and heat briefly in the microwave or a preheated 400°F oven.

Sweet Potatoes

Sweet potatoes are one of the most ancient, nutritious, and valuable food crops of the Americas. Not to diminish the value of white potatoes, but in comparison, sweet potatoes are substantially richer in nutrients. They are especially high in vitamin A and the major minerals. With their natural sweetness and glorious color, sweet potatoes lend themselves to simple preparations. And they are splendid as a side dish, simply baked or microwaved—as I recommend quite often in this book's menus.

White or Sweet Potato Oven "Fries"

4 SERVINGS

A terrific way to enjoy low-fat "fries," this is a great accompaniment for veggie burgers and soy hot dogs. Or see the menu with "Chili Dogs," page 148.

4 to 5 large potatoes, preferably red-skinned or Yukon gold, or 3 large sweet potatoes, or a combination

2 tablespoons light olive oil

Salt to taste

1 Preheat the oven to 425°F.

2 Peel the potatoes and cut them into long, ½-inch-thick fry-shaped strips. Combine them in a large mixing bowl with the oil and toss well to coat. Sprinkle with a little salt.

3 Transfer the fries to a nonstick baking sheet. Bake, stirring gently every 10 minutes, until the potatoes are lightly browned, 20 to 30 minutes. Serve at once.

Calories: 205 • Total fat: 7 g
Protein: 2 g • Carbohydrate: 34 g
Cholesterol: 0 mg • Sodium: 9 mg

Baked Potatoes the Classic Way

For those of us who lead hectic lives (and who doesn't these days?), the microwave is a boon for baking all types of potatoes. You can bake them in a fraction of the time it takes in the oven.

But if you find yourself home on a cold or drizzly day, consider baking a few white or sweet potatoes the old-fashioned way. Their flavor deepens and they bake much more evenly in the oven than they do in the microwave.

Preheat the oven to 400°F. Scrub the potatoes (especially well if you plan to eat the skins of white potatoes) with a vegetable brush. Cut off any eyes that have begun to sprout. Conventional wisdom says to poke a few times with a fork to allow steam to escape to prevent exploding, but to be honest, I never do this. Instead, I wrap the potatoes individually in aluminum foil and arrange them on an oven rack. Bake until a knife pierces through easily, about 1 hour.

Curried Sweet Potatoes with Spinach and Chickpeas

6 SERVINGS

2 large sweet potatoes

One 16-ounce can chickpeas, drained and rinsed

One 14- to 16-ounce can low-sodium diced tomatoes

10 to 12 ounces fresh spinach, well washed, stemmed, and coarsely chopped

1 to 2 teaspoons good-quality curry powder, or to taste

Salt to taste

Calories: 152 • Total fat: 1 g
Protein: 6 g • Carbohydrate: 28 g
Cholesterol: 0 mg • Sodium: 231 mg

I just love sweet potatoes spiced with curry—what a superb fusion of flavors! This and the following recipe will help prove my point.

1 Bake or microwave the sweet potatoes in their skins until done but still firm. When cool enough to handle, peel, and cut into large dice.

2 Combine the chickpeas and tomatoes in a large saucepan or stir-fry pan and bring to a simmer over medium heat.

3 Add the spinach and cover. Cook briefly, just until the spinach wilts, and stir in the sweet potatoes, curry, and salt. Stir together and cook over low heat for 5 minutes, and serve.

MENU

Curried Sweet Potatoes with Spinach and Chickpeas *(this page)*

or

Curried Sweet Potatoes with Green Peas *(page 195)*

Cucumbers and Tomatoes in Yogurt *(page 39)*

Corn on the cob

Warm pita bread

Curried Sweet Potatoes with Green Peas

6 SERVINGS

Serve this with the menu on page 194 or with Fruited Bulgur Salad (page 48) and some sliced bell peppers.

3 large sweet potatoes

2 cups frozen green peas, thawed

One 14- to 16-ounce can low-sodium diced tomatoes

1 to 2 teaspoons good-quality curry powder, or to taste

2 to 3 tablespoons minced fresh cilantro

Salt to taste

1 Bake or microwave the sweet potatoes in their skins until done but still firm. When cool enough to handle, peel, and cut into large dice.

2 Combine the peas and tomatoes in a large saucepan or stir-fry pan and bring to a simmer over medium heat.

3 Stir in the sweet potatoes and curry. Cook over low heat for 5 minutes, stir in the cilantro, and serve.

Calories: 116 • Total fat: 0 g
Protein: 4 g • Carbohydrate: 25 g
Cholesterol: 0 mg • Sodium: 13 mg

Candied Sweet Potatoes

6 SERVINGS

2 tablespoons nonhydrogenated margarine, melted

Juice of 2 oranges (½ to ¾ cup)

⅓ cup maple syrup

1 teaspoon pumpkin pie spice (or substitute 1 teaspoon cinnamon if unavailable)

5 large sweet potatoes, peeled and sliced ¼ inch thick

Calories: 245 • Total fat: 5 g
Protein: 2 g • Carbohydrate: 51 g
Cholesterol: 0 mg • Sodium: 58 mg

This is a variation on the classic recipe more often referred to as "candied yams." Did you know that calling sweet potatoes "yams" is actually a misnomer? Yams are rarely sold in this country, so quite often, what you see sold as yams are actually sweet potatoes. I make this dish for nearly every Thanksgiving dinner.

1 Preheat the oven to 375°F.

2 Combine the first 4 ingredients in a large mixing bowl. Stir until well combined. Add the sliced potatoes, stir well, and transfer to a shallow 1½-quart round or 9 by 13-inch oblong baking dish.

3 Cover and bake until the sweet potatoes are just tender, about 40 minutes. Stir once or twice during that time to distribute the liquid over the potatoes. Bake, uncovered, until the glaze thickens, an additional 10 to 15 minutes. Cover and keep warm until ready to serve

Veggies on the Side

CHAPTER 9

As a child, I never had to be urged to eat my vegetables, even though most of the time they were hopelessly overcooked. I've rarely had a vegetable I didn't like. It wasn't until my early teens, believe it or not, that I had my first taste of a very lightly sautéed vegetable at the home of a friend. As I recall, it was zucchini, and having it that way was a major revelation for me—vegetables need not be boiled to death! From that point on, I began to take things into my own hands, preparing more vegetable-filled meals for my brother and myself (both of us were incredibly squeamish about eating meat), which led to our becoming full-fledged vegetarians.

If grains, beans, and soy foods are the foundation of a vegetarian diet, fresh vegetables are the building blocks, providing a dazzling array of vitamins, including the valuable anti-oxidants, and numerous nutrients proven to prevent disease.

As a parent, I've noticed how insidious media messages train kids to think of vegetables as "yucky." How sad! As a result, I've tried to consciously foster a positive attitude toward vegetables in my two vegetarian sons. Like most kids, they can be finicky about one thing or another, so I serve an assortment of simply prepared vegetables at dinner. That way, they can try this one or that, or even a little of everything, if I'm lucky. An array of fresh vegetables on the table contributes to a feeling of abundance, enhancing everyone's enjoyment of the meal.

Mini-Lexicon of Broccoli Varieties (and Some Tips)

I've mentioned here and there in this book that broccoli is a favorite vegetable in my family. When I no longer have any in the vegetable drawer, I know it's time to go shopping for produce. But even the healthiest of pleasures can get tired if they are overindulged, so to keep from getting into a broccoli rut, I occasionally buy one of the few variations available.

Broccoli: The familiar kind of broccoli is one of the most healthful vegetables, ranking just behind spinach and sweet potatoes. I often steam bite-size pieces in a large saucepan on the stovetop or in a casserole dish in the microwave with a little water. We like it just a little beyond tender-crisp, but still bright green. After draining it, I stir in just a touch of natural margarine or whipped butter and a dash of salt. I usually buy broccoli crowns without too much stem. Precut broccoli is convenient but more expensive, and, to my taste, not as flavorful. If you have a chance to cook some straight from the garden, you'll have the ultimate broccoli experience!

Broccoflower™: A hybrid of cauliflower and broccoli, it looks like light green cauliflower. Its flavor is closer to cauliflower, with a hint of broccoli's sweetness. Steam it as described above for broccoli.

Broccoli Rabe (also called broccoli raab or rapini): Much loved in Italian cuisine, this variety is leafier than broccoli, with smaller florets. The flavor is more pungent—slightly bitter, in fact. A good way to prepare it is to cut it into 2- to 3-inch lengths and sauté in olive oil with garlic until it is tender-crisp or done to your liking.

Broccolini: This newer variety of broccoli has long, tender stems (that need not be scraped) and small floret heads. It has the same mild, slightly sweet flavor of broccoli and adds a graceful visual note to the dinner plate.

Steamed Broccoli and Cauliflower

4 TO 6 SERVINGS

I have long enjoyed combining these two cruciferous vegetables. Broccoli takes slightly more time to cook than cauliflower, so it is given a head start.

2 medium broccoli crowns, cut into bite-size pieces

1 small head cauliflower, cut into bite-size pieces

1 tablespoon nonhydrogenated margarine

Pinch of salt

1 Combine the broccoli in a large, deep saucepan or 1½-quart casserole dish with about 1 inch of water. Steam over medium heat or microwave for 2 minutes to 3 minutes, just until it begins to turn bright green.

2 Stir in the cauliflower and continue to steam or microwave until both are done to your liking, 4 to 6 minutes. Drain, and return to the casserole dish or a serving container. Stir in the margarine to melt, season with salt, and serve.

Calories: 49 • Total fat: 2 g
Protein: 2 g • Carbohydrate: 5 g
Cholesterol: 0 mg • Sodium: 51 mg

Broccoli and Baby Corn Stir-Fry

4 TO 6 SERVINGS

Here's a colorful side dish to serve with Asian-style rice, noodle, or tofu dishes.

1 teaspoon dark sesame oil

¼ cup sherry or dry white wine

4 cups bite-size broccoli florets

1 large carrot, peeled and sliced diagonally

One 15-ounce can baby corn, drained

Pinch of salt

1 Heat the oil and sherry together in a stir-fry pan, and add the broccoli and carrot. Stir-fry over medium-high heat until the broccoli is bright green and tender-crisp.

2 Add the baby corn and salt. Stir-fry until the baby corn is heated through, and serve.

Calories: 108 • Total fat: 1 g
Protein: 3 g • Carbohydrate: 18 g
Cholesterol: 0 mg • Sodium: 32 mg

Egg-Dipped Cauliflower or Broccoflower

4 TO 6 SERVINGS

6 cups bite-size cauliflower or broccoflower florets

2 eggs, beaten

Light olive oil for frying

Salt to taste

Calories: 66 • Total fat: 2 g
Protein: 5 g • Carbohydrate: 6 g
Cholesterol: 109 mg • Sodium: 45 mg

This is one of the only vegetable dishes from my childhood in which the vegetable in question (in that case cauliflower—broccoflower is a relatively recent innovation) was not completely overcooked, and indeed, still had a nice resistance to the bite. Now, my kids like it, too.

1 Combine the cauliflower florets in a large, deep saucepan or 1½-quart casserole dish with about 1 inch of water. Steam over medium heat or microwave for about 2 minutes, at which time it should be quite underdone, and drain.

2 Stir the cauliflower pieces into the beaten egg until evenly coated.

3 Heat just enough oil to coat the bottom of a wide skillet. When hot, arrange some of the cauliflower pieces in the skillet in a single layer (you'll need to cook them in 2 or 3 batches). Cook over medium heat, turning frequently until the pieces are golden and crisp. Season with salt. Keep each batch warm in a covered container while preparing the next, and serve.

Broiled Mushrooms Teriyaki

4 TO 6 SERVINGS

Served in small side portions, this aromatic preparation complements Asian noodle or rice dishes.

3 tablespoons low-sodium teriyaki sauce

1 teaspoon dark sesame oil

1 tablespoon rice vinegar or white wine vinegar

1 tablespoon honey or brown rice syrup

12 to 16 ounces fresh mushrooms, any variety (white, portabella, shiitake, cremini, baby bella, or a combination)

Calories: 52 • Total fat: 0 g
Protein: 2 g • Carbohydrate: 8 g
Cholesterol: 0 mg • Sodium: 192 mg

1 Preheat broiler (unless using a toaster oven).

2 Combine the first 4 ingredients in a mixing bowl and stir together.

3 Wipe the mushrooms clean. If using shiitakes, remove and discard the stems. Leave the mushrooms whole (unless you're using large portabellas; slice them ¼ inch thick).

4 Combine the mushrooms with the teriyaki mixture and stir together. Arrange in a shallow foil-lined pan and pour any excess marinade over them.

5 Broil in the oven or a toaster oven for 4 minutes, and stir. Broil until the mushrooms begin turning dark and are touched by charred spots, 4 to 5 minutes. Remove from the broiler and transfer to a serving container.

Mushrooms

Not long ago, when a recipe called for mushrooms, it meant white mushrooms. What else was there? Now, every supermarket and produce grocery offers a wide array of mushrooms and these can add charm to the simplest of dishes. Here are a few varieties that have become almost standard fare:

Baby bella: These medium-size, warm brown mushrooms are a smaller version of portabellas. They have a flavor that is deeper than white mushrooms, yet not quite as earthy as the larger kind.

Cremini: Mild-flavored and light brown, these are just a step away from white mushrooms, with the same size and shape, but a slightly more distinct flavor.

Portabella: Once the exclusive domain of upscale restaurants, these are now widely available. You can buy the whole caps, which are 3 to 4 inches in diameter, or sliced. These deep brown, earthy mushrooms are exceptional for grilling and broiling.

Shiitake: These earthy brown mushrooms have broad, thin caps with a pleasantly chewy texture. Among the most nutritious of mushrooms, they are commonly available both fresh and dried. Trim away the tough stems before use. Fresh shiitakes are delightful in Asian-style soups and stir-fries, as well as in vegetable sautés and pasta dishes. Dried shiitakes are most useful to impart flavor to soup stocks and sauces.

Broiled Portabella Mushrooms

4 SERVINGS

A wonderful accompaniment to the salad course of a special meal, served on a separate plate. These also make great "meaty" fillers for burger buns with lettuce, tomato, and your favorite condiments.

2 tablespoons dry white wine

1 tablespoon light olive oil

1½ tablespoons balsamic vinegar

Pinch of salt

4 large portabella caps

Oregano for sprinkling, optional

1 Preheat broiler (unless using a toaster oven).

2 Combine the wine, oil, vinegar, and salt in a small mixing bowl and stir together.

3 Wipe the mushrooms clean and arrange, smooth side up, on a small foil-lined baking sheet. Brush them with the marinade.

4 Broil in the oven or a toaster oven for 4 to 5 minutes, then turn and broil until the mushrooms are touched by charred spots, 4 to 5 minutes. Remove from the broiler, sprinkle with oregano if desired, and serve.

Calories: 45 • Total fat: 2 g
Protein: 3 g • Carbohydrate: 3 g
Cholesterol: 0 mg • Sodium: 1 mg

Napa Cabbage and Mushroom Stir-Fry

4 TO 6 SERVINGS

1 tablespoon peanut oil

1 teaspoon dark sesame oil

¼ cup dry white wine

1 medium head napa cabbage, leaves halved lengthwise and thinly sliced

8 to 10 ounces cremini or baby bella mushrooms, cleaned and cut in half

Salt and freshly ground pepper to taste

Calories: 66 • Total fat: 4 g
Protein: 2 g • Carbohydrate: 6 g
Cholesterol: 0 mg • Sodium: 19 mg

Napa cabbage is a leafier relative of bok choy. This is compatible with Asian rice, noodle, and tofu dishes.

Heat the oils and wine in a stir-fry pan. Add the cabbage and mushrooms, and stir-fry over medium-high heat until the cabbage is tender-crisp and the mushrooms tender, 6 to 8 minutes. Season with salt and pepper, and serve.

Variation: Make this dish with a small head of thinly shredded savoy cabbage in place of the napa.

Sautéed Cabbage and Onions

6 SERVINGS

1½ tablespoons light olive oil

1 large onion, quartered and thinly sliced

¼ cup dry white wine

One 16-ounce package shredded coleslaw cabbage

Salt and freshly ground pepper to taste

Calories: 63 • Total fat: 2 g
Protein: 1 g • Carbohydrate: 6 g
Cholesterol: 0 mg • Sodium: 14 mg

Convenient shredded coleslaw cabbage is put to good use in this simple sauté. Try to use a blend with a little red cabbage and carrot for added color. This makes a good side dish for potato dishes and veggie burgers. Use leftovers on sandwiches with soy "bacon" and deli slices.

1 Heat the oil in a stir-fry pan or soup pot. Add the onion and sauté over medium-low heat until it is translucent. Stir in the wine and cabbage. Cover and cook until the cabbage is limp, about 10 minutes.

2 Raise the heat to medium, uncover and cook, stirring often, until the cabbage is lightly and evenly golden, about 5 minutes longer. Season with salt and pepper, and serve.

Roasted Italian Vegetables

4 TO 6 SERVINGS

This makes an excellent side dish for pasta. See the menu accompanying Farfalle with Mushrooms (page 76).

2 small zucchini

4 small Japanese eggplants

4 to 6 ounces sliced portabella mushroom caps

2 large red bell peppers, cut into long, wide strips

½ cup good-quality balsamic vinaigrette

Salt and freshly ground pepper to taste

1 Preheat the oven to 425°F.

2 Stem the zucchini and eggplants. Quarter the zucchini lengthwise, then cut them in half crosswise. Cut the eggplants into eighths lengthwise, then cut them in half crosswise.

3 Combine the zucchini and eggplant with the mushrooms and bell peppers in a large roasting pan (foil-lined if you prefer). Pour the vinaigrette over them, season with salt and pepper, and stir.

4 Bake, stirring gently every 5 minutes or so, until the vegetables are tender and lightly browned, 20 to 25 minutes. Serve at once.

Calories: 94 • Total fat: 0 g
Protein: 3 g • Carbohydrate: 22 g
Cholesterol: 0 mg • Sodium: 212 mg

Roasted Root Vegetables

4 TO 6 SERVINGS

2 medium turnips

1 medium rutabaga (see note)

2 medium parsnips

2 tablespoons light olive oil

½ teaspoon salt-free herb-and-spice seasoning mix, optional

Salt and freshly ground pepper to taste

Calories: 99 • Total fat: 6 g
Protein: 1 g • Carbohydrate: 11 g
Cholesterol: 0 mg • Sodium: 36 mg

I'd like to champion these underused (and often maligned) vegetables by urging you to try them roasted. Roots are naturally sweet and become even more so during the roasting process.

1 Preheat the oven to 425°F.

2 Slice turnips and rutabaga ½ inch thick, then peel the slices. Cut into thick finger-shaped pieces. Peel and slice the parsnips ½ inch thick.

3 Combine the vegetables with the oil, optional seasoning mix, and salt and pepper in a large mixing bowl, and stir together. Transfer to a roasting pan (foil-lined if you prefer).

4 Bake, stirring gently every 10 minutes, until the vegetables are tender and lightly browned, about 30 minutes. Serve at once.

Note: If you haven't got a really sharp knife, don't even think about using rutabaga. A good substitution would be two medium sweet potatoes, peeled and sliced ¼ inch thick.

MENU

WINTER COMFORT

Barley with Mushrooms and Browned Onions *(page 101)*

Roasted Root Vegetables *(this page)*

Simple tossed salad

Maple Baked Pears *(page 254)*

Maple-Roasted Carrots

6 SERVINGS

Here's an easy way to enjoy a roasted effect with no cutting involved. It's a good side dish to make while something else, like Shake-and-Bake Tofu, is in the oven (see the menu on page 138). This is one children are likely to go for.

1 pound carrots, peeled and cut into thick, 2- to 3-inch-long sticks, or one 16-ounce bag baby carrots

2 tablespoons maple syrup

1 tablespoon light olive oil

Pinch of cinnamon

Pinch of salt

Calories: 69 • Total fat: 2 g
Protein: 1 g • Carbohydrate: 11 g
Cholesterol: 0 mg • Sodium: 27 mg

1 Preheat the oven to 425°F.

2 Combine all the ingredients in a mixing bowl and stir together. Arrange on a nonstick baking sheet. Bake, stirring gently every few minutes, until the carrots are tender and lightly browned, about 20 minutes, and serve.

Carrots

Carrots come out at or near the top of two different surveys. First, they're ranked among the most nutritious vegetables, following closely behind dark leafy greens, broccoli, and sweet potatoes; vitamin A and beta-carotene are their strong suits. Second, they are often named "favorite vegetable" by children. Sweet and crunchy, carrots are a vegetable worth having often, both raw and judiciously cooked.

Gingered Baby Carrots and Apricots

4 SERVINGS

1½ tablespoons nonhydrogenated margarine

One 16-ounce bag baby carrots

¼ cup undiluted frozen apple juice concentrate, thawed

½ teaspoon grated fresh ginger or ¼ teaspoon ground ginger

½ cup sliced dried apricots

Calories: 156 • Total fat: 5 g
Protein: 1 g • Carbohydrate: 27 g
Cholesterol: 0 mg • Sodium: 96 mg

I like to serve this with curries and grain pilafs. Try it with Long-Grain and Wild Rice Pilaf (page 99) or Fragrant Rice and Cashew Pilaf (page 100).

1 Heat the margarine in a large skillet. Add the carrots, apple juice, and ginger. Cover and cook for 15 minutes, or until the carrots are tender-crisp to your liking.

2 Stir in the apricots, and serve.

Sautéed Leeks and Carrots

4 TO 6 SERVINGS

1 tablespoon light olive oil

¼ cup dry white wine

3 medium leeks, white and palest green parts only, chopped and very well rinsed

4 large carrots, peeled and sliced

Pinch of nutmeg, optional

Salt and freshly ground pepper to taste

Calories: 109 • Total fat: 2 g
Protein: 1 g • Carbohydrate: 16 g
Cholesterol: 0 mg • Sodium: 36 mg

Leeks and carrots both have a natural sweetness that mingles nicely. This is a mild and pleasant side dish, good with pasta, potatoes, and soy dishes.

1 Heat the oil and wine in a wide skillet. Add the leeks and carrots, cover, and cook over medium-low heat for 8 to 10 minutes, or until tender-crisp.

2 Uncover and sauté, stirring frequently, until the leeks and carrots begin to turn golden. Stir in the optional nutmeg, season with salt and pepper, and serve.

Summer Squash and Corn Sauté

4 TO 6 SERVINGS

Here's a summer harvest dish that I absolutely love. Fresh corn kernels are a must if you want to get the full impact of the fresh flavors. This is great with veggie burgers, soy hot dogs, and tortilla specialties.

1½ tablespoons light olive oil

1 large green or red bell pepper, cut into short strips

2 medium yellow summer squash, halved lengthwise and sliced ¼ inch thick

1 to 1½ cups uncooked corn kernels (from 1 to 2 ears)

2 medium firm tomatoes, diced

Salt and freshly ground pepper to taste

1 Heat the oil in a wide skillet. Add the bell pepper and sauté over medium heat for about 2 minutes. Add the squash and corn and continue to sauté, stirring frequently, until all the vegetables are tender-crisp to your liking.

2 Add the tomatoes and continue to sauté briefly, just until they have lost their raw quality. Season with salt and pepper, and serve.

Calories: 97 • Total fat: 4 g
Protein: 2 g • Carbohydrate: 13 g
Cholesterol: 0 mg • Sodium: 7 mg

MENU

Summer Squash and Corn Sauté *(this page)*

Soy Sloppy Joes *(page 151)*

Bountiful tossed salad

Stone-ground tortilla chips

Asparagus, Squash, and Red Pepper Sauté

4 TO 6 SERVINGS

1½ tablespoons light olive oil

¼ cup dry white wine

2 medium red bell peppers, cut into short strips

2 medium zucchini or yellow summer squash, halved lengthwise and sliced ¼ inch thick

6 ounces slender asparagus, bottoms trimmed and cut into 1½-inch lengths

Salt and freshly ground pepper to taste

Calories: 73 • Total fat: 4 g
Protein: 1 g • Carbohydrate: 5 g
Cholesterol: 0 mg • Sodium: 5 mg

An appealing vegetable trio is enlivened by a wine-scented sauté.

Heat the oil and wine in a wide skillet. Add the bell peppers, squash, and asparagus, and sauté over medium-high heat, stirring frequently, until all the vegetables are tender-crisp to your liking, about 8 minutes. Season with salt and pepper, and serve.

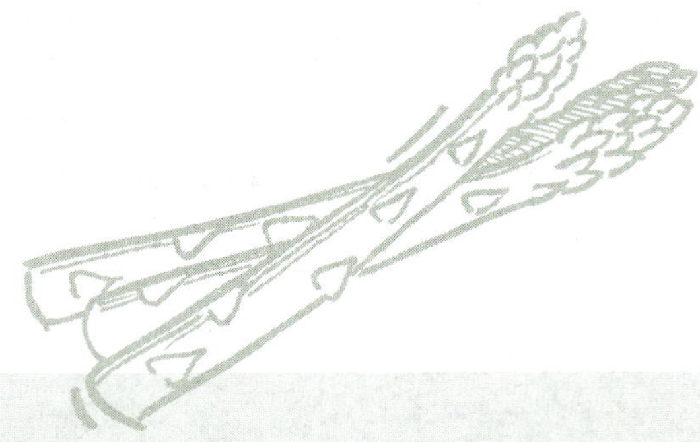

Asparagus

Now that the seasons for fresh produce have been stretched by imports, it's not quite as much of a thrill to see the first asparagus of early spring. A pity, since I once considered the arrival of asparagus to the market as much an awaited sign of spring as forsythia and robins. Still, I like to stick with vegetables that are in season by buying locally. Freshly picked, slender asparagus is more agreeable to my eyes and palate than thick, stringy imported winter asparagus.

Spring asparagus needs to have only about half an inch trimmed off the bottom of the stalks; scraping is unnecessary when the stalks are slender. Asparagus makes a good side dish, simply steamed, with a tiny bit of nonhydrogenated margarine or whipped butter added. Microwave cooking yields good results; place the stalks in a small casserole dish with just enough water to keep them moist. Cover and cook until tender-crisp to your liking. How long this takes depends on the quantity and quality of the asparagus, so test often and serve right away.

Another great way to prepare slender asparagus is to cut it into 2- to 3-inch lengths and sauté it in olive oil with minced garlic.

Sautéed Turnips and Red Peppers

4 TO 6 SERVINGS

1½ tablespoons light olive oil

3 to 4 medium turnips, cut into ½-inch-thick rounds, peeled and sliced into strips

2 medium red bell peppers, cut into short strips

2 to 3 tablespoons minced parsley, dill, or scallion

1 cup green sprouts (such as baby pea shoots), optional

Salt and freshly ground pepper to taste

Raw turnips have a pleasantly bitter bite like radishes, but sautéed they are delectably sweet.

1 Heat the oil in a wide skillet. Add the turnips and bell peppers, and sauté over medium heat, stirring frequently, until the vegetables are tender-crisp to your liking, about 8 minutes.

2 Stir in the herbs and optional sprouts, season to taste with salt and pepper, and serve.

Calories: 60 • Total fat: 4 g
Protein: 1 g • Carbohydrate: 5 g
Cholesterol: 0 mg • Sodium: 48 mg

Sautéed Bell Peppers

4 TO 6 SERVINGS

2 tablespoons extra-virgin olive oil

5 to 6 medium to large green, red, or yellow bell peppers or a combination, cut into long strips

1 tablespoon balsamic vinegar, optional

Pinch of salt

Use a variety of peppers to make this side dish colorful. Use leftovers to make sandwiches on fresh bread with spreadable goat cheese.

1 Heat the oil in a wide skillet. Add the peppers, cover, and cook over low heat, about 10 minutes, stirring occasionally.

2 Uncover and sauté, stirring frequently, until the peppers are tender and lightly browned, 15 to 20 minutes. Stir in the optional vinegar, season with salt, and serve.

Calories: 67 • Total fat: 6 g
Protein: 1 g • Carbohydrate: 4 g
Cholesterol: 0 mg • Sodium: 2 mg

6 SERVINGS

Contemporary Creamed Spinach

1½ to 2 pounds fresh spinach, well washed, stemmed, and coarsely chopped

One 12.3-ounce container firm silken tofu

1½ tablespoons nonhydrogenated margarine

1 tablespoon minced fresh dill or 1 teaspoon dried dill

Salt and freshly ground pepper to taste

Calories: 88 • Total fat: 4 g
Protein: 6 g • Carbohydrate: 6 g
Cholesterol: 0 mg • Sodium: 135 mg

In this updated version of creamed spinach, you get the goodness of soy, but not the bother of cooking a flour-thickened sauce. It's a feast for spinach fans!

1 Steam the spinach in a large pot, in batches if need be, just until it wilts. Just the water clinging to the leaves is sufficient. Drain, then place on a cutting board and chop finely.

2 Puree the tofu in a food processor until completely smooth.

3 Combine the pureed tofu with the remaining ingredients in a medium saucepan and stir together. Heat slowly over medium-low heat, stirring occasionally, until hot, and serve.

Spinach

A recent study I read ranking vegetables in order of their nutritional quality put spinach at the top of the list (next were the other dark leafy greens, then sweet potatoes, broccoli, and carrots). It's packed with nutrients, notably iron and vitamin A. For convenience, I use frozen chopped spinach in soups and stews, especially when a large quantity is needed, but when spinach is the highlight of a dish, I much prefer fresh organic spinach.

Often, I will simply steam the spinach (with just the water clinging to the leaves) and remove it from the heat the minute it wilts down. After draining it, I stir in the customary pat of natural margarine that I like on steamed green vegetables, plus a pinch of salt.

Curried Spinach and Eggplant

6 SERVINGS

Both spinach and eggplant are compatible with curry seasoning, so teaming the two vegetables makes this stew-like side dish twice as nice. This is delicious on its own or over couscous.

1 recipe Versatile Steamed Eggplant (page 215)

One 14- to 16-ounce can low-sodium diced tomatoes

2 teaspoons good-quality curry powder, or to taste

10 to 12 ounces fresh spinach, well washed and stemmed

Salt to taste

1 When the eggplant recipe is done, add the tomatoes and curry and bring to a simmer.

2 Add the spinach, cover, and cook just until it wilts down, 1 to 2 minutes. Give the mixture a good stir, season with salt, and serve in shallow bowls.

Calories: 57 • Total fat: 0 g
Protein: 2 g • Carbohydrate: 12 g
Cholesterol: 0 mg • Sodium: 55 mg

Broiled Japanese Eggplant

6 SERVINGS

2 tablespoons hoisin sauce (see note)

1 tablespoon dark sesame oil

½ teaspoon grated fresh ginger, or to taste

1 teaspoon honey or maple syrup

6 small Japanese eggplants, rinsed, stemmed, and cut in half lengthwise

Calories: 53 • Total fat: 2 g
Protein: 1 g • Carbohydrate: 7 g
Cholesterol: 0 mg • Sodium: 339 mg

An intensely flavored (but not overpowering) accompaniment for Asian-style dishes, this adds an enticing visual accent to the dinner plate as well.

1 Preheat the broiler.

2 Combine the first 4 ingredients in a medium mixing bowl and stir together.

3 Arrange the eggplants, cut side up, on a foil-lined baking sheet or roasting pan and distribute the marinade over them.

4 Broil until the eggplants begin turning dark and are touched by charred spots, 6 to 8 minutes. Serve at once.

Note: Hoisin is a pungent sauce commonly used in Chinese cookery. You will find it in most supermarkets, shelved near soy sauce and other Asian condiments.

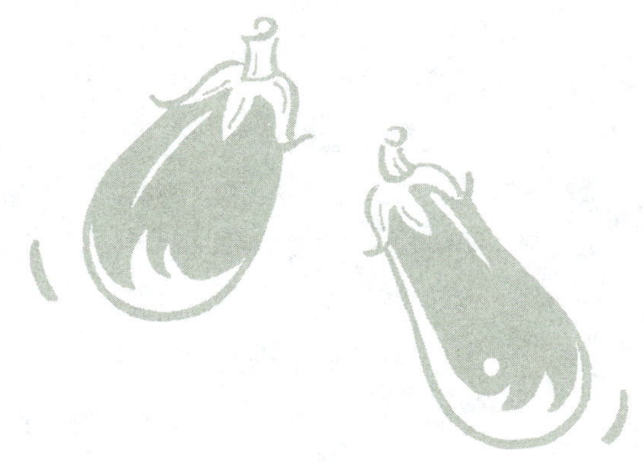

Versatile Steamed Eggplant

4 SERVINGS

1 medium onion, quartered and thinly sliced

1 medium-large eggplant (about 1 pound)

Salt and freshly ground pepper to taste

Calories: 44 • Total fat: 0 g
Protein: 1 g • Carbohydrate: 10 g
Cholesterol: 0 mg • Sodium: 6 mg

Use this preparation in stews, for topping pizza, on French bread sandwiches topped with mozzarella cheese, spread with goat cheese, or in wraps. See Curried Spinach and Eggplant (page 213) or Eggplant Parmigiana Wraps (page 177).

1 Combine the onion with ¼ cup water in a deep saucepan or stir-fry pan. Bring to a simmer, cover, and cook over medium-low heat while preparing the eggplant.

2 Cut the eggplant into ½-inch-thick slices, then peel it. Cut each slice in half crosswise, then slice into ¼-inch-thick strips. Add to the saucepan along with another ½ cup water. Cover and steam, stirring occasionally, until the eggplant is tender but not mushy, about 8 minutes. Keep the bottom of the saucepan moist, but not too liquidy, using a little more water if needed. Season with salt and pepper.

Eggplant Lover's Lament

Eggplant lovers, I have good news and not-so-good news. The good news is that eggplant comes in an increasing number of varieties, from tiny Japanese to white and magenta types. The bad news? When analyzed, eggplant often ranks dead last among vegetables in terms of fiber content, vitamins, and minerals. Even white mushrooms top it!

But I still love eggplant. It's not as if it's really bad for you, like jelly donuts. And I don't think any of my fellow eggplant enthusiasts will turn away from this palatable yet hapless vegetable, either. In Italy, where it is treasured, its name, *melanzana,* translates loosely as "mad apple." A seventeenth-century European herbalist proclaimed that "doubtless these Apples have a mischievous qualitie." Bad reputation and mediocre nutrition aside, we eggplant lovers are loyal, and you'll likely relish these basic recipes.

Winter Squash

Winter squashes epitomize the fall harvest season. Since I live in the Northeast, they adorn my kitchen from October through March. I'll admit that a big old winter squash may not be a practical choice when you come home starving at 6:30; and they can be cumbersome to work with unless you have good, sharp knives.

Squashes are quintessential Native American vegetables. I particularly appreciate that they are truly seasonal, local produce. Few people get the urge to bake a butternut squash in July, so their season is rarely extended artificially through imports.

I've noticed a proliferation of squash varieties over the last few years. Before that, butternut, acorn, and the occasional sugar pumpkin were the extent of the choices, but now, you are likely to encounter golden acorn (a sweeter, smoother cousin of the green variety), banana squash, delicata, turban, hubbard, delicious, and others.

While all these winter squashes have some variation in flavor, all have deep yellow to orange flesh that can be characterized as mild, smooth, and slightly sweet. The exception is spaghetti squash, whose flesh comes out in spaghetti-like strands when done (see the recipes on pages 220 and 221). Some varieties (like delicata and golden acorn) are small, making them easier to cut and quicker to bake than larger squashes.

Here are a few tips for making good use of winter squash:

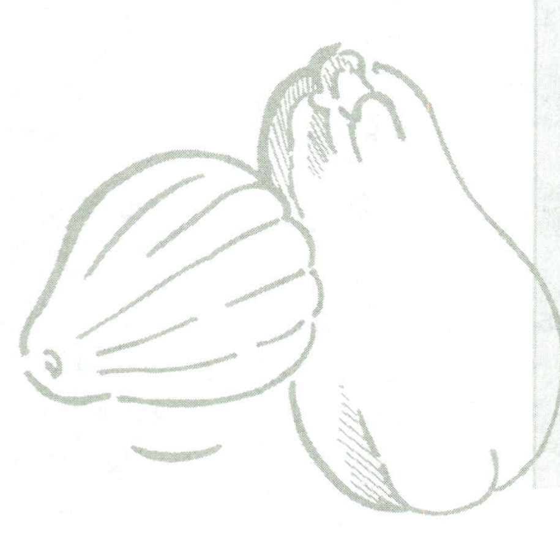

- Fresh winter squashes will keep at room temperature for 2 to 3 weeks. Refrigerating them may alter their flavor and texture, so it's not recommended.
- If you don't want to struggle with cutting a large, thick-skinned squash, bake the whole squash at 375° for a half hour or so. When cool enough to handle, you will find it easier to cut in half.
- After pre-baking whole large squashes, cut them in half lengthwise once cool enough to handle, then place the cut side up in a baking dish with about ½ inch of water at the bottom, and cover each half tightly with foil.

Soy and Honey-Glazed Winter Squash

6 SERVINGS

A sweet-and-salty glaze gives this squash dish a pleasant Asian spin.

2½ to 3 pounds small winter squash (carnival, golden acorn, delicata, or other)

2 tablespoons honey

¼ cup apple juice

2 tablespoons soy sauce, or to taste

1 teaspoon dark sesame oil

1 The squashes may be baked in the oven or microwave. If you are going to use the oven, preheat it to 375°F.

2 Cut the squashes in half lengthwise. Place the halves, cut side up, in a baking dish with about ½ inch of water, and cover each half tightly with foil. Bake until easily pierced with a knife but still firm, 30 to 45 minutes, depending on the type and size of squash used. Or microwave, using 4 to 7 minutes each as a rule of thumb per small squash or 10 minutes for a butternut. Test occasionally to make sure they don't overcook.

3 When the squashes are cool enough to handle, scoop out and discard the seeds. Peel the squashes and cut into 1-inch chunks.

4 Combine the remaining ingredients in an extra-wide skillet or stir-fry pan and heat gently, stirring together. Add the squash and turn up the heat to medium-high. Cook, stirring, until the liquid reduces and the squash is nicely glazed, 8 to 10 minutes. Serve at once.

Calories: 116 • Total fat: 1 g
Protein: 2 g • Carbohydrate: 23 g
Cholesterol: 0 mg • Sodium: 338 mg

Bake for an additional 30 to 50 minutes, depending on size, until the flesh is easily pierced with a knife.

- It's easier to scoop out the seeds from a squash that is done than an unbaked one.
- Smaller squashes like delicata and golden acorn can be microwaved successfully (see the specifics in some of the recipes that follow). For larger squashes, I like to stick with oven baking. The flavor develops better, and they cook more evenly. Don't even think about microwaving spaghetti squash. Twice they have exploded in my microwave, leaving me with an incredible mess to clean!

Red Onion and Almond-Stuffed Winter Squash

4 SERVINGS

4 small winter squashes (carnival, acorn, golden acorn, delicata, or other)

1 tablespoon nonhydrogenated margarine

1 large red onion, chopped

¼ cup finely chopped toasted almonds

½ teaspoon grated fresh ginger or ¼ teaspoon ground ginger

Salt and freshly ground pepper to taste

Calories: 208 • Total fat: 7 g
Protein: 3 g • Carbohydrate: 31 g
Cholesterol: 0 mg • Sodium: 43 mg

An appetizing preparation, this will invigorate the winter-worn palate.

1 The squashes may be baked in the oven or microwave. If you are going to use the oven, preheat it to 375°F.

2 Cut the squashes in half lengthwise. Place the halves in a baking dish, cut side up, with about ½ inch of water, and cover with foil. Bake until easily pierced with a knife but still holding their shape, 30 to 40 minutes, depending on the type and size of squash used. Or microwave, using as a rule of thumb 4 to 7 minutes each for each squash. Test occasionally to make sure they don't get overcooked.

3 When the squashes are cool enough to handle, scoop out and discard the seeds. Scoop out the pulp and transfer to a mixing bowl, leaving a sturdy shell of about ¼ inch thick all around.

4 Heat the margarine in a medium skillet. Add the onion and sauté over medium heat until golden. Add the almonds and continue to sauté until they give off a toasty aroma.

5 Combine the onion mixture with the squash pulp. Add the ginger, season with salt and pepper, and stir together. Stuff back into the squash shells. Reheat in the microwave or oven, just until heated through, and serve.

Butternut Squash Puree

6 SERVINGS

Despite all the wonderful varieties of winter squash, I still like butternut best for basic preparations like this one. This smooth puree will add color to your plate and comfort your palate.

1 large butternut squash

1½ tablespoons nonhydrogenated margarine or whipped butter

Pinch of nutmeg

Pinch of salt

Calories: 80 • Total fat: 2 g
Protein: 1 g • Carbohydrate: 13 g
Cholesterol: 0 mg • Sodium: 39 mg

1 The squash may be baked in the oven or microwave. If you are going to use the oven, preheat it to 375°F.

2 Cut the squash in half lengthwise. Place the halves in a baking dish, cut side up with about ½ inch of water, and cover with foil. Bake until easily pierced with a knife, 45 to 50 minutes. Or microwave until easily pierced with a knife, about 10 minutes.

3 When the squash is cool enough to handle, scoop out and discard the seeds. Scoop out the pulp and transfer to a serving container. Add the margarine, and stir in to melt. Mash the squash until smooth. Stir in the nutmeg and season with salt. Reheat in the microwave or oven just until heated through, and serve.

Stewed Spaghetti Squash

6 SERVINGS

1 medium-large spaghetti squash (about 2½ pounds)

1½ tablespoons nonhydrogenated margarine

2 medium red or yellow onions, halved and sliced

2 garlic cloves, minced

One 28-ounce can low-sodium stewed tomatoes, with liquid

Salt and freshly ground pepper to taste

Calories: 121 • Total fat: 3 g
Protein: 2 g • Carbohydrate: 20 g
Cholesterol: 0 mg • Sodium: 80 mg

I consider spaghetti squash a "fun" vegetable and enjoy serving it to anyone who has never tried it. Everyone seems delighted by this unique squash and its spaghetti-like flesh. This is delicious accompanied by Long-Grain and Wild Rice Salad (page 50).

1 Preheat the oven to 400°F.

2 Cut the squash in half lengthwise; remove the stem and seeds. Place, cut side up, in a casserole dish with ½ inch of water. Cover tightly with foil and bake until easily pierced with a fork, 40 to 45 minutes. When the squash is cool enough to handle, scrape it lengthwise with a fork to remove the spaghetti-like strands of flesh.

3 Heat the margarine in a large skillet. Add the onions and sauté over medium heat until translucent. Add the garlic and continue to sauté until the onions are golden.

4 Break the tomatoes up with your hands and add them and the squash to the skillet. Cover and simmer over low heat for 8 to 10 minutes, stirring occasionally. Uncover and cook until the liquid in the skillet is reduced, 5 to 8 minutes. Season with salt and pepper, and serve.

Cranberry Spaghetti Squash

6 SERVINGS

Served in its shell, this makes a dramatic presentation as part of a winter meal.

1 medium-large spaghetti squash (about 2½ pounds)

2 tablespoons nonhydrogenated margarine

2 scallions, thinly sliced

½ cup dried cranberries

¼ cup finely chopped toasted walnuts or slivered almonds

Salt and freshly ground pepper to taste

1 Preheat the oven to 400°F.

2 Cut the squash in half lengthwise; remove the stem and seeds. Place, cut side up, in a casserole dish with ½ inch of water. Cover tightly with foil and bake until easily pierced with a fork, 40 to 45 minutes. When the squash is cool enough to handle, scrape it lengthwise with a fork to release all the spaghetti-like strands of flesh.

3 Combine the spaghetti squash with the remaining ingredients in a mixing bowl and toss well. Stuff back into the squash shells.

4 Return the filled squash shells to the baking dish and reheat just until heated through, about 10 minutes. Season with salt and pepper, and serve, scooping a small amount out of the shells for each serving.

Calories: 130 • Total fat: 7 g
Protein: 1 g • Carbohydrate: 14 g
Cholesterol: 0 mg • Sodium: 79 mg

MENU

A COLORFUL HARVEST MEAL

Any of the winter squash recipes in Chapter Nine *(pages 217–221)*

Long-Grain and Wild Rice Pilaf *(page 99)*

Mixed Greens with Beets and Walnuts *(page 50)*

Green Delicacies

Fresh fava beans and green soybeans are two vegetables that I consider delicacies but which I don't often serve—mainly because I don't find them too frequently. Fresh fava beans enjoy only a relatively short season in midsummer. And as for fresh green soybeans, I've only been able to buy them frozen rather than truly fresh, and I grab them on those rare occasions when I spot them in a natural foods market.

FRESH FAVA BEANS

Also known as Windsor beans, broad beans, and horse beans, favas are a popular legume in the Mediterranean and in South America. However, these large, flattish beans have not captured the fancy of North Americans to any great extent. Their appearance and taste are similar to lima beans, and like limas, they have a stronger flavor when fresh.

Preparing fava beans is an exercise in mindfulness, akin to the pleasure of shelling fresh spring peas. Remove their outer shell and plunge into boiling water for 1 minute. Drain, then slip off the outer skins when cool enough to handle. Cook in gently simmering water until just tender, about 5 minutes. Drain, and if you'd like, add a touch of natural margarine or butter and a pinch of salt. The delicate, fresh flavor is a welcome treat, if only once a year.

FRESH GREEN SOYBEANS

Fresh green soybeans are nothing like the dried white soybeans that take forever to cook, and which are basically best for making soymilk and tofu. They are a delicate green encased in a pea-like pod, with a flavor most like fresh fava beans. Simply follow package directions for cooking—they're usually done in about 5 minutes. Serve them just as they are, letting everyone shell their own pods. I like them as an appetizer, unsalted, unbuttered, just soy bliss in and of themselves

Green Vegetable Frittata Parmesan

4 TO 6 SERVINGS

Here's a super way to use up leftover cooked green vegetables.

3 eggs, beaten

1½ cups frozen green peas, thawed, or 1½ to 2 cups finely chopped and steamed broccoli florets, sliced zucchini, or asparagus cuts

¼ cup grated fresh Parmesan cheese

Salt and freshly ground pepper to taste

Light olive oil

1 Combine the first 3 ingredients in a mixing bowl and stir together. Add a little salt and pepper and stir again.

2 Heat just enough oil to coat the bottom of a 9-inch nonstick skillet. When hot, pour in the egg mixture. Cover and cook over medium heat until the bottom is golden brown and the top is fairly set, about 5 minutes.

3 Slide the frittata out onto a plate. Invert the skillet over the plate and quickly flip over so that the frittata goes back into the skillet, uncooked side down. Remove the plate, return the skillet to the heat, and cook the second side, uncovered, until golden brown.

4 Slide the frittata back onto the plate, let cool for a few minutes, cut into wedges, and serve.

Calories: 115 • Total fat: 5 g
Protein: 9 g • Carbohydrate: 8 g
Cholesterol: 167 mg • Sodium: 18 mg

Frittatas

I never make egg dishes as entrées for dinner. Occasionally, though, I like to make these vegetable frittatas to serve on the side when the main fare is light. Served in wedges, they're especially compatible with light pasta and potato dishes, or with certain soups. You will also find a Spanish Potato Frittata, in Chapter Eight, page 185.

Corn Frittata Parmesan

4 TO 6 SERVINGS

3 eggs, beaten

1½ cups frozen corn kernels, thawed

¼ cup grated fresh Parmesan cheese

Salt and freshly ground pepper to taste

Light olive oil

Calories: 115 • Total fat: 4 g
Protein: 8 g • Carbohydrate: 10 g
Cholesterol: 167 mg • Sodium: 119 mg

This is good at room temperature as well as warm. Try it out on kids; leftovers are good to pack in brown-bag lunches.

1 Combine the first 3 ingredients in a mixing bowl and stir together. Add a little salt and pepper and stir again.

2 Heat just enough oil to coat the bottom of a 9-inch nonstick skillet. When hot, pour in the egg mixture. Cover and cook over medium heat until the bottom is golden brown and the top is fairly set, about 5 minutes.

3 Slide the frittata out onto a plate. Invert the skillet over the plate and quickly flip over so that the frittata goes back into the skillet, uncooked side down. Remove the plate, return the skillet to the heat, and cook the second side, uncovered, until golden brown.

4 Slide the frittata back onto the plate, let cool for a few minutes, cut into wedges, and serve.

MENU

Corn Frittata Parmesan *(this page)*

Garlicky Black Beans *(page 113)*

or

Green Chili Black Beans *(page 114)*

Sautéed Bell Peppers *(page 211)*

Simple tossed salad

Spinach or Swiss Chard Frittata Parmesan

4 TO 6 SERVINGS

This is good with either of these greens, but try it in late summer or early fall when gardens are overflowing with Swiss chard.

10 to 12 ounces fresh spinach or Swiss chard, well washed and stemmed

3 eggs, beaten

¼ cup grated fresh Parmesan cheese

Salt and freshly ground pepper to taste

Light olive oil

1 Steam the spinach or chard in a large covered pot with only the water clinging to the leaves, until just wilted down. This will take about a minute for the spinach and 3 to 4 minutes for the chard; drain. When cool enough to handle, chop the leaves.

2 Combine the eggs, spinach or chard, and Parmesan in a mixing bowl and stir together. Add a little salt and pepper and stir again.

3 Heat just enough oil to coat the bottom of a 9-inch nonstick skillet. When hot, pour in the egg mixture. Cover and cook over medium heat until the bottom is golden brown and the top is fairly set, about 5 minutes.

4 Slide the frittata out onto a plate. Invert the skillet over the plate and quickly flip over so that the frittata goes back into the skillet, uncooked side down. Remove the plate, return the skillet to the heat, and cook the second side, uncovered, until golden brown.

5 Slide the frittata back onto the plate, let cool for a few minutes, cut into wedges, and serve.

Calories: 88 • Total fat: 4 g
Protein: 8 g • Carbohydrate: 2 g
Cholesterol: 167 mg • Sodium: 165 mg

MENU

Spinach or Swiss Chard Frittata Parmesan *(this page)*

Pasta with Triple Red Sauce *(page 74)*

Bountiful tossed salad

Dilled Spinach and Feta Frittata

4 TO 6 SERVINGS

10 to 12 ounces fresh spinach, well washed, stemmed, and coarsely chopped or one 10-ounce package frozen chopped spinach, thawed and well drained

3 eggs, beaten

½ cup crumbled feta cheese

2 tablespoons minced fresh dill

Salt and freshly ground pepper to taste

Light olive oil

Calories: 130 • Total fat: 9 g
Protein: 10 g • Carbohydrate: 3 g
Cholesterol: 184 mg • Sodium: 344 mg

The addition of feta cheese gives this frittata a rich, pungent flavor.

1 If using fresh spinach, steam it in a large covered pot with only the water clinging to the leaves, until just wilted down, and drain.

2 Combine the spinach, eggs, feta cheese, and dill in a mixing bowl and stir together. Add a little salt and pepper and stir again.

3 Heat just enough oil to coat the bottom of a 9-inch nonstick skillet. When hot, pour in the egg mixture. Cover and cook over medium heat until the bottom is golden brown and the top is fairly set, about 5 minutes.

4 Slide the frittata out onto a plate. Invert the skillet over the plate and quickly flip over so that the frittata goes back into the skillet, uncooked side down. Remove the plate, return the skillet to the heat, and cook the second side, uncovered, until golden brown.

5 Slide the frittata back onto the plate, let cool for a few minutes, cut into wedges, and serve.

MENU

A SAVORY BRUNCH

Dilled Spinach and Feta Frittata *(this page)*

Leek and Red Pepper Hash Brown Potatoes *(page 183)*

Platter of black olives and sliced tomatoes

Fresh breads and spreads of your choice

Tropical Fruit Medley *(page 244)*

CHAPTER 10

Simple Sauces, Dips, and Sandwich Spreads

Here for your healthy snacking and sandwich enjoyment is a collection of dips and spreads, plus a couple of useful sauces for good measure. We are a culture that snacks too much (hence the emphasis on healthful dips—but watch what you use for dipping!) yet eats lunch on the run, if at all. These sandwich spreads might invite you to slow down and enjoy the midday meal.

I rely on several of these recipes when expecting daytime company. "Tuna"-Style Tofu Spread, for instance, is one of my standard lunch dishes. It doesn't matter what my guests think of tofu; I don't say a word, and it gets devoured. I barely get to taste it when others are around, so I try to make it once in a while for myself and my family. Bean spreads, too, are terrific antidotes to the sandwich rut, whether you are packing a brown-bag lunch or eating at home. Dips are great for inspiring kids (and adults, too) to eat more raw veggies. As long as the dip itself is healthful and low in fat, why not?

I think of these as easy, everyday recipes, but you might also consider giving this chapter a look when you need to serve a number of appetizers, around the holidays or for a special celebration.

Peanut Butter or Cashew Butter Sauce

MAKES ABOUT 1¼ CUPS (6 SERVINGS)

½ cup peanut butter or cashew butter

3 to 4 tablespoons low-sodium teriyaki or soy sauce, or to taste

1 to 2 tablespoons rice vinegar or white wine vinegar, or to taste

1 teaspoon freshly grated ginger or ½ teaspoon ground ginger

Cayenne pepper or any hot sauce, to taste, optional

Calories: 136 • Total fat: 9 g
Protein: 7 g • Carbohydrate: 6 g
Cholesterol: 0 mg • Sodium: 409 mg

A delectable sauce to serve over noodles, grains, or green vegetables. Cashew butter is a luscious treat. Look for it in natural foods stores. It is also, as you may imagine, a delicious change of pace from peanut butter in sandwiches. This recipe doubles easily if you'd like a larger quantity.

Combine all the ingredients in a food processor with ½ cup water. Go easy on the hot stuff, unless you definitely want a spicy sauce. Process until smoothly pureed. Heat gently in a small saucepan and use as desired.

Mushroom Gravy

MAKES ABOUT 1½ CUPS (4 TO 6 SERVINGS)

1 tablespoon nonhydrogenated margarine

8 to 10 ounces white or cremini mushrooms, cleaned and sliced

2 tablespoons unbleached white flour

1 cup canned vegetable stock

Salt and freshly ground pepper to taste

Calories: 47 • Total fat: 2 g
Protein: 1 g • Carbohydrate: 4 g
Cholesterol: 0 mg • Sodium: 88 mg

A simply delicious sauce to serve over grains, veggie burgers, green vegetables, or mashed potatoes.

1 Heat the margarine in a medium saucepan. Add the mushrooms and cook, covered, until they are done to your liking.

2 Dissolve the flour in enough cold water to make a smooth paste. Add it to the saucepan along with the vegetable stock and whisk together. Bring to a simmer, and cook gently until the mixture has thickened. Season with salt and pepper, and serve.

Hummus

MAKES ABOUT 2 CUPS
(6 TO 8 SERVINGS)

A classic Middle Eastern dip for scooping onto wedges of pita bread.

Combine all of the ingredients in a food processor with ¼ to ⅓ cup water. Process until smoothly pureed. Transfer to a serving bowl. Serve at room temperature.

One 16-ounce can chickpeas, drained and rinsed

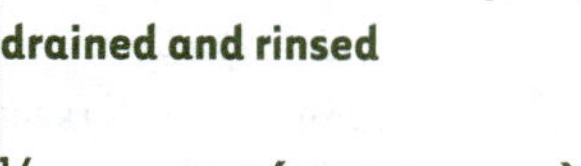

⅓ cup tahini (sesame paste)

Juice of 1 lemon

1 teaspoon ground cumin

1 garlic clove, crushed, or ¼ teaspoon garlic powder

Salt and freshly ground pepper to taste

Calories: 140 • Total fat: 6 g
Protein: 5 g • Carbohydrate: 16 g
Cholesterol: 0 mg • Sodium: 162 mg

MENU

A MIDDLE EASTERN FEAST

Hummus *(this page)*

Baba Ghanouj *(page 230)*

or

Roasted Eggplant and Yogurt Dip *(page 231)*

Israeli Salad *(page 39)*

Fruited Couscous *(page 106)*

Warm pita bread, cut into wedges for dipping

MAKES ABOUT 2 CUPS
(6 TO 8 SERVINGS)

Baba Ghanouj

2 medium eggplants (about 2 pounds)

1 tablespoon light olive oil

3 to 4 garlic cloves, minced

¼ cup tahini (sesame paste)

Juice of ½ to 1 lemon, or to taste

Salt and freshly ground pepper to taste

Calories: 102 • Total fat: 6 g
Protein: 2 g • Carbohydrate: 11 g
Cholesterol: 0 mg • Sodium: 12 mg

Like the previous recipe, this classic dip is delicious scooped up on wedges of pita bread.

1 Preheat the oven to 475°F. Arrange the whole eggplants on a foil-lined baking sheet. Bake, turning with tongs once or twice, until the eggplants have completely collapsed, 40 to 50 minutes. Remove and let cool. When cool enough to handle, remove the stems and slip off the peels.

2 Heat the oil in a skillet. Add the garlic and sauté over low heat until golden, about 2 minutes.

3 Combine the eggplant pulp, garlic, tahini, and lemon juice in a food processor. Process until the mixture is a slightly chunky puree (if you don't have a food processor, you can finely chop the eggplant by hand, transfer to a serving container, and stir in the remaining ingredients). Transfer to a serving container, season with salt and pepper, and serve at room temperature.

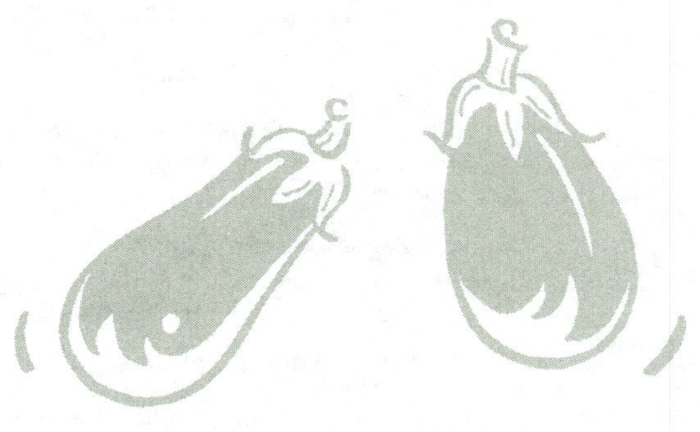

Roasted Eggplant and Yogurt Dip

MAKES ABOUT 2 CUPS (6 TO 8 SERVINGS)

Smoky roasted eggplant is tempered by yogurt in this Middle-Eastern-inspired dip. This is good for spreading on fresh bread as well as scooping up on pita.

1 large or 2 medium-small eggplants (about 1½ pounds)

1 tablespoon light olive oil

2 to 3 garlic cloves, minced

1 cup low-fat plain yogurt or soy yogurt

¼ to ½ cup minced fresh parsley

Salt and freshly ground pepper to taste

1 Preheat the oven to 475°F. Arrange the whole eggplant or eggplants on a foil-lined baking sheet. Bake until completely collapsed, 40 to 50 minutes. Remove and let cool. When cool enough to handle, remove the stems and slip off the peels. Chop the pulp into small bite-size chunks.

2 Heat the oil in a skillet. Add the garlic and sauté over low heat until golden, about 2 minutes.

3 Combine the chopped eggplant with the garlic, yogurt, and parsley in a serving container. Season with salt and pepper, and stir together. Serve at room temperature.

Calories: 67 • Total fat: 3 g
Protein: 3 g • Carbohydrate: 9 g
Cholesterol: 2 mg • Sodium: 31 mg

Yogurt "Tartar Sauce" or Dip

MAKES ABOUT 1 CUP (6 SERVINGS)

This is especially good as a sauce for Shake-and-Bake Tofu (page 138). You can also use it as a sauce or spread with veggie burgers, or try it as a dip for crisp raw vegetables.

¾ cup low-fat plain yogurt or soy yogurt

2 tablespoons soy mayonnaise

1 tablespoon pickle relish

1 to 2 teaspoons prepared mustard, or to taste

Combine all of the ingredients in a small bowl and stir together until well blended.

Calories: 36 • Total fat: 1 g
Protein: 2 g • Carbohydrate: 4 g
Cholesterol: 2 mg • Sodium: 88 mg

Spinach and Yogurt Dip

MAKES ABOUT 1½ CUPS (4 TO 6 SERVINGS)

1 tablespoon light olive oil

1 small onion, minced

2 to 3 garlic cloves, minced

10 to 12 ounces fresh spinach, well washed, stemmed, and coarsely chopped

1 cup low-fat plain yogurt or soy yogurt

Salt and freshly ground pepper to taste

Calories: 97 • Total fat: 4 g
Protein: 5 g • Carbohydrate: 9 g
Cholesterol: 4 mg • Sodium: 107 mg

Here's a nourishing dip for whole-grain crackers or pita bread.

1 Heat the oil in a large skillet. Add the onion and garlic and sauté over low heat until lightly golden.

2 Add the spinach, in batches if need be, cover, and cook briefly, just until it wilts. Remove from the heat, and stir in the yogurt. Season with salt and pepper, and serve.

Spinach-Miso Pesto Spread

MAKES ABOUT 1 CUP (6 SERVINGS)

One 10-ounce package frozen chopped spinach, thawed and squeezed

¼ to ½ cup fresh basil leaves

2 tablespoons extra-virgin olive oil

2 tablespoons miso, any variety, or to taste

¼ cup walnuts

Calories: 94 • Total fat: 7 g
Protein 2 g • Carbohydrate: 4 g
Cholesterol: 0 mg • Sodium: 301 mg

Serve as a spread on whole-grain crackers, crisp lavash, or wedges of pita bread. For more information on miso, a pungent soyfood, see page 21.

Combine all of the ingredients in a food processor. Process until the mixture becomes a coarse, even puree. Transfer to a serving bowl. Cover and refrigerate until needed or serve at once.

Dilled Yogurt-Tahini Dip or Dressing

MAKES ABOUT 1¼ CUPS (6 SERVINGS)

Use this as a dip for vegetables or small crackers or as a dressing for salads or pita sandwiches.

Combine all of the ingredients in a small bowl and stir together until well blended.

1 cup low-fat plain yogurt or soy yogurt

¼ cup tahini (sesame paste)

2 to 3 tablespoons minced fresh dill

½ teaspoon ground cumin

Calories: 84 • Total fat: 5 g
Protein: 4 g • Carbohydrate: 6 g
Cholesterol: 3 mg • Sodium: 37 mg

Silken Tofu and Olive Dip

MAKES ABOUT 1¼ CUPS (6 SERVINGS)

Silken tofu makes a perfect base for a good, dairy-free dip.

1 Combine the olives, bell pepper, and scallions in a food processor. Pulse on and off until they are finely and evenly chopped, but not pureed. Transfer to a small serving container.

2 Blend the tofu in the food processor until it is smoothly pureed. Combine with the chopped olive mixture and stir together. Add a few grindings of optional pepper, and serve.

½ cup pitted pimiento-filled or cured green olives

½ medium red bell pepper, diced

1 to 2 scallions, chopped

One 12.3-ounce package firm silken tofu

Freshly ground pepper, optional

Calories: 46 • Total fat: 3 g
Protein: 4 g • Carbohydrate: 2 g
Cholesterol: 0 mg • Sodium: 202 mg

MAKES ABOUT 1¼ CUPS
(6 TO 8 SERVINGS)

Light Cheese Dip

1 cup low-fat cottage cheese

¼ cup light cream cheese or Neufchâtel cheese

1 teaspoon salt-free herb-and-spice seasoning blend

2 tablespoons minced fresh parsley or dill

1 scallion, minced, optional

Calories: 53 • Total fat: 3 g
Protein: 6 g • Carbohydrate: 2 g
Cholesterol: 10 mg • Sodium: 162 mg

Here's a dip that could inspire your family to eat more raw vegetables. It's great for informal gatherings and cold buffets, too. Serve this with an array of colorful vegetables, including broccoli florets, baby carrots, red bell peppers, and halved cherry tomatoes.

Combine all of the ingredients in a food processor. Process until smoothly pureed. Transfer to a serving bowl. Cover and refrigerate until needed or serve at once.

MENU

A BUFFET OF EASY APPETIZERS

Light Cheese Dip *(this page)*

with a platter of raw vegetables

Hot Bean Dip *(page 235)*

with stone-ground tortilla chips

Dried Tomato Tapenade *(page 240)*

with crisp breads or toasted Italian bread

Spinach and Yogurt Dip *(page 232)*

with whole grain crackers

Hot Bean Dip

MAKES ABOUT 2 CUPS
(8 OR MORE SERVINGS)

This spicy dip makes a filling snack for a crowd. Serve with stone-ground tortilla chips.

One 16-ounce can vegetarian spicy fat-free refried beans

One 4- to 7-ounce can chopped mild or medium-hot green chilies

1 teaspoon ground cumin

1 cup grated cheddar or Monterey Jack cheese, or cheddar- or Jack-style soy cheese

1 Combine the beans, ¼ cup water, the chilies, and cumin in a mixing bowl and stir until well combined.

2 Transfer the mixture to a shallow 1-quart container and sprinkle with the cheese. Cover and microwave until the beans are hot and the cheese is melted, about 4 minutes. Serve hot.

Calories: 107 • Total fat: 4 g
Protein: 6 g • Carbohydrate: 11 g
Cholesterol: 13 mg • Sodium: 199 mg

No-Fuss Guacamole

MAKES ABOUT 1½ CUPS
(6 SERVINGS)

Using prepared salsa to make guacamole is an easy way to incorporate the flavors of tomatoes, onions, and chilies. Serve with stone-ground tortilla chips.

1 large avocado, peeled and mashed

½ cup red or green salsa (salsa verde)

2 to 3 tablespoons minced fresh cilantro

1 to 2 tablespoons fresh lemon or lime juice, or to taste

½ teaspoon ground cumin, optional

Pinch of salt

1 Combine all the ingredients in a serving container and mix together well.

2 Serve at once. Store leftover guacamole in an airtight container and use the next day.

Calories: 64 • Total fat: 4 g
Protein: 1 g • Carbohydrate: 6 g
Cholesterol: 0 mg • Sodium: 202 mg

Salsa Ranchera (Tomato Salsa)

MAKES ABOUT 2 CUPS
(8 OR MORE SERVINGS)

2 cups chopped flavorful tomatoes, or one 16-ounce can diced or stewed tomatoes, lightly drained

1 small onion, quartered, optional

One 4-ounce can chopped mild green chilies or 1 to 2 fresh jalapeño peppers, seeded and coarsely chopped

Several sprigs fresh cilantro

1 to 2 tablespoons fresh lemon or lime juice, or to taste

¼ teaspoon salt, or to taste

Calories: 13 • Total fat: 0 g
Protein: 0 g • Carbohydrate: 3 g
Cholesterol: 0 mg • Sodium: 4 mg

Store-bought salsas are generally quite good (I always have some on hand, both for using as a dip and as a shortcut to great flavor in recipes). However, for an occasional treat, nothing equals homemade salsa, especially one made with fresh tomatoes. Serve with tortilla chips or as a condiment with Mexican-style dishes.

To prepare in a food processor, combine all the ingredients and pulse on and off until coarsely pureed. To prepare by hand, finely chop the tomatoes, onion, chilies, and cilantro. Stir in the lime juice and salt, and serve.

Note: The use of one jalapeño will result in a hot salsa, while two will make this fairly incendiary. Those with more experienced palates are free to use as many jalapeños as they'd like. Store remaining salsa in an airtight jar. This will keep for several days, but it's best fresh.

Tomato-Mango Salsa

MAKES ABOUT 2 CUPS (8 OR MORE SERVINGS)

A somewhat more exotic salsa, this jazzes up meals with a tropical beat. See the menu with Gingered Coconut Rice, page 96. Serve with tortilla chips or as a condiment with spicy dishes.

1 cup coarsely chopped ripe tomatoes

1 medium to large mango, pitted, peeled, and coarsely chopped

One 4-ounce can chopped mild green chilies or 1 to 2 fresh jalapeño peppers, seeded and coarsely chopped (see note, page 236)

Several sprigs fresh cilantro

1 to 2 tablespoons fresh lime or lemon juice, or to taste

To prepare in a food processor, combine all the ingredients and pulse on and off until coarsely pureed. To prepare by hand, finely chop the tomatoes, mango, chilies, and cilantro. Stir in the lime juice and serve.

Note: Store remaining salsa in an airtight jar and use within two days.

Calories: 24 • Total fat: 0 g
Protein: 0 g • Carbohydrate: 5 g
Cholesterol: 0 mg • Sodium: 3 mg

Curried Tempeh Spread

6 SERVINGS

Tempeh is a chewy, fermented soy food. For more information, see page 146. This spread is comparable to a curried chicken salad, though if you already like tempeh, you need not compare it with anything; just enjoy it on fresh whole-grain bread or crackers.

One 8- to 10-ounce package tempeh

⅓ cup soy mayonnaise

1 teaspoon prepared mustard

1 teaspoon good-quality curry powder, or to taste

1 scallion, minced, optional

1 Using your hands, finely crumble the tempeh into a serving bowl.

2 Combine the remaining ingredients in a small bowl and stir together. Pour over the tempeh and mix together well. Serve at once.

Calories: 115 • Total fat: 5 g • Protein: 7 g
Carbohydrate: 8 g • Cholesterol: 0 mg
Sodium: 109 mg

"Egg Salad"-Style Tofu Spread

6 SERVINGS

1 pound soft or medium-firm tofu

⅓ cup soy mayonnaise

1 to 2 teaspoons prepared mustard, or to taste

½ teaspoon good-quality curry powder, or to taste

1 large celery stalk, finely diced

Salt to taste

Calories: 90 • Total fat: 5 g
Protein: 5 g • Carbohydrate: 3 g
Cholesterol: 0 mg • Sodium: 130 mg

Whenever I make this for lunch I always think, "I should make this more often." It's a pleasant change-of-pace spread that can be served on fresh bread or, better yet, stuffed into pita.

1 Using your hands, finely crumble the tofu in a serving bowl.

2 Combine the mayonnaise, mustard, and curry powder in a small bowl and stir together. Pour over the tofu and add the celery. Mix well, season with salt, and serve.

"Tuna"-Style Tofu Spread

6 SERVINGS

One 8-ounce package baked marinated tofu

½ cup soy mayonnaise

1 large celery stalk, finely diced

1 scallion, minced, optional

Calories: 127 • Total fat: 8 g
Protein: 9 g • Carbohydrate: 4 g
Cholesterol: 0 mg • Sodium: 299 mg

When I serve this to lunchtime company, even tofu skeptics love it! For me, it's a throwback to tuna salad, something I gave up many years ago, though I still liked its taste. This is especially good served in warm pita bread. I also like to mix leftovers with macaroni for a "tofuna"-noodle salad. For more information on baked marinated tofu, see page 136. For this recipe, it's best to use a baked tofu product that comes in large chunks like Soy Boy's Tofu Lin, rather than the type that comes in small cutlets.

1 Using your hands, finely crumble the tofu in a serving bowl.

2 Add the remaining ingredients, mix well, and serve.

Chickpea Spread

6 TO 8 SERVINGS

This is excellent stuffed into or spread on pita bread, as well as on crispbreads and crackers. I like it best on fresh pumpernickel bread.

One 16-ounce can chickpeas, drained and rinsed

⅓ cup soy mayonnaise

½ green bell pepper, finely diced

1 tablespoon fresh lemon juice

½ teaspoon ground cumin

1 Mash the chickpeas coarsely (either by hand with a fork, or pulse on and off in a food processor until coarsely mashed—don't puree!).

2 Combine the mashed chickpeas in a serving container with the remaining ingredients. Mix together well, and serve.

Calories: 121 • Total fat: 4 g
Protein: 4 g • Carbohydrate: 17 g
Cholesterol: 0 mg • Sodium: 264 mg

White Bean and Dried Tomato Spread

6 TO 8 SERVINGS

This is fantastic on fresh pumpernickel or rye bread for lunch; or spread it on fresh Italian bread to serve with light pasta dishes.

One 16-ounce can large white beans (Great Northern or cannellini), drained and rinsed

¼ cup oil-cured sun-dried tomatoes

2 tablespoons chopped fresh parsley or scallions

1 teaspoon salt-free herb-and-spice seasoning mix

1 tablespoon fresh lemon juice

Freshly ground pepper to taste

Combine all the ingredients in a food processor and process until coarsely pureed. Transfer to a serving container, and serve at room temperature.

Calories: 104 • Total fat: 2 g
Protein: 4 g • Carbohydrate: 16 g
Cholesterol: 0 mg • Sodium: 182 mg

Dried Tomato Tapenade

MAKES ABOUT 1 CUP (6 TO 8 SERVINGS)

¾ cup sun-dried tomatoes (not oil-cured)

⅓ cup toasted slivered or sliced almonds

1 tablespoon extra-virgin olive oil

1 tablespoon fresh lemon juice

1 tablespoon minced fresh basil or ½ teaspoon dried basil

Salt to taste

Calories: 98 • Total fat: 7 g
Protein: 3 g • Carbohydrate: 6 g
Cholesterol: 0 mg • Sodium: 7 mg

Spread this luscious concoction on toasted Italian bread or whole-grain crackers and serve as an appetizer or as an accompaniment to pasta dishes.

1 If the dried tomatoes you are using aren't moist, first soak them in hot water for about 10 minutes, then drain.

2 Combine the dried tomatoes with the remaining ingredients and ⅓ cup water in a food processor. Pulse on and off until the mixture is coarsely but evenly pureed, with a texture similar to pesto. Add a few more drops of water if needed, and salt.

3 Transfer the mixture to a small crock and use as a spread.

CHAPTER 11

Fundamental Fruits

Fruits entice me with their sensuous shapes and scents. But I must admit that if a bowl of beautiful whole fruits is on the table, I am more likely to look at them than eat them. I forget that they are not merely a still life for my visual enjoyment. On the other hand, a platter of fruit that has been cut up, glistening seductively or gently embellished, as in the recipes in this chapter, will be devoured without a second thought.

In *Tassajara Cooking,* Edward Espé Brown's 1973 classic, he says of fruits that they are "a deceptively potent food: refreshing, invigorating, cleansing." In many cuisines, fruit is served with the main part of the meal, rather than as an afterthought or dessert. Come to think of it, I've often made fruit salads like Tropical Fruit Medley (page 244) or Pineapple-Orange Ambrosia (page 244) to serve with lunch or brunch, especially when serving guests. Interspersing bites of fruit with foods of contrasting tastes, the sweet flavors do indeed refresh and cleanse the palate. I've started serving fruit with dinner more often—smoothies with pizza, strips of mango with spicy bean dishes, apples and pears in salads. That *is* invigorating.

Choose good, ripe fruits, ones that are truly in season. Imports help foster variety, but there's nothing like a strawberry in June, a peach in late August, or a pear in October. That way, little embellishment is needed to highlight a fruit's luscious gifts.

Fruit and Yogurt Parfaits

4 SERVINGS

Two 8-ounce containers low-fat vanilla yogurt or soy yogurt (or try lemon- or orange-flavored yogurt)

2 cups fresh fruit (see variations below)

Grated semisweet chocolate, toasted sliced almonds, or low-fat granola for topping

Calories: 127 • Total fat: 1 g
Protein: 7 g • Carbohydrate: 21 g
Cholesterol: 6 mg • Sodium: 82 mg

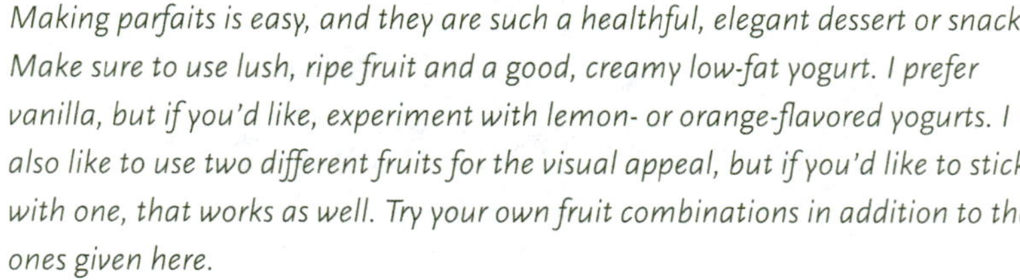

Making parfaits is easy, and they are such a healthful, elegant dessert or snack. Make sure to use lush, ripe fruit and a good, creamy low-fat yogurt. I prefer vanilla, but if you'd like, experiment with lemon- or orange-flavored yogurts. I also like to use two different fruits for the visual appeal, but if you'd like to stick with one, that works as well. Try your own fruit combinations in addition to the ones given here.

1 Use 4 parfait dishes if you have them; if not, medium-size glass tumblers will do. For each serving, layer ¼ cup each of yogurt and fruit in the parfait dish; repeat each layer, then do the same for the other parfaits.

2 Sprinkle with the topping of choice, and serve.

Parfait Variations:

Strawberries: Remove the hulls from 1 pint of very sweet strawberries and slice them.

Strawberries and blueberries: Combine 1 cup of strawberries, hulled and sliced, with 1 cup fresh blueberries.

Peaches or nectarines with berries: Combine 1 cup diced peach or nectarine, with 1 cup of berries.

Mango and berries: Combine 1 cup diced mango, with 1 cup of blueberries, raspberries, or sliced strawberries.

Mango and banana: Combine 1 cup diced mango, with 1 cup thinly sliced banana.

Fresh apricot: Use 2 cups (about 6) sliced fresh apricot. Or combine 1 cup of sliced fresh apricot with 1 cup of small seedless grapes or berries.

Miniature Fresh Fruit Tarts

6 SERVINGS

My kids would never eat pies until I began making them with graham cracker crusts. I've also lost the taste for pastry crust (who needs all that fat?). The miniature size is perfect for fruit fillings that need not be baked or that wouldn't hold together in a large crust.

1 package miniature graham cracker pie shells (6 small shells)

1 recipe Chunky Applesauce (page 250), Sugared Strawberries (page 249), or Fresh Berry Sauce (page 247)

Low-fat vanilla yogurt or soy yogurt, optional

1 Preheat the oven or toaster oven to 350°F. Bake the pie shells according to package directions, remove from the oven, and allow to cool.

2 Divide the filling of your choice among the shells. Top each with a small dollop of yogurt, and serve.

Calories: 290 • Total fat: 12 g
Protein: 2 g • Carbohydrate: 44 g
Cholesterol: 0 mg • Sodium: 239 mg

Tropical Fruit Medley

4 TO 6 SERVINGS

One 20-ounce can unsweetened pineapple chunks, well drained

2 kiwi fruits, peeled and sliced

1 large mango, pitted, peeled, and diced

1 medium papaya, pitted, peeled, and diced, or 1 large banana, sliced

One 8-ounce container lemon or lime low-fat yogurt or soy yogurt

Calories: 175 • Total fat: 0 g
Protein: 3 g • Carbohydrate: 38 g
Cholesterol: 1 mg • Sodium: 25 mg

This sunny combination of fruits will ease the monotony of winter's limited fresh fruit choices.

1 Combine the first 4 ingredients in a mixing bowl and stir together.

2 Serve in individual dessert bowls with a dollop of the yogurt on top.

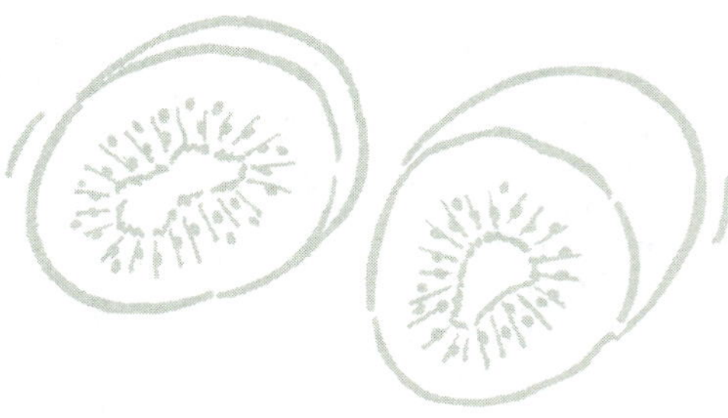

Pineapple-Orange Ambrosia

4 TO 6 SERVINGS

One 20-ounce can unsweetened pineapple chunks, well drained

4 clementines or other small seedless oranges, peeled and sectioned

½ cup dried cranberries

One 8-ounce container low-fat vanilla yogurt or soy yogurt

Granola for topping, optional

Calories: 161 • Total fat: 0 g
Protein: 3 g • Carbohydrate: 35 g
Cholesterol: 2 mg • Sodium: 27 mg

This recipe will perk up your taste buds during winter's long fruit drought.

1 Combine the first 4 ingredients in a serving container and stir together.

2 Serve in individual dessert bowls, topping each serving with a sprinkling of optional granola.

Mango and Banana or Pear Smoothie

2 SERVINGS

Some days, I need little more than this or the following refreshing smoothie for lunch. My younger son wanted readers to know that he came up with the mango and pear combination at the age of seven. It's unbelievably good—thanks, Evan!

Combine all the ingredients except optional ice in a food processor or blender and process until smoothly pureed. Serve at once in tall glasses, over ice if desired.

1 mango, peeled, pitted, and coarsely chopped

1 banana, peeled and cut into several pieces, or 2 large ripe juicy pears (preferably Bartlett), peeled, quartered, and cored

One 8-ounce container low-fat vanilla yogurt or soy yogurt

½ cup orange juice, or as needed

Ice, optional

Calories: 240 • Total fat: 1 g
Protein: 7 g • Carbohydrate: 49 g
Cholesterol: 6 mg • Sodium: 74 mg

Mango-Strawberry Smoothie

2 SERVINGS

Smoothies are superb served with pizza meals. Try this or any of the other smoothies in this chapter the next time you make pizza. I've suggested these smoothies as part of some of the menus in Chapter Six, A Flash in the (Pizza) Pan.

Combine the first 4 ingredients in a food processor or blender and process until smoothly pureed. Serve at once in tall glasses, over ice if desired.

1 mango, peeled, pitted, and coarsely chopped

1 cup sweet strawberries, hulled

One 8-ounce container low-fat vanilla yogurt or soy yogurt

½ cup tropical juice blend or orange juice, or as needed

Ice, optional

Calories: 210 • Total fat: 1 g
Protein: 7 g • Carbohydrate: 41 g
Cholesterol: 6 mg • Sodium: 74 mg

Orange-Vanilla "Creamsicle" Smoothie

1 TO 2 SERVINGS

1 cup fresh orange juice

½ cup low-fat vanilla yogurt or soy yogurt

¼ cup seltzer or sparkling water

Dash of vanilla extract, optional

Ice, optional

Calories: 144 • Total fat: 1 g
Protein: 5 g • Carbohydrate: 28 g
Cholesterol: 4 mg • Sodium: 57 mg

I remember buying creamsicles from the ice cream truck as a child. The combination of the orange and vanilla flavors was wonderfully refreshing. Here's a healthy, natural re-creation of those flavors in an invigorating beverage.

Combine the first 4 ingredients in one or two tall glasses. Stir vigorously with a spoon until well blended. If you'd like a frothier version, combine the ingredients in a food processor or blender and process until smoothly blended and slightly frothy. Serve at once, over ice if desired.

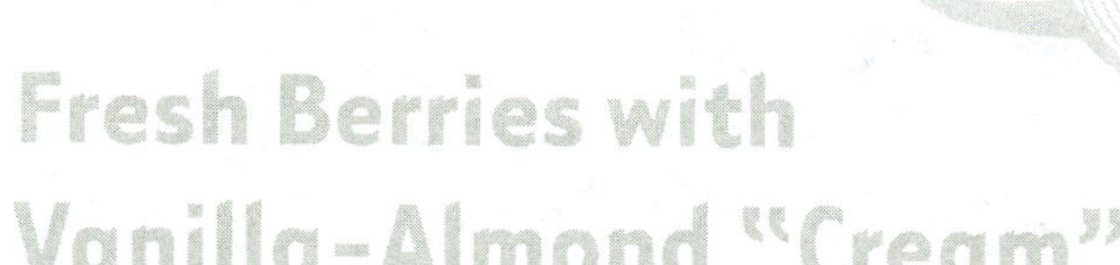

Fresh Berries with Vanilla-Almond "Cream"

4 TO 6 SERVINGS

2 cups (1 pint) fresh berries (blueberries, blackberries, raspberries, or any combination)

Two 8-ounce containers low-fat vanilla yogurt or soy yogurt

1 teaspoon vanilla extract

Pinch of nutmeg, optional

⅓ cup toasted sliced or slivered almonds

Calories: 137 • Total fat: 5 g
Protein: 6 g • Carbohydrate: 15 g
Cholesterol: 4 mg • Sodium: 50 mg

Whichever berry or berries please you most, here's a tasty way to enjoy them.

1 Divide the berries among 4 to 6 dessert bowls.

2 Combine the yogurt, vanilla, and optional nutmeg in a small mixing bowl and stir together until creamy.

3 Spoon the yogurt mixture over the berries, sprinkle with the almonds, and serve.

Fresh Berry Sauce

6 SERVINGS

This versatile topping is great for cakes, pies, ice cream, and regular or frozen yogurt.

2 cups fresh berries (blueberries, strawberries, raspberries, or any combination)

½ cup apple juice

2 teaspoons cornstarch or arrowroot

1 tablespoon natural granulated sugar, or to taste, optional

1 Wash the berries well. Use small berries such as blueberries or raspberries whole; remove hulls and chop strawberries into approximately ½-inch chunks.

2 Combine the berries in a medium-size saucepan with the apple juice. Bring to a simmer, cover, and cook gently until all the berries have softened and burst, 5 to 10 minutes.

3 Dissolve the cornstarch in ¼ cup cold water. Stir slowly into the berry mixture and simmer until it has thickened, about 1 minute. If you'd like the sauce to be sweeter, stir in the optional brown sugar to taste. Let cool to room temperature before serving.

Calories: 28 • Total fat: 0 g
Protein: 0 g • Carbohydrate: 6 g
Cholesterol: 0 mg • Sodium: 1 mg

Life Is Just a Bowl of Berries

The song says life is just a bowl of cherries. But there's no better time than midsummer to look at life as a bowl of *berries*.

Take advantage of the abundance of strawberries and blueberries. Scour farmers' markets and specialty groceries for gooseberries, red currants, blueberries, blackberries, and raspberries. Go to a farm where you can pick your own fruit—it makes a great family outing.

However you get your berries, use them up quickly once at home—they're highly perishable. Mix two or three varieties in a bowl for eating plain, and set some aside for these easy recipes.

Amaretto Strawberries

4 TO 6 SERVINGS

1 pint flavorful fresh strawberries, hulled and sliced

3 tablespoons amaretto (almond liqueur)

Low-fat vanilla yogurt, frozen yogurt, soy yogurt, or non-dairy frozen dessert

Calories: 55 • Total fat: 0 g
Protein: 0 g • Carbohydrate: 8 g
Cholesterol: 0 mg • Sodium: 1 mg

This simple preparation for fresh strawberries has long been a favorite of mine. The almond flavor of amaretto melds perfectly with the sweetness and aroma of lush, ripe strawberries.

1 Combine the strawberries with the amaretto in a serving container and stir together. Crush about ¼ cup of the strawberries with a fork, and mix again.

2 Let the mixture stand for about 30 minutes before serving (if you are planning to let it stand any longer than that, cover and refrigerate). Serve over yogurt or frozen yogurt in dessert bowls.

Strawberries

The season for good, locally grown strawberries is fleeting, unless you live in California. Though it's possible to buy them nearly all year, mass-produced strawberries are the equivalent of flavorless hothouse tomatoes. There's nothing like the real thing, freshly picked.

I'm fortunate to live in the Hudson Valley region of New York state, where both cosmopolitan and rural pleasures abound. Thriving small farms yield lush seasonal produce, with many outlets for picking your own. I love to take my sons to pick our own produce—it's a great way to appreciate the connection between the land and the kitchen. We especially like to pick berries. The first time we picked strawberries, one of my boys kept putting his head in the bucket to take a deep breath, saying, "It smells so relaxing!" As he grows older, I'm sure that the scent of strawberries will spur pleasant memories.

Sugared Strawberries

4 TO 6 SERVINGS

This is what I do most often with fresh strawberries. Sprinkling the sweet strawberries of late spring to early summer with just a little sugar, then letting them stand, draws out their delicious juice. They become almost an instant sauce, perfect for serving over yogurt and frozen yogurt, or to simply enjoy on their own. This is also delicious as a filling for Miniature Fresh Fruit Tarts (page 243).

1 pint flavorful fresh strawberries, hulled and sliced

1 to 2 teaspoons natural granulated sugar, or to taste

Combine the strawberries with the sugar in a serving container. Let the mixture stand for about 30 minutes before serving (if you are planning to let them stand any longer than that, cover and refrigerate). Serve in small dessert bowls or as suggested above.

Calories: 23 • Total fat: 0 g
Protein: 0 g • Carbohydrate: 5 g
Cholesterol: 0 mg • Sodium: 1 mg

Chunky Applesauce

4 TO 6 SERVINGS

6 to 8 large sweet cooking apples, such as Cortland or Rome, peeled and cut into ½-inch dice

½ cup apple juice

2 tablespoons natural granulated sugar, or to taste

Cinnamon to taste

Calories: 155 • Total fat: 0 g
Protein: 0 g • Carbohydrate: 36 g
Cholesterol: 0 mg • Sodium: 3 mg

This is the perfect thing to make after you've gone apple-picking or to celebrate the first crop of apples at the local farmers' market. This is a delightful filling for Miniature Fresh Fruit Tarts (page 243).

1 Combine the apples and juice in a large saucepan. Bring to a simmer, cover, and cook over low heat, stirring occasionally, until the apples are soft, 20 to 30 minutes.

2 Add the brown sugar and cinnamon, and allow to cool. Serve warm or at room temperature.

Apple Brown Betty

4 TO 6 SERVINGS

4 heaping cups peeled, diced sweet apples

½ cup natural granulated sugar

½ teaspoon cinnamon

2 tablespoons nonhydrogenated margarine

4 cups fresh bread crumbs

Calories: 307 • Total fat: 7 g
Protein: 4 g • Carbohydrate: 58 g
Cholesterol: 16 mg • Sodium: 192 mg

Apple Brown Betty is an old-fashioned dessert that looks and tastes as wholesome as can be.

1 Preheat the oven to 350°F.

2 In a mixing bowl, combine the apples with the sugar and cinnamon, and stir together.

3 In a 9 by 9-inch nonstick baking pan, arrange layers of half of the apple mixture. Dot with half of the margarine, then sprinkle with half of the bread crumbs. Repeat the layers, then sprinkle ¼ cup water over the top.

4 Cover and bake for 30 minutes. Uncover and bake until the top is golden brown, about 10 minutes more. Serve warm.

Baked Apples with Yogurt

6 SERVINGS

Baked apples are a splendid example of "nursery food," and children as well as adults deserve this sort of comfort on a regular basis. To ease preparation, you need a very sharp, short knife for coring the apples.

6 medium sweet cooking apples, such as Cortland

⅓ cup natural granulated sugar

1 teaspoon cinnamon

¼ cup finely chopped walnuts, optional

1 cup low-fat vanilla yogurt or soy yogurt

1 Preheat the oven to 350°F.

2 Core the apples carefully with a small sharp knife, and place them in a baking pan.

3 Combine the brown sugar and cinnamon and optional walnuts in a small bowl and stir together. Divide the mixture among the hollows of each apple.

4 Fill the baking pan with about ½ inch of water. Cover with foil and bake until the apples are tender, about 45 minutes.

5 Allow the apples to cool until just warm, fill the hollows with a little yogurt, and serve.

Calories: 146 • Total fat: 0 g
Protein: 2 g • Carbohydrate: 32 g
Cholesterol: 2 mg • Sodium: 30 mg

Simple Summer Fruit Medleys

Winter fruits—apples, bananas, pears—are fine with me, but while they offer nourishment during the cold seasons, I can't say they cause my palate any excitement. It's summer's lush, ripe fruits that entice me far more. Summer fruits need little or no embellishment. These past few summers I have enjoyed teaming two or three fruits whose colors and flavors synergize well. Truly, you don't need quantities, but I give some only as a guideline. Once the fruit is washed and/or cut up (obviously you need not cut berries, with the exception of strawberries, and not even those if they are small), it should be eaten right away.

Mango and blueberries: What a dramatic pairing of colors! Depending on how many people you're serving, combine 1 or 2 peeled, diced mangos (large chunks are fine) with 1 to 2 cups blueberries.

Strawberries and blueberries or blackberries: Hull about 1 pint sweet, fresh strawberries. Cut them in half and combine with 1 cup or so of blueberries or blackberries. Gorgeous!

Honeydew or cantaloupe and raspberries: The pretty red of raspberries adds a decorative punctuation to the pale green or orange of the melons. Cut up half of a large, lush honeydew or a whole cantaloupe into bite-size chunks (or use some of each), and combine with about a cup of raspberries.

Peaches or nectarines and berries: If the fruit is perfectly ripe, this is heavenly. Use late-summer peaches or nectarines from a farmers' market, not those that arrive at the supermarket as hard as stones. Use 4 to 6 peaches or nectarines, pitted and diced, and a cup or two of whatever late summer berry you can find.

Greengage plums, apricots, and red grapes: Greengage plums are a beautiful green. No, they are not unripe, and they are sweet, rather than tart, as their color might suggest. Combine 2 or 3 pitted and diced greengage plums with 3 or 4 pitted and diced fresh apricots and a good-sized bunch of crisp red grapes, taken off their stems, of course.

Cantaloupe and black plums: Combine a lush cantaloupe, cut into bite-size chunks, with a few of those wonderful black plums that have the deep, sweet red flesh.

Cantaloupe, watermelon, and blueberries: Here's a classic trio for midsummer. For ease, I like to use seedless watermelon. Use about half of a lush cantaloupe and a quarter of a good-sized watermelon, both cut into large, bite-size chunks, and a cup or so of blueberries.

Yellow watermelon and berries: Try finding yellow watermelon—it's becoming more prevalent. Its flavor is not that different from the more common type of watermelon, but its cheery color makes it even more appealing. Combine about a quarter of a large melon or half of a small one with a cup or two of whatever midsummer berry you'd like. This is attractive with blackberries.

4 SERVINGS

Maple Baked Pears

4 to 5 medium firm pears, preferably Bosc

¼ cup maple syrup

Cinnamon

¼ cup finely chopped walnuts

Low-fat vanilla frozen yogurt or non-dairy frozen dessert, optional

Calories: 221 • Total fat: 4 g
Protein: 2 g • Carbohydrate: 42 g
Cholesterol: 0 mg • Sodium: 4 mg

There's something refined about baked pears. The subtle maple flavor suits them perfectly.

1 Preheat the oven to 350°F.

2 Quarter the pears lengthwise, and remove the cores and stem ends. Cut each quarter in half lengthwise. Arrange in a 9 by 9-inch nonstick baking pan.

3 Drizzle the syrup over the pears, and sprinkle with a little cinnamon. Scatter the walnuts over the pears.

4 Bake until the pears are tender but not overcooked, 25 to 30 minutes. Stir the mixture well about 15 minutes into the baking time. Serve warm in shallow bowls or over frozen yogurt if desired.

Variation: Omit the walnuts; sprinkle the pears with about ¼ cup semisweet chocolate chips once out of the oven.

Index